*Place and Memory
in the Singing Crane Garden*

Penn Studies in Landscape Architecture

John Dixon Hunt, Series Editor

This series is dedicated to the study and promotion of a wide variety of approaches to landscape architecture, with emphasis on connections between theory and practice. It includes monographs on key topics in history and theory, descriptions of projects by both established and rising designers, translations of major foreign-language texts, anthologies of theoretical and historical writings on classic issues, and critical writing by members of the profession of landscape architecture. The series was the recipient of the Award of Honor in Communications from the American Society of Landscape Architects, 2006.

Place and Memory
in the
Singing Crane Garden

Vera Schwarcz

PENN

University of Pennsylvania Press

Philadelphia

Publication of this volume was aided by a grant from Wesleyan University.

Published by
University of Pennsylvania Press
Philadelphia, Pennsylvania 19104-4112

Printed in the United States of America on acid-free paper
10 9 8 7 6 5 4 3 2 1

Library of Congress Cataloging-in-Publication Data
Schwarcz, Vera, 1947-
  Place and memory in the Singing Crane Garden / Vera Schwarcz.
    p. cm. — (Penn studies in landscape architecture)
  Includes bibliographical references and index.
  ISBN-13: 978-0-8122-4100-6 (hardcover : alk. paper)
  ISBN-10: 0-8122-4100-2 (hardcover : alk. paper)
  1. Ming He Yuan (Beijing, China)—History. I. Title.
  SB466.C53M567 2008
  712'.6 0951156—dc22

                                                    2007043620

Contents

Preface

Thinking about gardens leads naturally to an alchemy of mind.
—*Diane Ackerman,* Cultivating Delight

It is rare to be able to date the birth of a book. I feel grateful that I can point to the day, month, and hour: October 16, 1993–10:30 A.M. A brisk wind was blowing this Saturday across Beijing University. I was taking a walk on wooded paths in the northwest corner of campus I have come to know intimately over the past twenty-five years. I had lived at Beida (the shortened name of Beijing University), I had returned for yearly visits, and I had written about its history in the 1910s and 1920s. This morning in October, I was unprepared for discovery. I was just strolling and thinking about the dense layers of friendship that bind me to this familiar ground.

Suddenly I was accosted by a new building. It was located among the old Yenching University structures that I knew quite well. They connected the Beida of the Communist era back to the distinguished institution of liberal learning founded by American missionaries in the 1920s. Those buildings have more beauty, more history than the cement dormitories and classrooms built after 1949. The new building blended into the Yenching style, yet was far more graceful in its proportions, in the details of the paintings under its winged roofs. When I came to the front of the building I was surprised by the sign: Arthur M. Sackler Museum of Art and Archaeology. How could this museum appear so suddenly? After all, I knew each part of this campus like the palm of my hand. True, I had not returned for a few years after the shock that followed the violent suppression of student demonstrations in June 1989.

I entered the museum to chat with the ticket seller. It being Saturday, I was not carrying money, in keeping with my practice as an observant Jew. Having no cash, I had more time for conversation. In the colloquial language that has become one of my "mother tongues," I asked the old man in the ticket booth: "What was here before? This is my *mu xiao* [my "mother school"—I chose the Chinese intentionally to signal my intimacy with our shared space]. I know it too well for such a surprise!" The septuagenarian with a kind smile full of wrinkles turned out to be a retired manual laborer, a former groundskeeper at Beida. He answered me as if we had been old friends: "Oh, this was the place of the *niu peng*. The shacks where they herded all those brainy professors during the Cultural Revolution."

Niu peng—the "ox pens." This then was the site that my old friends at Beida had hinted about so often, yet had refused to identify over two decades of friendship and interviews. Almost everyone I knew among the highly educated intellectuals in China had spent time in the niu peng. I had heard much whispering about the brutalities committed in the first prison, set up at Beida. But I never knew exactly where my friends had suffered their humiliation and terror.

On this day of Shabbat, I backed away from the Sackler Museum and went to sit in a nearby pavilion, also new. A flood of questions came to my mind: How does Jewish money (I knew of Arthur Sackler's background) come to provide a haven for architectural fragments that survived the Cultural Revolution? Is it an atrocity to have an art museum on the very ground where there had been so much suffering? Can art ever be a meaningful container for historical trauma? In the next hour I faced all the dilemmas that frame this book. I knew before I left the garden setting outside the Sackler Museum that I was willing to dedicate years to wrestling with those dilemmas. Even without being a historical geographer, I knew that I wanted to write a narrative about this layered terrain. In my journal, on Sunday night, I wrote: "A sense of congealed time, blood on the surface of deep waters. I bring with me a lot of Jewish history. I also realize with gratitude that a new subject has found me on my first Shabbat back in China. The new building, oddly perfect. Its simple doors studded with gilded knobs, like the noblemen's mansions of old. The marble Qing sundial in front of the Sackler—a remnant of the old Yuan Ming Yuan (Summer Palace). A coming-out of Beida's hidden treasures. And the ache. The guard who speaks about the ox pens, does he hear all the whispered cries behind the art? Inside the museum today, I glimpsed a broken vessel. The careful piecing together of a broken past. This is my own task now."

In the weeks following the discovery of the new Sackler Museum I had ample occasion to savor what Diane Ackerman called "an alchemy of mind." Different fragments of my past connection to Beida began to coalesce into a new angle of vision about both Chinese space and Chinese time. I did not yet know that my subject would become the garden. I had noticed only the museum. I had just begun to reconstruct the fabric of its connectedness to the painful events of the 1960s. The idea of a special refuge in the midst of terror had not become central to my thinking yet. Ming He Yuan—the Singing Crane Garden with its own history of ruination and remembrance in the nineteenth century—would take root in my mind later. For now, I concentrated on the museum and the ox pens. That was alchemy enough to start with.

Drawing upon many years of trusted intimacy at Beida, I used my remaining weeks in 1993 to interview as many of the old professors still alive who recalled, and were willing to talk about, their experiences during the Cultural Revolution. In less than twenty days, I was privileged to talk at length with historian Zhou Yiliang, biologist Chen Yuezeng, economist Chen Zhenhan, and the well-known Sanskrit scholar Ji Xianlin. Having previously written a book based on oral history, I found that doors of conversations opened more readily than I had expected. Professor Ji brought a unique intensity to our conversations. He led me to understand that he was planning to write his own memoir of the ox pens at Beida, but that the time was not yet ripe. In 1998, when this work, *Niu peng za yi* (Recollections of the Ox Pen), saw the light of day, my task in writing this book became much easier.

Ji Xianlin's writing filled in one layer of the ground I came to explore in this book. An older strata was illuminated for me by the work and friendship of Hou Renzhi, the eminent geographer who pioneered the historiography of Beijing. A graduate of Yenching University, Professor Hou brought to his studies a scrupulous and lively imagination. His book *Yan Yuan Shihua* (Tales from Yan Yuan Garden) became my guide in this project. His detailed evocation of the Singing Crane Garden led me to want to know more about the Manchu noblemen who built up this terrain in the nineteenth century. Hou Renzhi's friendship and interest in my work opened paths of inquiry I could not have imagined possible in October 1993. Aware that I wanted to link the old Ming He Yuan to the history of the ox pens and the Sackler Museum, he introduced me to two scholars who quite literally changed the shape of this book: Jiao Xiong and Yue Shengyang.

Jiao Xiong is a retired archivist who specializes in garden history. He is also a talented painter who agreed to reproduce for me the topography of all the princely gardens in northwest Beijing. Aided by his detailed paintings, I was able to enter the garden world of the nineteenth century. Yue Shengyang drew for me a detailed map of the ruins of the Ming He Yuan visible on the Beida campus today. On May 10, 1998, these two scholars accompanied me on a walk to trace the periphery of Singing Crane Garden. We started in front of the Sackler Museum. Dr. Yue quickly sketched for me a map of the niu peng—an enclosure he knew as a boy when he visited his imprisoned parents. This map revealed darker meanings of the "garden" than I had been able to fathom before. The end of our stroll took us to the entrance of the nineteenth-century garden—residence 75 behind the Sackler Museum.

There, another surprising illumination awaited me. This was the same courtyard that I had visited frequently in 1979–80, when I first came to live as an exchange scholar at Beida. This was the home of Wang Yao, a well-known historian of modern literature who became a friend and mentor. I knew he had been beaten severely during the Cultural Revolution (missing teeth and a care-worn face testified to the abuse).

As I stood outside Wang Yao's old residence, his widow came out to greet me. It was this much-aggrieved woman who pointed out the defaced pillars that framed the entrance to Wang Yao's study. It had not been enough to drag her husband away to the ox pens. Traces of history that linked this courtyard to Confucian gentlemen and Manchu princes had to be erased as well. Here, in the May sunshine, I came to understand a little better why willful ruination would become a central theme in this book.

The more evidence of devastation I uncovered, the more significance I attached to Arthur Sackler's passion for cultural preservation. To trace the history of his life and his museum-building efforts around the world was not a simple proposition. A prominent psychiatrist, collector, and businessman, Dr. Sackler had many admirers and detractors. I have been especially fortunate in this project to be able to interview his close associates, each revealing a new facet of a man who came to build the art museum at Beida. In Jerusalem, Meir Meyer, acquisition director for the Israel Museum, was the first to discuss with me Arthur Sackler's commitments as a Jew and as a man dedicated to the preservation of the Chinese heritage in art. This alchemy of mind was further elaborated in my conversations with Heather Peters, Lo Yi Chan, Lois Katz, and Curtis Cutter. All of them worked closely with Arthur Sackler and were familiar with the history of the Beijing museum. Jill Sackler, Dr. Sackler's widow, shared with me her own reflections about the past and future of the museum in Beida. The man who opened up the Sackler story in the most intimate way was a doctor by training: Hu Qimin (Tommy Hu) worked with Arthur Sackler from the first medical conference that the

Sackler Foundation sponsored in China to the establishment of the *China Medical Tribune* and the Sackler Museum at Beida. I am grateful to him for letting me know that this history mattered not just for Western academics but for Chinese survivors of the ox pens as well.

Professors Zhang Zhuhong and Zhang Zhilian from the history department of Beijing University have also been greatly encouraging in this research. Each provided access to written sources and interviews that enriched the framework of analysis presented here. With their help and with support from the Office of the Vice President and the Foreign Students' Department at Beida, I was able to develop a comprehensive chronology of events before, during, and after the Cultural Revolution. My goal, as Chinese scholars and friends have come to understand, was never to besmirch the reputation of Beijing University. Its centrality in the events of the 1960s, its link to Yenching and to the princely gardens of the nineteenth century, is no accident. The very excellence of the minds that congregated in this corner of China made it repeatedly vulnerable to the designs of those bent upon destroying the tradition of refuge and reflection embodied by the old Ming He Yuan.

The Singing Crane Garden became for me, too, an oasis in times of turmoil. I began full-time research on this project a year before I became enveloped by administrative duties at Wesleyan University. Continued research for this book anchored me during the ravage of September 11, 2001. Working on ruined Chinese gardens has been a constant reminder of the fragility and importance of historical memory. Every time I reentered this work, I became more appreciative of the spaces for reflection that historical research provides. Not unlike works of art, history invites and creates a stillness in the midst of public frenzy.

At Wesleyan University, I have had four excellent Chinese research assistants: Yu Huan, Xie Yinghai, Michael Chang, and Chen-Wei Chung. They helped me find and translate key documents, including many nineteenth-century garden poems. Two members of the Asian Literature Department also provided help: Ellen Widmer with sources about Yenching, and Zhang Xiashen with translations from the Chinese. Debbie Sierpinski has once again worked with patience on the word-processing challenges of this project—our sixth manuscript together. John Wareham provided expert technical advice and help in reproducing all the images in this book. At Wesleyan, too, I have benefited from a Meiggs Grant that enabled me to take a leave of absence to bring this project to fruition. At the University of Pennsylvania Press, I have been privileged to work with John Dixon Hunt, an expert editor and path-breaking scholar of garden theory. It was his expertise and generosity of spirit that brought this work into the series on the history of landscape studies.

Finally, I want to pay tribute here to my family and friends who helped nourish the garden that became this book. Over the decade that it took to sort out the various histories of the Singing Crane Garden, they were tireless in sending me poems, tapes, cards, and essays about gardens, art, and suffering. Each helped flesh out the ideas that first accosted me outside the Sackler Museum on October 16, 1993. Each helped me realize that the garden is not only a physical space, but a spiritual opportunity as well. To dwell in landscaped spaces is to savor a delight that goes beyond flowers, lakes, trees, and rocks. It is to taste the eternal in the ephemeral. This is the main theme of the Song of Songs as well. I can think of no better way to show my gratitude to all who have helped me craft this book than to use the language of the Song of Songs in praise of garden lore:

You, who dwell in the garden,
Know that friends wait
To hear your voice,
Let it be heard now.

Introduction

A Garden Made of Language and Time

. . . It is not death
Has drawn me to this desolate world
I defy all waste and degradation

—These swaddling clothes
Are a sun that will not be contained in the grave

—Yang Lian, "Apologia to a Ruin"

Gardens are not merely earthly stuff. They occupy grounds in the mind as well. Some reach there by the beauty of their design, some by the power of their cultural symbolism. Many use both. Other gardens take up no space at all. Yet even as ruins, or as memories of ruins, they have the power to breathe life into worn words. They create spaciousness in dark times. This book explores strategies for creating spaciousness by translating what I have learned from the history of gardens into the garden that is history. It takes as its starting point a corner of China that managed to survive repeated devastation through fragile means such as language and the integrity of recollection. If the Singing Crane Garden (Ming He Yuan) can speak to us today, it is because its ruination was defeated by imagination, because voices from a distant past continue to speak about our predicament today.

The specific site that launched this inquiry lies in northwest Beijing. Removed from the bustle of the Tian An Men Square by several highways that ring the capital of China, the grounds of the Singing Crane Garden occupy a picturesque site at the heart of Beijing University (figure 1). A visitor who survived traffic-clogged streets and managed to gain entrance to the tightly guarded campus would have to continue on a northwest axis before reaching any sign of the Singing Crane Garden. A gray, new boulder in front of the

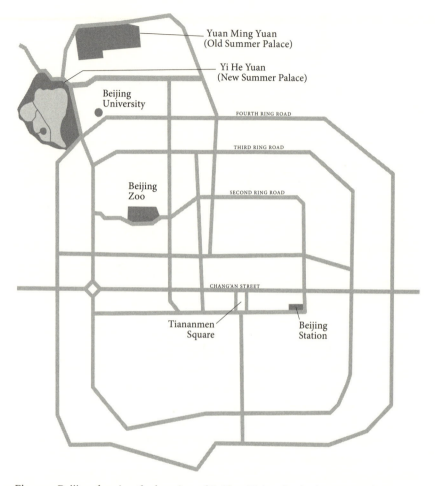

Figure 1. Beijing showing the location of Beijing University in the northwest area of the city. Drawn by Yishuo Hu.

Arthur M. Sackler Museum of Art and Archaeology commemorates the garden's name in bold characters and little historical detail (figure 2). This stone hints at a princely retreat of the nineteenth century while remaining quite mute about the atrocities that took place on these grounds in the 1960s. Cultural memory is evoked and dismissed all at once.

This double gesturing is limited not to one rock, one courtyard at Beijing University, or one city in China. Rather, such layered connotations have

Figure 2. New stone boulder inscribed with the characters "Ming He Yuan" (Singing Crane Garden). The calligraphy was done by Qigong, a surviving relative of the Manchu imperial family, who also suffered considerable persecution during the Cultural Revolution. The base of the boulder is set in a marble pedestal that commemorates the generosity of Jill Sackler in donating funds to the renovation of the grounds around the Arthur M. Sackler Museum of Art and Archaeology.

been exposed and explored by scholars of Chinese and Western gardens alike. Denis Cosgrove, the British geographer, for example, wrote about the iconography of landscapes with just such attentiveness to the "curtain" that veils culturally organized spaces. His argument, simply put, is that landscapes beckon us to practice a distinctive mode of seeing—"a way in which some Europeans have represented themselves and the world about them and their social relationship with it, and through which they have commented on social relations."[1] China, too, has a complex history of looking at the meanings of landscaped spaces. The Ming He Yuan boulder at Beijing University does not quite fit into these notions of representation. The paucity of physical evidence combined with politically informed reticence makes "reading" this garden a particularly interesting challenge.

The Chinese scholar Feng Jin hinted at this predicament in a recent essay about the concept of "scenery" in the Chinese garden. Although his focus is not on the Singing Crane Garden in Beijing, he does note that the shortage of material remains has forced scholars to reconstruct garden-making on the basis of literary sources scattered throughout a vast body of ancient documents. The reason for this shortage is mentioned at the end of Feng Jin's lengthy essay. The meanings of classical Chinese gardens, he suggests, are hard to decode "because the monopoly of the theory of class struggle prohibited any mention of literati culture."[2] That is to say, the intellectuals who both built and appreciated gardens have been smeared with political disapproval in the late twentieth century. Whereas Denis Cosgrove is free to piece together the iconography of the English landscape, Chinese scholars have made their way to this same subject hampered by the repressive politics of the Maoist era. Not only are there fewer gardens left to study, but the very language for their explanation has been decimated by decades of propaganda and murderously real class struggle.

Reading a garden such as the Ming He Yuan, therefore, requires narrative strategies that circle its muted terrain, that give voice to all that has been silenced through violence and indirect commemoration. Poetry is repeatedly used in this book because it is well suited for indirection. To be sure, Chinese gardens have always been at home in words. There is a long tradition of poetry about landscaped spaces. Poems, in turn, appeared all around the garden: on rocks, walls, corridors, pavilions, and even mountainsides. With war and revolution, however, both gardens and the refined literati consciousness that nurtured them came under attack. What is left is just words: fragile, halting snippets that mark a longing for leisure and contemplation in the very places where bamboo, chrysanthemums, and gingko no longer flower at ease. In this study, poems from the Chinese have been rendered into idiomatic English, often altering shape and sound, to convey to a twenty-first century reader a wordless yearning to make sense of loss and devastation.

Such a yearning may be discerned, for example, in the poetry of Yang Lian, a writer whose youth had been marred by the Cultural Revolution of the 1960s. A former Red Guard, Yang was part of a generation of artists who sought out the ruined landscape of northwest Beijing in order to come to terms with the ravage in their own lives. Shortly after the death of Mao Zedong in 1976, these artists congregated in the rice paddies that lay north, beyond the walls of Beijing University. Since the landscape outside had been intensely politicized, they sought out ruins to articulate their own severed connection to history. The broken stones of the old Summer Palace (Yuan Ming Yuan) provided an alternative to the denuded cultural imagination fostered in the university under the guidance of the Communist Party. Heading ever north, they created gardens of the mind out of words alone. Yang Lian's poem "Apologia to a Ruin" speaks to this ravaged landscape directly. Seeking what is no longer there, Yang asserts that the journey is nonetheless worth taking:

. . . the only hope that illuminated me
Faint star out of its time . . .
Pitiless chiaroscuro of my soul.[3]

Yang Lian was part of a generation intentionally heading north, away from the ardor of the Maoist era that had been identified with the red sun. Yang's friend and collaborator, the poet Bei Dao, even incorporated the idea of "north" into his pen name, which means "northern island." Away from the enforced collectivism of class struggle, these poets sought and found language for other landscapes. The visual evidence of the ruins in northwest Beijing became a fulcrum for meditations about loss and desolation—as well as about renewal. Yang Lian's poem concludes not with death, but with a willingness to defy "these swaddling clothes," with a desire to excavate "a sun that will not be contained in the grave."[4]

The history of the Singing Crane Garden is similarly illuminated by devastation. Around the gray boulder inside the exuberantly developing Beijing University, absence reigns. To map this terrain, one must learn to walk a little slower, listen more closely as time unfolds in guarded words. Like Yang Lian, I was also drawn to the northwest corner of Beijing by a darkened sun. I knew the traumatic history of the burning of the Summer Palace in 1860. I had studied the brutal impact of the Cultural Revolution upon Beijing University in the 1960s. But it was not death that pulled me on this project. Rather it was the possibility of cultural renewal in traumatized spaces. My ambition was to take the idea of the garden out of the ground and into the realm of history and language. In the end, the Singing Crane Garden may be no more than time and words. Yet in encompassing this space, both history and language may acquire new spaciousness, fresh meaning.

Winged Eaves and Liquid Light

The browning carapace of a pagoda may not seem like an auspicious place to think afresh about language and time. My own first glimpse of the Pavilion of Winged Eaves (Yi Ran Ting) in 1989 did not suggest the possibilities of

Figure 3. The Pavilion of Winged Eaves (Yi Ran Ting) in 1989.

renewed cultural imagination that thrive here. It was late May when I came upon the site, in the company of my five-year-old son. Most of our days in that spring of 1989 were engulfed by student demonstrations in Tian An Men Square. I was following the unfolding events with consuming interest. Having written a great deal about the struggle for science and democracy in modern China, I witnessed the tragic suppression of the student movement with dread and familiarity. The campus of Beijing University was, as many times before in the twentieth century, at the heart of student activism. To give my son a bit of relief from loudspeakers and protest posters, I took him for bike rides along the more isolated paths in the northwest corner of Beida. At first, the Pavilion of Winged Eaves was hardly visible among the weeds. It took the excited explorations of a five-year-old to uncover the broken slabs of stone leading to a square viewing area. Pillars that had once been painted bright red were now the color of dried blood. As I looked out from beyond the terrace railing, all I saw was scrawny trees and a tangle of electric wires (figure 3). Nothing here suggested that we had stumbled upon one of the most cherished meditation spots of the old Singing Crane Garden.

Nothing, except perhaps the ceiling. This was home to fifty identical *grus japonensis*—red-crowned cranes. Each painted bird filled to the brim a blue circle framed by an artfully subdued square of green. Each crane had its wings spread to the very edge of the formal, geometrical sky—a perfect image of frozen time. Below the masters of this dancing yet stationary heaven was a series of carefully brushed images of marble bridges, carved lions, and more buildings with winged eaves (figure 4). Nothing in the shadowy interior of the pagoda informed the visitor that these were scenes from the campus of Yenching University, the American-sponsored institution that had occupied these grounds before 1952, before the national Beijing University was moved out north, away from the neighborhood of the Forbidden City.

A decade after our discovery, in 1998, all that changed. China's foremost educational institution was celebrating its centenary, consciously laying claim both to the old Imperial University founded in 1898 as well as to the twentieth-century campus of Yenching. The brownish carapace was gone. Reddish pillars had been painted a sinewy green. Broken railings had been replaced with a simplified version of "veranda"-style woodwork that was tinted with a jarring red. The stone steps had been repaired (figure 5). The artificial hillock was reconstructed with new bricks. The cranes, too, had been touched up and looked more frozen in their broken flight. The scenic spots from the Yenching campus were repainted too, made more schematic,

Figure 4. Painted ceiling of the Pavilion of Winged Eaves, 1989.

Figure 5. Renovated Pavilion of Winged Eaves as it appeared in the summer of 1999.

more recognizable for the many alumni and visitors walking around with a newly published school map. At the entrance of the pavilion was a formal slab to mark the place of dead beauty (figure 6):

XIAO JING TING—SCHOOL SCENES PAVILION

The original name of the School Scenes Pavilion was Yi Ran Ting, which was part of the Singing Crane Garden refurbished in 1926 after the founding of Yenjing University, when it was decorated with ten famous spots of Yenjing University—hence its name of "School Scenes Pavilion." This name was retained during the restoration that begun in 1984.[5]

The official and repetitious language conveys the bare bones of the history buried here. Only two dates are carved in stone: 1926 and 1984. The decades before and after are consigned to silence. The gray marker erected in 1998 makes no mention of the *niu peng*—"ox pens"—erected at the foot of the pagoda to incarcerate and torture eminent professors during the 1960s. It is equally reticent about 1860, when the Singing Crane Garden was scorched by British armies on their way to the burning of the Summer Palace. It does not even nod toward the Sackler Museum of Art and Archaeology established on

Figure 6. Stone tablet installed in front of the Pavilion of Winged Eaves as restorations began in 1984. Photograph by the author.

the grounds of the former ox pens, and it keeps utterly quiet about the struggles that accompanied its design after the Tian An Men massacre of 1989. The School Scenes Pavilion is, like a child standing on good behavior, properly warned against talking to strangers. It keeps family secrets buried behind a naively verdant exterior.

To excavate voices that celebrated beauty and mourned its desolation on these grounds, one has to practice what the Italian chemist-writer Primo Levi called "hard listening." A survivor of Auschwitz, Levi knew how easily history swallows the evidence for its own existence. It is not only massive atrocities like the Holocaust that stifle our access to the past. The very passage of time (invariably codified and manipulated by political authorities) brings to us only the freshly painted bones of garden history. One has to dig below stone markers and refurbished monuments to hear what Levi called "the hoarse voices of those who can no longer speak."[6]

On the campus of Beijing University, such voices are marked by a reticent attachment to the old sites, old names, old knowledge. One of the most eloquent among them belongs to Hou Renzhi, a British-educated historical geographer who has been quietly reconstructing the history of Beijing and its princely gardens. In a slim, bilingual volume dedicated to the history of Bejing University, he includes a line drawing of the Yi Ran Ting that speaks volumes for the beauty that once thrived and was squelched here. A solitary pine and the winged roof give voice to the seasoned memory of a scholar who had been forced to repent for the historical knowledge that had set him apart from "revolutionary masses." Politically persecuted in 1957 and during the Cultural Revolution, this eminent graduate of Yenching University writes about his beloved campus in roundabout terms. Whereas European geographers such as Denis Cosgrove are able to stretch disciplinary boundaries with intellectual ease and theoretical verve, Hou Renzhi has undertaken the same project in China against great odds. For Cosgrove, the iconography of landscape is an opportunity to map relations of power and of perception across the history of English elites. Hou Renzhi's scholarly life, by contrast, has been characterized by political campaigns during which the Communist Party kept denouncing the literati values that once nourished garden spaces. Hou's book about the history of Beijing University is dedicated to a new, post–Cultural Revolution generation of undergraduates. It seeks to awaken in them an appreciation for the ground that lies beneath their feet. Hence the artful drawing of the Yi Ran Ting.

Within the political limitations of the 1980s (when the book was first published), the learned historian managed to hint at the pain buried around the pagoda with the winged eaves. In a particularly poignant and muted passage, the author departed from the obligatory optimism of socialist historiography. Having championed the expansion of geography into the realm of history and literature (much like Cosgrove), Hou Renzhi now speaks directly to those who will shape the iconography of landscape in the future, when cultural memory may be accessed more freely: "If we do not recall the past, we can hardly believe what a painful experience this quiet corner on our campus has undergone. We are sure, the past is not to be forgotten."[7] The explicit historical reference here is to 1860, which also ravaged the old Ming He Yuan. But with an informed ear one can hear a subtle reference to the suffering inflicted on Chinese intellectuals at Beijing University during the Cultural Revolution. Hou Renzhi knows that without recalling the past, without providing glimpses of the Yi Ran Ting, future generations will not be able to converse with the landscape, with history, with language itself.

A similarly muted reference to the Yi Ran Ting appears in an essay by Ji Xianlin, the eminent Sanskrit scholar who was also incarcerated in the ox pens of Beijing University. Like Hou Renzhi, Ji Xianlin has paid dearly for all the knowledge accumulated abroad, for his long-standing attachment to cultural memory. During the darkest years of the Cultural Revolution, he shared his incarceration quarters with Hou Renzhi, as well as another eminent scholar, Zhu Guanqian. A philosopher by training, Zhu had written extensively about the history of tragedy before he actually lived through one in the 1960s. In an essay dedicated to the memory of this "pen-mate," Ji Xianlin records the solace that landscaped spaces—or better yet, the informed memory of a vanishing world—provided during weeks and months of beatings and torture. Ji's essay describes how the garden helped Zhu Guanqian to preserve his sanity under duress.

Language was not much help in this nightmare. Each word, spoken or written, could become a liability in the eyes of Red Guards who monitored the activities and thoughts of aged prisoners. All that remained was the possibility of looking out of the window with informed eyes: "At night, after the lights were turned off, Zhu tossed and turned in his bed studying the famous Yi Ran Ting pavilion glimpsed through a window. . . . In the morning, he would run to a corner and practice *tai ji quan*. One time he was discovered by the so-called 'staff to promote reform.' They beat him fiercely. In the eyes of these young lords, our bodies and souls had committed grave sins."[8]

More than a century after its destruction, this remnant of the Singing Crane Garden provided comfort to the knowing eye. Like Hou Renzhi's drawing, it is a sliver of an ample past. Yet it sufficed to stem the tide of despair. Ji Xianlin even goes so far as to suggest that the spiritual practice of looking beyond the window of the ox pens, combined with the risky regime of martial arts, enabled Zhu Guanqian to overcome the temptation of suicide—a terrible desire to which many of their fellow intellectuals succumbed during the Cultural Revolution.

This evocative power of fragments is also explored by the American sinologist Stephen Owen in his path-breaking work on Chinese cultural memory. Far from needing an entire landscape to activate imagination, Owen argues, Chinese poets, writers, and thinkers were able to reconstruct entire worlds from snippets, from an old arrow head, from a nameless skull.[9] Why not the Yi Ran Ting? Why not use the fading light provided by this pavilion to begin to imagine how landscaped spaces can inform, enrich, and indeed heal the wounds of history?

The very name of this pavilion weaves it into a history that used to sanction and cherish reflection. Yi Ran Ting harks back as far as the Song dynasty, when scholar-official Ou-Yang Xiu (1007–1072) used it to play with the phrase "winged eaves." Serving in central China where mountain peaks invite rooftops to follow their rhythm, Ou-Yang Xiu delighted in letting his eyes roam from hill to pavilion, and back. Just as the actual structure at Beijing University provided solace for pained minds, so too, Ou-Yang Xiu's idea of *yi ran ting* promised inner peace and relief from the din of public life. Warmed by the friendship of fellow poets, the Song statesman envisioned a place where thoughts, like mountains, could rise on winged words.[10]

It took the power and privilege of an emperor to bind place and name in the capital city of Beijing. By the time of the Qing dynasty (1644–1911), pavilions with winged eaves dotted north and south China alike. The most beautiful, most daring ones were located in south and central China. In the north, where Manchu rulers held the reigns of government, the landscape was less suitable for soaring cornices. Nonetheless, the idea of *yi ran ting* endured because it offered a verbal link to the imaginative landscape of the south. The Qianlong emperor (who reigned as Hongli from 1711 to 1795) stood at the apex of this aesthetic of cultural domination. Not content to encode the world beyond the Great Wall with his cultural authority, Qianlong took pride in visiting sites and writing poems about the gardens of the south as well.

Some 42,000 of his poems survived, each marking a place, a moment— not unlike the red seal on each item of his vast imperial art collection.[11] One such verse, titled "Yi Ran Ting," marks a specific spot in northwest Beijing. Located on the periphery of Qianlong's Summer Palace, this promontory was not unlike the one occupied by the School Scenes Pavilion today. Set apart from the main road leading to Yuan Ming Yuan and to the temple complex on Jade Mountain further north, this was a place to sit and contemplate the passage of time:

Meandering toward the west,
I came upon a pavilion.
Seated under its winged eaves,
I savor liquid light.
Blue seems near enough to touch,
Green beams afar, a taste of the untamed.[12]

Qianlong's words would echo throughout the centuries that followed the emperor's excursion to Yi Ran Ting. Liquid light and a taste of the untamed continued to attract princes and scholars alike. The fact that a famous ruler had stopped to notice nature here added cultural glory to an already gracious setting. Place and name were thus joined in an enduring bond. The Singing Crane Garden that came to house the old pavilion became part of a northern lineage of respite from the eventfulness of the public past. In ways that Qianlong could not have imagined, imprisoned intellectuals in the 1960s looked for and found here liquid light as well.

The character *yi* in classical Chinese has several meanings. It connotes "wings" as well as "refuge" and "assistance."[13] Space imaginatively reconstructed can aid the mind to soar. It can also shelter intellectuals from violent events. The Yi Ran Ting which stands on the cement hill at Beijing University today is a silent witness to both these possibilities. Its upturned roof protects more than the school scenes repainted in 1998. It frames the spaciousness of historical reflection possible on layered grounds.

The density of voices belonging to those who built, celebrated, mourned, and commemorated the Singing Crane Garden would be a meaningless cacophony without the Yi Ran Ting. This physical link between nineteenth-century princes and twentieth-century Red Guards allows us to decode different meanings of experiential time in one corner of China. It is as if one patch of a large quilt hinted at the design of the missing whole. We may never know the fullness of beauty that was the entire coverlet. But even a remnant, imaginatively grasped, expands the possibilities of historical understanding. In the words of Gaston Bachelard (a French philosopher who explored the interstices between physical and temporal existence), "Space that has been seized upon by the subject is not an object to be measured by the estimates of the surveyor. It has been lived in . . . with all the partiality of the imagination."[14]

To Still the Burning Fires of the Mind

Bachelard's insight about the role that imagination plays in expanding the boundaries of space is especially useful in mapping the garden that once surrounded Yi Ran Ting. The space occupied by the Singing Crane Garden depended upon and nourished subjectivity. To study it, in turn, one has to call to mind more than the structures that occupied the grounds surrounding the Pavilion of Winged Eaves. The surveyor of this site has to take into account the accelerating pace of an increasingly brutal history. It is in that framework that the respite provided by the Ming He Yuan begins to take shape in both words and time. This enlarged site may be understood in terms of Denis Cosgrove's "symbolic landscapes"—but only if we grasp how metaphorical thinking became an increasingly endangered activity in nineteenth- and twentieth-century China. Encoding and decoding iconographies depends upon a safe historical distance from the subject under scrutiny. The distance diminished rapidly for Chinese intellectuals enmeshed in social revolution.

When Cosgrove cites Erwin Panovsky and John Ruskin to develop a paradigm for the social formation of landscapes, he is appealing to an intelligentsia that did not fear for its life, that contemplated the legacy of the past with a certain amount of equanimity. Hou Renzhi, by contrast, paid dearly for every bit of scholarly work that did not fit the paradigm of class struggle. Similarly, such noted garden historians as Chen Congzhou and Hu Dongchu were repeatedly persecuted for their efforts to document classical spaces where contemplation thrived. Chen Congzhou's masterful study of Suzhou gardens published in 1956 was amply illustrated with poetic allusions to underscore the symbolic significance of the landscape. For this accomplishment, Chen was condemned as a "rightist," demoted from his university position and ostracized until the 1980s. Hu Donchu, the author of the 1981 work *The Way of the Virtuous: The Influence of Art and Philosophy on Chinese Garden Design,* had paid his dues as well. A survivor of the Cultural Revolution, imprisoned in the ox pens, Hu had to bide his time until Mao died before he could turn to scholarship and the possibility of linking space and thought.

China's scorched terrain, however, is not the only place where a garden of history took root as contemplative spaces vanished from sight. Simon Schama's monumental inquiry *Landscape and Memory* also took its inspiration from a wounded imagination. Journeying back to Germany and Poland, where Jews and their cultured attachment to the past had been brutally extinguished, Schama acknowledges that he is constructing a refuge in the mind, an imaginary landscape to house what is missing in space. His study gives absence a presence. It seeks, in Schama's own words, to see how "through a mantle of ash can emerge a shoot of restored life."[15]

The Manchu prince Mianyu, owner of the Singing Crane Garden, would have understood this metaphor quite well. He lived through times in which ashes consumed much of his garden, but not the mind that cherished possibilities of cultural renewal. Mianyu was born to privilege and power. At that time of his birth in 1814, his father had already reigned for fourteen years as the Jiaqing emperor. By the time of Mianyu's death in 1865, the Mandate of Heaven had been sorely tested by conflict with the West and by internal rebellion within. Physical spaces for imperial refuge had been assaulted, most notably the burning of the Summer Palace. Leisurely meditation on the harmony between man and nature had vanished with the pressure to defend the country and the court by force of arms. Prince Mianyu witnessed and took part in all this. His garden, though short lived, was part of a survival strategy that went beyond the space it occupied in a northwest corner of the imperial capital. It became, in the embroidering of memory, a shoot of restored life.

As the fifth, and youngest, son of the Jiaqing emperor, Mianyu had little hope of ruling China directly. When his father died in 1820, the six-year-old boy was elevated to prince of the second rank with the title of Hui Jun Wang. In 1839, in the middle of the Opium War, his princedom was elevated to the first degree with the title Hui Qin Wang. By 1853, when the Taiping Rebellion threatened to overthrow the war-weakened dynasty, Mianyu took charge of the forces defending the imperial capital—with the augmented title of "Feng ming da jiang jun" (Worthy Military General in Charge of Sustaining the Mandate).[16] It was with such heavy burdens in mind that Prince Hui designed and cherished the Singing Crane Garden.

The site for this refuge was granted to him in 1835 by his second brother, who reigned as the Daoguang emperor from 1821 to 1850. Granting gardens to close kin had been a Manchu practice for more than a century before Mianyu came to own the Singing Crane Garden. These special gifts were marks of imperial favor, down payments on loyalty and service expected from those who became neighbors of the emperor's Summer Palace. The actual plot of land occupied by Mianyu's garden had been part of an imperial enclosure called Spring's Mirror Garden (Jing Chun Yuan), which his father began to subdivide for his children (figure 7). A small, eastern portion was granted by the Jiaqing emperor to his favorite daughter in 1802. After his death, the Daoguang emperor saw fit to grant the much larger, western section to his brother, Prince Hui. Five years before China's defeat in the first Opium War, eighteen years before he placed the fate of the capital in the hands of Mianyu, the supreme ruler of China understood the necessity of having a skilled and loyal brother nearby in the outskirts of Beijing.

The physical terrain of the Singing Crane Garden, and that of neighboring princely retreats, will be explored in more detail later. For now, it is the symbolic landscape that has to be brought into focus. As a Manchu prince, Mianyu was prepared to live with the past in mind. Coming from a nomadic

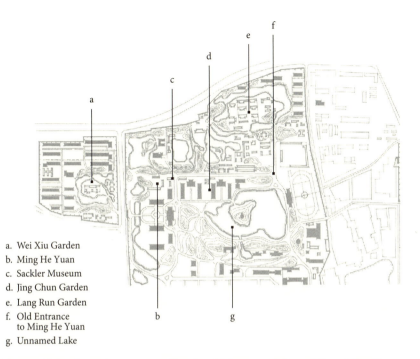

a. Wei Xiu Garden
b. Ming He Yuan
c. Sackler Museum
d. Jing Chun Garden
e. Lang Run Garden
f. Old Entrance
   to Ming He Yuan
g. Unnamed Lake

Figure 7. Princely gardens surrounding the old Summer Palace of Yuan Ming Yuan as noted inside the campus of Beijing University. Original map courtesy of Professor Hou Renzhi. This section redrawn by Yishuo Hu of the University of Pennsylvania School of Design.

tribe that occupied China in 1644, he had been schooled to value both Manchu traditions and the Chinese classics. Fluent in both languages, this nobleman lived in several cultural universes at once. When traveling beyond the Great Wall to the imperial hunting grounds of Jehol, he became a Manchu tribesman mindful of his authority among Mongol and Tibetan allies who also shared his Lamaist Buddhist faith. In the Forbidden City of Beijing or near the Summer Palace, he was a Confucian official, prepared to serve with virtue the ruler of the realm.

In both worlds, Mianyu lived quite literally in the light of the past. In his posthumous collection entitled *Ai ri zhai ji* (Collection from the Studio of Cherished Days), the owner of the Singing Crane Garden summarized some of the wisdom he gained in his garden as well as in his more public life as an imperial kinsman. Addressing himself to a new generation of princes corrupted by wealth, opium, as well as the growing threat of internal rebellion and war with the West, Mianyu wrote: "Patience and the power of words can make or unmake a man. Haste in the pursuit of honor, like ill used words, place one's virtue at risk. Ordinary folk rush about to try to outwit fate and believe everything they hear. A gentleman learns to still the burning fires of his mind. Therefore, his words reflect his heart."[17] Burning fires were anything but metaphorical by the time Mianyu's descendants edited his works. Nonetheless, the power of words endured. Even if gardens could no longer house patience and virtue, the mind held on to them even as political and cultural change made them increasingly obsolete.

The tenacity of this attachment to cultural memory has also been noted by Craig Clunas in his study of Ming dynasty scholar gardens in the lower Yangtze area. Here, too, landscaped spaces occupied a double life between the physical and the symbolic. In contrast to Ming gardens, however, Qing princely retreats were not owned by Confucian literati. Their "cultural syntax," to borrow from Clunas, was more mixed and multivocal. The Yangtze delta gardens of scholar-officials were anchored in the agriculture, poetry, and painting of the south. They were "fruitful sites" in ways that Mianyu's garden never hoped to be.[18] Imperial retreats bred dreams of leisure and hopes for respite from the increasingly arduous (and increasing unsuccessful) effort to reestablish Manchu authority over a war-shattered China. Gardens that had once been part of a complex cultural arrangement came to stand for the waning possibility of quieting the burning fires of the mind.

To understand this second, nonphysical life of the garden, we have to look beyond the conventional parameters of landscape history. John Dixon Hunt, a pioneer in garden theory, has argued that we must turn our focus to a broader spaciousness that he terms "the art of the millieu." In *Greater Perfections: The Practice of Garden Theory,* Hunt points out that designed spaces are "both a physical object and a place experienced by a subject . . . the idea of a garden is at the same time paradoxically composed of perceptions of gardens in many different ways and different people and different culture and periods."[19] Lest this angle of vision become too diffuse, Hunt goes on to anchor the idea of the garden in the soil of language itself. Building upon the work of previous garden historians, he points out that most words for "garden" are rooted in the simple, important idea of enclosure. Whether one starts with "yard" in English, "hof" in Dutch, "gradina" in Romanian, the path leads directly to the idea of a fenced-in space (from the Indo-European *gher* [fence]).[20]

Figure 8. Chinese character *yuan*—originally suggesting an open park, later connoting a "garden" that encloses lakes, artificial hills, and pavilions.

The Chinese ideograph for "garden" mirrors this idea with its own multiple connotations. *Yuan* originally referred to an open park, a hunting preserve of the rich and the powerful (figure 8). Later, in the course of Chinese history, lettered gentlemen developed a taste for more intimate enclosures. Consequently, *yuan* took on the meaning of a cultivated space where one planted seeds of thought as well as seeds of plants. This evolution from a broad, nearly public *yuan* to a bordered, more private universe replete with lakes, hills, fir trees, lotus flowers, pavilions, and courtyards parallels the rise of the Confucian literati in the long centuries from the Han dynasty through the Song.[21]

Confucius himself hinted at the harvest of insight possible in a garden when he told his disciples: "The wise enjoys the streams, the benevolent the mountains; the wise are active, the benevolent passive, the wise are happy and the benevolent live long."[22] For the Master of the *Analects,* as for the Manchu Prince Mianyu in the nineteenth century, the natural universe served as a mirror for the moral virtues of men. The four lines that border the character *yuan* came to symbolize the walls (both of stone and of time) that enclosed the garden. Inside the four walls of the garden, we find the radical for "earth/soil," which is the essential precondition for any garden. The small square at the center evokes lakes and ponds, which mirror both the sky and the mind of the observer.[23] The play of strokes below the waters suggests trees and rocks that give the garden its distinctive character. Seen in this way, the garden is a frame within a frame. It demands discrimination (and often privileged education and leisure time) for the slow-paced unfolding of the carefully constructed vistas and cultural symbols.

The study of history also demands borders and boundaries. Inquiry into an event depends upon a fixed temporal framework. Like the hedge around the garden, the historian's angle of vision must be initially constricted in order to give evidence its full weight. The Singing Crane Garden in this study is an example of such a framing device. Starting with the garden walls erected by Prince Hui and ending with the construction of the Sackler Museum of Art and Archaeology at Beijing University, this history uncovers various voices that give this corner of China its experiential depth.

Had the Singing Crane Garden been a walled pleasure palace alone, it would not have generated the many ripples of grief and insight that endured throughout the nineteenth and twentieth centuries. The fertility of experience found on its scarred grounds is the result of the subtleness of imagination already apparent when Prince Mianyu wrote about fires of the mind. The Pavilion of Winged Eaves, as well as other physical remains that dot the campus of Beijing University today, are part of the framework that helps us understand both Prince Hui as well as inmates of the "ox pens" such as Ji Xianlin and Zhu Guanqian. Each found this site to be a protected space where language and time could unfold multiple meanings unhindered by the brutality of the public past.

Jing and *Dong*: Stillness and Motion in the Garden of History

The garden of historical memory thus took the place once occupied by historical gardens. As freedom to move through graceful spaces contracted over time, other skills of artful reflection came to the fore. The wealth of contemplative possibilities nurtured by classical landscaped spaces allowed Chinese intellectuals to survive long periods of spiritual desecration. Gardens, after all, had been places where mental discipline had been a central concern. In the words of Dorothy Graham, an American traveler who roamed the princely estates of Beijing in the 1930s, the limited enclosure of the yuan was designed to "calm the raging seas, temper the wind and adjust nature to the scale of man's encompassing will."[24] For Graham, the turbulence tamed by Chinese gardens was largely metaphorical. Even the descendants of Manchu noblemen whom she visited and chatted with before the outbreak of war with Japan were able to stand a bit to the side of turbulent events. As distance from history vanished in the 1940s, the challenge of calming minds grew ever more intense.

Fortunately, that challenge had been embedded in classical garden design and provided a lexicon for living through, living with turbulence. *Jing* and *dong* are two aspects of the classical garden that are particularly useful in mapping the symbolic terrain of the Singing Crane Garden. The first suggests stillness, the second motion. Their layered and joined connotations go far beyond angles of vision provided by standing still or perambulating through a classical Chinese garden. Jing and dong are aspects of space, of persons and of history as well. Each has at least two faces, two phases, two voices—or better put, this duality hints at a multifaceted predicament that the garden mirrors and evokes.

Jing centers on the idea of unruffled waters. A smooth lake, a well-designed work of art, the echo of a temple bell are all part of the idea of jing. There are several Chinese homonyms for stillness that use this sound. Two that may be most useful here are one that has the "standing" radical built into it and another that combines the radical for "verdant" combined with the idea of "grasping." The first *jing* is a classical phrase used to suggest quiet, tranquility, as well as the willpower to pacify a rebellion in an unruly border area. The second *jing* (identical in pronunciation and tone) suggests calm and stillness, as in a sea after the storm.

Garden viewing had long depended on jing, upon quiet watching—which meant that one literally had to stop walking, still the mind, allow a scene to emerge out of carefully structured greenery in an unhurried fashion. Jing depends upon—and creates—an inner quietude analogous to the introspection of the historian who seeks to make sense out of the discrete, fragmented pieces of evidence that frame a subject of inquiry.

Like a guest who has crossed the garden gate, the student of the past must also slow down, bend a bit to try on an angle of contemplation that may do justice to the complex, shadow-laden terrain. Standing still, one may be able to better fathom one corner of the garden of history. Jing is a quality of attentiveness used in this study to focus on specific sites within the old Singing Crane Garden, and within the gracefully designed Yenching University that thrived in northwest Beijing in the 1930s. Jing also helps illuminate moments of historical memory that offered solace to such beleaguered intellectuals as Zhu Guanqian during their incarceration in the ox pens.

Stillness in the garden, as in history, is short lived. It is necessarily followed by dong—a concept that suggests more than physical motion through shifting landscapes. At its core, this character centers on the idea of "power"—a muscle grown tough by heavy exertion. In garden viewing, dong is a gentle invitation to proceed along enclosed corridors dotted with windows that invite the eye to roam across artfully framed scenes. On the terrain of the Singing Crane Garden, however, another more violent idea of *yun dong*—"political mobilizations"—has reigned for decades. Especially during the terror of the Red Guards, "movement" was a heavy-handed form of enforced ambulation, of required dislodgement from loyalties to the past, a violent uprooting of historical memories. The historian who would map this landscape has to partake of dong as well. Motion, in this project, implies more than the effort required to gather new sources, add new voices to a complex event such as the conflagration of 1860 or the Cultural Revolution of the 1960s. It requires, as this study shows, a reexamination of past certainties and conventional notions about the causality of both war and revolution.

Without jing, neither the garden nor history would make sense. Stillness and contemplation are prerequisites for the creation of meaning. Yet this is also true for dong, the effortful extension of vision beyond what is close at hand. This double challenge lies at the heart of garden viewing as well. Chen Congzhou, a seasoned survivor of many historical upheavals, describes mobility and stillness as two facets of a singular garden experience:

When looked at from a fixed position, the beauty of the changing seasons changes with the mood of man. . . . A garden without water, clouds, shadows, sounds, morning twilight and sunset is a garden devoid of natural beauty. For these, though ethereal, set off the actual scenes of a garden. Motion also exists in repose. Sitting in front of a rockery complete with horizontal and vertical holes . . . one would have an illusion of motion though the hill is at rest. The surface of water looks mirror-calm despite ripples. Likewise, a painting may look dead on the surface but is alive and moving all the same. A thing in repose is motionless if it is without vitality. Hence, we have the key to garden design in the relationship between in-motion [*dong*] and in-position [*jing*] garden viewings.[25]

Three and a half centuries before this Shanghai-based intellectual was free to ruminate about jing and dong, another Chinese scholar had begun to codify the various elements that lend complexity to garden viewing. Ji Cheng was the seventeenth-century author of *Yuan Ye* (The Craft of Gardens). Ji was an impoverished scholar from the picturesque and wealthy province of Jiangsu. By the time he published his compendium on garden design in 1634, the Ming dynasty was on the verge of collapse. Hard times had reached far south of the Great Wall. Manchu nomads already dreamt of a change in the mandate of heaven. Nonetheless, one decade before the end of the Ming, Ji Cheng took it upon himself to articulate the accumulated wisdom of classical aesthetics specifically as it related to its physical expression in landscaped spaces. He coupled the well-known concept of "yuan" with the less artful expression of "craft" (*ye*) to suggest practical strategies for garden design. Previous scholars had bought, designed, painted, and versified gardens, while leaving details about beams, stones, waterways, and plantings to professional gardeners who had a lower social status. By contrast, Ji Cheng set out to document technical aspects of design in a way that would flesh out the aspirations of his educated contemporaries. Craft, he argued, was the concrete way to create a garden that would enable one to nourish the mind: "to live as a hermit in the midst of the town."[26]

A Daoist or a Buddhist hermit would have no difficulty nourishing the mind in the harmonious setting of a mountain temple. Scholar-officials of the Ming, and later Manchu princes, however, were weighed down by the cares of office and palace politics. Ji Cheng had understood the dilemmas of the rich and the powerful and found ingenious ways to articulate various strategies that would combine motion and stillness, experiences of nature with the numinous beyond.

Drawing upon a large literature that linked gardening arts with artful contemplation, *Yuan Ye* played with the intermingling of scenery and sentiment in a way that expanded the meaning of both. One specific technique codified by Ji Cheng was "borrowed views." This was a scheme for drawing into the limited enclosure of the garden trees, mountains, vistas from far beyond so as to inspire the eye and the mind to seek out a vastness within. In borrowing views, a contemporary scholar points out, "the designer's intentions and scenery are co-arising," and the garden with "borrowed views" enjoins visitors to new occasions of "co-presenting and approaches their experience half-way in further conjunctions of sentiment and scenery."[27]

In effect, Ji Cheng's crafted structuring of vision created an event out of the physical stuff within and beyond the garden gates. It created a temporal flow, much like the historical narrative of a historian who seeks to anchor her subject in the shifting sands of time. An event is not merely a fixed moment of time when something happens. Even as dramatic and devastating an occurrence as the burning of the Summer Palace cannot be seen in isolation. The historian, too, depends on borrowed views, on the voices and memories of subjects close to the fiery vortex created by Lord Elgin's troops in October 1860. In this book, I have used the voice of a neighboring witness, Prince Yi-huan (1840–1849)—owner of the garden next to the Singing Crane Garden—to paint a more complex picture of what was lost and what endured in northwest Beijing. This history of ruination in nineteenth- and twentieth-century China draws upon the same wellspring of experience as Ji Cheng did, while expanding the idea of "borrowed views" to intellectual history as well.

In Ji's classic there was ample room for motion and stillness, for presence as well as emptiness. In fact, one of the key themes illustrated in *Yuan Ye* are structures ranging from wooden pillars to stone tiles—all surrounding a "central void"—a space framed by markers arranged in a way that invites the visitor to contemplate what is missing at the core.[28] By 1644, the empty center was no longer a poetic way of envisioning garden design. The "center" of power in Beijing had literally become emptied by rebels and invaders, and a new dynasty was taking shape among the ruins of the old. Here, too, an aspect of landscape design became extended into historical experience.

The "central void" was no longer a space to be contemplated with equanimity, but a trauma to live through, to give voice to. What was once an artful space bounded by pillars and stones had to be mapped with language instead. Historical memory took the place of garden design, much like the fate of Ji Cheng's own manuscript—which disappeared from circulation until it was discovered by a Chinese scholar at Tokyo's Imperial University in 1921. Uprooted, dislodged in both time and place, *Yuan Ye* made its way back to China in the 1930s just as war was breaking out and intellectuals began to cope with political disintegration once again.[29] The idea of living "like a hermit in town" became even less tangible than it had been at the end of the Ming. The tenacity of its appeal, however, lies in the very history that spelled disaster for physical gardens. What once flourished in space now took root in the mind.

The devolution of the physical garden can easily be mistaken as death. And indeed, there are many signs in China today of this phenomenon as chronicled in John Minford's essay "The Chinese Garden: Death of a Symbol." Minford's focus is on cluttered, crowded spaces such as apartment houses in Hong Kong and formerly gracious gardens in Suzhou where all that lingers from the past are poetic names, now gutted of affective meaning.[30] In contrast to Minford's bleak assessment, this book reveals an enduring search for cultural meaning in the very places where ruination appeared to be most extreme. On the very site of the destroyed Singing Crane Garden and the ox pens of the Cultural Revolution, the quest for self-knowledge grew ever more acute over time. In the midst of chaos and disorder, seeds of renewed vision arose from the ground up.

What began to wane at the end of the nineteenth century is the very idea of a retreat from politics. Techniques used to muffle the sound of public events temporarily lost their efficacy—and soon thereafter, their legitimacy. Nonetheless, words that framed that longing endured. On the grounds of the old Singing Crane Garden, it was a foreign architect—Henry K. Murphy (1877–1954)—who brought back some of the structural elements codified by Ji Cheng. Using winged roofs and cinnabar pillars, Murphy managed to create Yenching University, a campus for liberal learning where an attachment to historical memory was both sanctioned and valued. Although the Maoist revolution attacked both the ideal of liberal learning and the physical structures of Yenching, the site retained its capacity for "envelopment." This is a concept developed by philosopher Edward Casey in his book *The Fate of Place*. Envelopment describes the tenacity of solace in certain locations that goes far beyond material elements. Drawing upon a wide range of sources, Casey calls upon historians to go past "the hard shell of containing surfaces" in order to unearth the process through which a place surrounds us "no longer as an airtight, immobile limit—but as envelopment itself."[31]

This history of the Singing Crane Garden uses Casey's concepts to map a terrain beyond the immobile (and nearly forgotten) shards of an imperial pleasure palace. My goal here is not only to document events that gave birth to Mianyu's garden in the 1830s and its ruination in the 1860s and 1960s. Rather, I hope to evoke the spaciousness of imagination that survived in the midst of trauma and destruction. Making sense of envelopment in the midst of disaster depends upon a slow-paced, circuitous inquiry. Hou Renzhi hinted at this process in his own book about the gardens of Beijing University. Addressing himself to a new generation of career-minded, politically savvy Chinese students, the aged scholar argued for a change of pace, for a little less dong, a bit more jing—or better yet, for more attentiveness to the gravity of historical memory in the very place where forgetfulness had reigned for so long: "As you roam around the Unnamed Lake, appreciating the scenic beauty reflected in the water and feeling relaxed and delighted after hours of intensive study, have you ever asked yourself how the lake came to be what it is? And when you step out of the library or the laboratory and stroll by yourself, totally refreshed, among woods surrounding the lake, have you ever wondered who built the secluded paths?"[32]

Give Voice to the Past

Hou Renzhi asked these questions in the 1980s, when Beijing University was just beginning to recover from the atrocities of the Cultural Revolution. The Pavilion of Winged Eaves had not yet been renovated. It sat as a mute, browning witness to a past that had no place in the official recollections of the university. Plans for the Sackler Museum of Art and Archaeology had not been finalized, though discussions between party officials and the foreign donor had begun. Professor Hou was an enthusiastic supporter of the project, a consultant about the history of the Singing Crane Garden and a quiet accomplice to the unmentionability of the ox pens that had occupied these grounds in the recent past. All that Hou Renzhi could do is orient the forthcoming project in relationship to the landscape he knew so well: "A new exhibition hall for archaeology is to be built southwest of the Yi Ran Pavilion with the aid of the American Dr. Sackler Foundation. This is a step forward in the remarkable progress made recently by our university in its international exchange programs."[33]

This cheerful tone was meant to encourage officials to proceed with the project, despite their reservations about bringing funding from the capitalist West onto the Beida campus. In the early 1980s, Hou Renzhi could not have anticipated the derailment—and near death—of the Sackler Museum project in the wake of the political turbulence of 1989. All that the learned geographer could do is to place markers, a framework of physically anchored historical memory, around the museum project. The new archaeology museum, Hou Renzhi eagerly noted, would be linked in spirit and in location to the Yenching archaeology department, which had been dismantled and absorbed by the new Beijing University after the establishment of communist rule in 1949. With the new museum, Hou Renzhi foresaw, would come further sanctions for a fuller, scholarly engagement with a past that had been so often attacked.

After the opening of the Sackler Museum in May 1993, Beijing University's archaeology department did indeed fulfill the muted hopes expressed a decade earlier. In fact, when the museum mounted an exhibition of the history of archeological studies in Beijing, the visual link between past and present was made amply clear. The old Yenching exhibition hall was portrayed alongside the new museum with the aid of classical Chinese phrases. An aged, gray stone structure seemed to reach out to the colorful, winged roof of the Sackler institution while a Confucian saying guided the viewer in interpreting the message: *wen gu er zhi xin, ji wan kai lai*—"cherish the past to know the present, continue to march toward the future." Nine carefully chosen Chinese characters summed up the public version of historical memory at Peking University. Yes, the past is to be treasured, but only if it leads to a full-hearted appreciation of the new. The point was to move forward, with confidence—and one assumes, faith in a socialist future shaped by the guidance of the Communist Party. The new museum of art and archaeology served as a useful framework for an inspirational narrative about a history in which shadows had to remain unnamed.

This didactic message had nothing to say about the ravage that destroyed the old Summer Palace, or about Henry Murphy's efforts to gather relics in northwest Beijing. The new archaeology museum was designed, as we shall see, as a gracious home for shards of the ancient past. At the same time, it had to remain reticent about what happened to those remnants during the Cultural Revolution, what happened to scholars who were attacked simply for doing research about a past that had been condemned as "feudal" and as "bourgeois." A new museum was born out of a covenant to say little about the destructions that surrounded it.

Memory and mourning had no place in the new, beautiful building that stood on the grounds of the Singing Crane Garden. To go beyond the formulaic injunction of *wen gu er zhi xi, ji wang kai lai,* one has to turn to older voices that once surrounded the Ming He Yuan. One such voice that helps illuminate the past is that of Prince Yihuan, nephew and neighbor of the owner of the Singing Crane Garden. In the decades after the ravage of 1860, this younger Manchu prince continued to visit the ruined gardens of northwest Beijing in a conscious effort to articulate a grief that had no room in the public life of the Qing dynasty. A man deeply implicated in the politics of his day, Yihuan nonetheless knew that poetry was the only way to mark the void that remained in China's landscape and identity in the wake of historical trauma. In a work entitled "Visiting Ming He Yuan in the Company of My Ninth Brother," he instructs a still younger man in the art of memory and mourning:

Airy pavilions and stately halls—
ground into oblivion.

White mulberries swallowed by the blackest seas,
and you don't grieve?

Still seeking miracles? A rescuing dragon?
Nothing but bitter dreams.

No matter how fierce the tiger of regret,
we can defy it still.

Come, sit under these winged eaves,
give voice to what is gone.[34]

Written in the fall of 1860, this poem reaches beyond the grounds of the Singing Crane Garden. It comes forward to challenge and console those who seek knowledge of a missing past. Unlike the classical slogans that framed the exhibition about archaeological studies in the Sackler Museum, this use of classical language leaves room for doubt, for grief, for all the ruins that have no home in physical structures. The garden that was destroyed in space acquired a second life in the words of those committed to give voice to what is gone.

A historian of ruined landscapes, like Prince Yihuan, has to translate a past of wood and stone into a tapestry of words. The sinologist Frederick Mote suggested that this task is made easier for us by the Chinese tradition itself, which had long accustomed itself to translation from the broken remains of living history to the fragile, enduring medium of linguistic narrative. China, Mote notes, has the longest, most complex documentation of mankind's past precisely because it "constantly scrutinized the past as recorded in words and caused it to function in the life of the present."[35] The problem that became acute on the site of the Singing Crane Garden was how to revive the past through words that had also come under attack.

Much like the Singing Crane Garden in its time, a narrative that would contain its ravage and its renewal needs a framework that goes beyond conventional history. Were the narrative too close to fiery events, memory would have no room to speak its halting tale. Dori Laub, a psychiatrist who has written about the "art of trauma," suggests ways to listen to what is being said, and also silenced, by the words of history: "Indirect pointing to past meanings is an essential element in the art of trauma, in which the aim is not to come to an 'objectively real' depiction of an event but to create a protected space wherein the remembrance of traumatic experience can begin, if only haltingly, to occur."[36]

I also used indirect pointing in this study by moving my narrative back and forth around the fulcrum that is the Singing Crane Garden. I have not shied away from the traumatic events that changed the shape of the garden and the fate of those who lived and studied on its terrain. At the same time, I have chosen to approach those events, through the voices and lives of a wide range of dramatis personae. Some were close to the epicenter of disaster, some quite far away. My goal has been to bring the past forward in time. Like the poet Yang Lian, I have been lingering among ruins (and ruined lives) not for the sake of death, but to illuminate a landscape that remains shadowy even today.

Chapter 1
Singing Cranes and Manchu Princes

a place where thought
can take its shape
as quietly in the mind
as water in a pitcher . . .
—Wendell Berry, *"The Thought of Something Else"*

You do not have to be a Confucian scholar or a Manchu prince to know the value of a place where thought can take its shape at ease. Wendell Berry, a contemporary American poet of the South, likens the garden to water in a pitcher. Nothing is simpler, less adorned, less hard to find, yet more difficult to design. A garden, if well planned, is a place where one can get away from the clutter of daily life. An effective garden scours the mind and the soul. Contemplating what the Chinese call the "bones" of the garden—be they rocks, trees, water, or flowers—one is brought close to the architecture of the self. If one is truly fortunate, one is able to reshape one's innermost being in the presence of the garden.

This transformation was the goal and privilege of men like Mianyu and Yihuan. What made gardens even more precious in their lifetime was the fact that quietude of mind was hard won and difficult to hold on to. The more violent the events that marked their days, the more tenacious became the dream of a place where thought could take shape like water in a pitcher. Such a longing for stillness in the midst of chaos may be glimpsed visually in the photographs of Chinese gardens taken by Oswald Siren at the end of World War II. His masterful study, *Gardens of China*, was first published in 1949 on the eve of Mao Zedong's conquest of the mainland. Siren's camera captured possibilities for reflections that were being destroyed by political upheaval. In the midst of war and revolution, these black-and-white images convey both

Figure 9. "Gourd-shaped garden gateway in Cheng Wang Fu," Beijing. Photographed by Oswald Siren for *The Gardens of China* (New York, 1949), p. 78.

the decay of actual gardens as well as the imperishable ideals that nurtured their beauty.

One particular image speaks volumes about the subtle angles of light needed to see the garden in its own time. Simply labeled "Gourd-shaped garden gateway in Cheng Wang Fu, Peking," this photograph beckons the viewer to savor the spaciousness of historical images (figure 9). At first glance, you might think this is a study of gate architecture since the dark center of the image is indeed an artful opening that suggests an upright vegetable. It is not the gourd, however, that illuminates the image. The slanting sunlight from the end of the corridor beyond the gate is the real focus here. Peeling beams guard the passage, like so many silent witnesses to a slow-paced journey. The luminosity of the afternoon pours out of the gourd-gate with unrestrained generosity. It casts a bright halo on two slabs of well-worn rock. The "brush-handle" pattern of the outer balustrade echoes the bamboo grove that thrives beyond the gate.[1]

"Come in, amble," the image says. "Come in, stay a while," the garden says. "Come in, look beyond the material remains of the past," history says. Siren's gourd-shaped gateway is one remnant of the vanished world of Cheng Wang Fu. Its aged wood beams, like the browning carapace of the Pavilion of Winged Eaves before 1998, convey the barest hint of the splendor that once reigned in the gracious dwelling of Prince Cheng (Yunxing, 1752–1823), an uncle of the owner of the Singing Crane Garden. Both Cheng Wang Fu and the Ming He Yuan have vanished from the Chinese landscape. What remains of these pleasure palaces is nothing but slanting afternoon light. Siren's gift for indirect illumination inspires us to approach the garden slowly, mindful of thoughts that took shape here in times of upheaval and ravage.

To enter the world of the garden, it is not enough to document ownership and decay. One must, as Oswald Siren showed, take time for detours in the realm of the imagination. So much is missing from the material evidence of the past on the site of imperial gardens. So much depends on approaching absence with care. Edward Casey, in a different context, describes this journey as "indwelling"—a giving over of the self to the multilayered temporalities housed by the garden. This is not a space made up of only trees, water, and stone. It is, above all, a mood: "In gardens mood is an *intrinsic* feature, something that belongs to our experience of them. . . . In an empowered garden, I almost reside, yet I *also* walk about. . . . I dwell in multiple modes, in several registers and on many levels. This level leaves me on the *edge of dwelling*, just as gardens take me to the edge between built and natural places, or rather are that very edge."[2]

In-dwelling, in this sense, is a full-body experience, not merely an analytical goal. It enables one to go to the very edge of the familiar (be that in language or in space) and explore new modes of reflection.

Chinese gardens were designed to facilitate reflection. This goal is part and parcel of each element incorporated within the enclosure of the *yuan*. To walk the garden's paths, to contemplate its shifting vistas, was to embark upon an inner journey in which intentionally layered grounds were meant to quiet the mind. Even before disturbing events invaded the garden, chaos was made at home there. What Casey describes as the feeling of the "edge of dwelling" was experienced in a more upsetting fashion by Father Jean Denis Attiret (1702–1768), one of the first Westerners exposed to Qianlong's Summer Palace. A Jesuit who sought to bring the light of Christianity to the Qing court, Attiret was unprepared for the shadowy, odd spaces that thrived on the outskirts of Beijing. He stayed on as court painter and took the time to notice the unruly grace that enabled (indeed forced) new paths for reflection to develop in this strange land. He wrote back home to an audience unfamiliar with Chinese aesthetics. Contrasting what he saw in northwest Beijing with the mannered landscapes of Europe, Attiret concluded that Chinese gardens thrive on "Beautiful Disorder and wandering as far as possible from all Rules of Art . . . when you read this, you will be apt to imagine such Works as very ridiculous, and they must have a very bad Effect on the Eye: but once you see them, you would find it otherwise and would admire the Art, with which all this irregularity is conducted."[3] "Beautiful disorder" captured the subtle transition from chaos to cosmos attempted on the grounds of Ming He Yuan as well. A historian who would give voice to this terrain must also make room for all kinds of "irregularity"—for a flow of time that moves in and out of the language of memory, in and out of peace and war.

The Singing Crane Garden cannot be conceived primarily as a point in space. Rather it must be evoked in motion, through the movement of the mind's eye, as it were. One way to begin that journey may be to follow the shifting meanings of the word "crane"—a bird whose name was anything but an accidental adornment to Mianyu's retreat in northwest Beijing. The Manchu prince went as far as to commission the building of a whole section of the garden to house these large birds, known for heart-wrenching cries during their mating season. But it was not the physical birds that added reflective depths to Ming He Yuan. It was the visitor's presumed familiarity with all the classical poetry and art that gave these creatures wings in the reflective consciousness.

The ancient classic *Yi Jing* (The Book of Changes) was the first to note the unique associations of *ming he*. From this earliest text, the crane stands out because of its preference for solitary spaces. The song of the crane, according to the *Yi Jing*, "'thrives in the shade, while tigers roar on mountains.'"[4] This contrast between the boisterous tiger and the reticent crane continued to enrich Chinese cultural imagination in later centuries to the point that a special term, "crying crane scholar" (*he ming zhi shi*), developed during the Han dynasty to refer to men of learning who developed their talents—their song, as it were—in the "shade," away from the manifest rewards of political life.

Renowned for their moral character and careful use of language, such scholars must have appealed to Mianyu, a Manchu prince who sought to be an exemplar of Confucian virtues as well. *He ming zhi shi* were learned men who measured out speech, ethics, and aesthetics with exquisite care in realms beyond politics. A Han dynasty ruler was counseled by his advisers "to reject all those ministers who speak smooth words and to search far and wide for the Crying Crane Scholars."[5] Like hermits of old, *he ming zhi shi* were prized because they displayed the soul's music in obscure, lonely places where "only children follow." Sequestered from the din of public events, these men were certain that their woes would find a meaningful echo in the world. Purity of mind and a high threshold for solitude (indeed loneliness) were attributes of the crane that poets, artists, and garden builders sought to appropriate. Du Mu (803–853), a Tang dynasty luminary, phrased this longing as follows:

With pure note, he welcomes the evening moon,
With sad thoughts, he stands on cold bulrush.
Beneath jasper clouds, moving and stopping restlessly,
To him the spirit of the white egret is coarse.
All day long without the companionship of a flock,
By the side of the gully he laments his shadow's solitude.[6]

In a more contemporary idiom, Taiwanese painter Chen Ch'i-kuan tried to capture the crane's movements with a sparse calligraphy brush. Economic, bold strokes are used to lift the huge bird off the ground. Unlike the stiff, bold, nearly livid *grus japonesis* in the ceiling of the renovated Yi Ran Ting pavilion behind the Sackler Museum, Chen's masterful scroll is a visual pathway through timelessness. Chen's crane is nothing but bone, sinew, and ink. What was once an elongated leg becomes an arched head poised for cutting air. The cumbersome, earth-bound body has given way to largely empty space in which the painter allows himself a few bold scratches of the brush, as the crane soars, "its body and wings disappearing above the leaves with only dangling legs in the album. As the great bird glides, it fills three double-leaves! There is limitless imagination and joy in these powerful forms."[7]

To bring the Singing Crane Garden to life requires a similar effort. I was fortunate to savor this possibility on May 10, 1998, when I walked the periphery of the old Ming He Yuan in the company of two scholars, Jiao Xiong and Yue Shenyang. Educated men scorched by China's recent history, they opened for me vistas for reflection about gardens, cranes, historical tragedy, and much else along the way.

If You Love Pure Shadows

When we started our stroll on that windy spring morning, I had no way of knowing what winged moments of apprehension were to come upon us. I was prepared for scholarly conversation, not for the wordless understanding that ruined gardens such as the Singing Crane Garden demand, and foster. My two companions were polite, initially reserved. The older gentleman, Jiao Xiong, was a descendant of gardeners who once worked in the imperial Summer Palace. The younger man, Yue Shengyang, was a historical geographer who received his doctorate in Japan. I knew that Mr. Jiao was a well-known researcher about the history of princely gardens in northwest Beijing. I had seen some of his artful evocation of their landscapes in ink and brush. Dr. Yue arrived for our stroll with a gift: a map of the ruins of Ming He Yuan currently visible on the campus of Beijing University (figure 10). This careful drawing was faithful to the lay of the land and even evoked its former beauty by the nearly uninterrupted flow of water that Yue Shenyang conveyed in artful blue.

Following this map, we started out in the back of the Sackler Museum of Art and Archaeology, a site whose history I knew better than my companions. I had spent the previous year in interviews about Arthur Sackler and his complex connection to Beijing University. I shared this history to set my companions at ease, to signal that I understood the darker past of the Cultural Revolution, that I was familiar with the "ox pens" buried beneath these grounds. My goal was to invite them to share their own ruminations, if they so chose. Along the walk, they did.

Our first stop was a partly submerged rock platform. Yue Shengyang

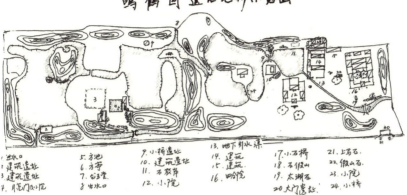

Figure 10. Map of the ruins of Singing Crane Garden as drawn for the author by Yue Shengyang in May 1998. Sites 1 and 2 lie on the north side of the Arthur M. Sackler Museum of Art and Archaeology. Site 16 marks the location of the former home of Wang Yao, while site 17 designates the marble bridge still in use today.

identified this as a piece of a moon viewing the terrace from the Ming He Yuan. Crossing a small alley we came to Red Lake (Hong Chi) , a pool renamed to draw attention to Beida's love of Chairman Mao. On the shores of Red Lake we came upon the remains of a moon gate from the nineteenth century. No afternoon light graced its empty, brittle wooden frame. The spaciousness of reflection that had been available to Oswald Siren in war-torn China had been erased from this corner of the Beijing University campus.

Once past this gate, we proceeded to a little island, which may have been one of the artificial features designed by Mianyu. It was on a hill near a weed-choked pond that Yue Shengyang whispered something about the forgotten history beneath this ground: "This was a preferred spot for committing suicide during the Cultural Revolution. If you tried to drown yourself in the larger, more famous 'Unnamed Lake' (Wei Ming Hu), the Red Guards would fish you right out. You would face additional beatings for having succumbed to anti-revolutionary pessimism. Here, at least no one found you. Here you could die in peace."[8]

When we reached site 14 on the map, marked simply as "building," Dr. Yue revealed that this had been the home of his own parents, graduates of Yenching University, who were sorely persecuted during the Cultural Revolution. As distinguished faculty members, they had been given a gracious, one-story

Figure 11. Site of the side entrance to the Singing Crane Garden, marked as "residence 79," as it appeared in the summer of 1998.

compound in the 1950s. By 1998, however, the Yue home had become a cluttered jungle of small rooms used by Beijing University's manual laborers. Here, Yue Shengyang began to share some memories of his teenage years when he had watched his mother being dragged to the nearby "ox pens" by Red Guards. It had been the young boy's painful duty to visit his incarcerated mother whenever possible. He was allowed to bring her a few necessities once in a great while. The grown man now recalled the humiliation, the swallowed rage. The Red Guards who tortured Yue Shengyang's mother used the courtyard of Democracy Hall to spread their dogmatic faith in Maoism. This place is not marked on Dr. Yue's map of ruins from the Ming He Yuan. It is inscribed in another, more durable fabric: that of historical memory. No sign appears on the Beida campus today to link Democracy Hall to the imprisonment of professors like Zhu Guangqian and Ji Xianlin. The building, used for the administrative offices of Beijing University, stands mute, almost innocent: a large, red building across the courtyard from the Sackler Museum of Art and Archaeology.

It was a relief to turn our attention to the nearby site marked "small courtyard" (site 12), which housed more gracious remains from the nineteenth cen-

Figure 12. Entrance to the home of Wang Yao's home, also identified as the entrance to the former Singing Crane Garden by Yang Chengyun in *Gu yuan cong heng* (The Journey of an Ancient Garden) (Beijing, 1998), p. 16.

tury. The past stood waiting here for us on that May day in the form of a worn wooden gate, topped with artfully carved lattice work and two marble pedestals. These were clearly Qing dynasty fragments—"used to dismount from horses," Jiao Xiong explains. Marked as "residence number 79" (figure 11), this gate was a side entrance to the Singing Crane Garden. My companions take pleasure in identifying this concrete link to our subject and strain to read the faded couplet still visible on the cracked, reddish boards. Where we might have expected traces of Maoist slogans, we read instead: *le tian zhi ming, an tu jiao ren* (Rejoicing in heaven, know fate. At peace with earth, impart humanness). The beautiful rhythms of classical Chinese soothe us, even as Yue Shengyang recalls that this courtyard was once the home of Yang Falu, an expert in ancient cultural studies, who also suffered greatly during the Cultural Revolution.

The end of our stroll takes us to site 16 on Yue Shengyang's map, the place that marks the main gate of the Singing Crane Garden. As I look up from the bluish paper, I stop in shocked recognition. This is residence 75—the home of my old teacher and dear friend, Wang Yao (figure 12). It was in this precise spot that I began my research in March 1979—when I went to visit for the first time China's most famous literary historian, a man who became my guide and mentor in the study of modern intellectual history. Although I had earned a Ph.D. in Chinese history, it was as if I knew nothing. When I began to study texts with Wang Yao, when I began to hear the story of his own journey and suffering during the Cultural Revolution, I finally began to fathom what it means to *live* with China's history.

I recall, as if it were yesterday, that chilly Thursday when I parked my recently bought bicycle near the marble bridge leading to Wang Yao's house. My companion in 1979 was Yue Daiyun, who had told me, "Look well, this is a compound right out of the eighteenth-century novel *Dream of the Red Chamber.*"[9] We had walked across the marble bridge and parked our bicycles near two stone lions—which even back then I knew were Qing period remains. Two decades later, I was quite literally back where I had begun. T. S. Eliot's words from the end of the "Four Quartets" come back to me:

And the end of all our exploring
Will be to arrive where we started
And to know the place for the first time.[10]

The marble lions still stand at the entrance of Wang Yao's house. Two smaller horse mounts are still in place. I recall the last time I saw Professor Wang here, in 1989, shortly before he died. Now, I am back with a new research project, but I do not have his trusted counsel, his seasoned view of literature and historical tragedy. I miss him as we cross the wooden threshold. To my great surprise, Wang Yao's widow is in the house. I had heard that she had moved out. It just so happens that she is back this Sunday, to pack up old books, mementos of long years spent in scholarship—and persecution.

We are old friends. She had hosted me for meals many times. She knows that I have heard her husband's stories of beatings during the Cultural Revolution. She greets me and my Chinese companions warmly. We speak about Wang Yao and the house that holds so many memories. I tell her that I am here to close a circle: I had begun my China studies with an abstract interest in intellectual history. I am back now to add flesh to the history that unfolded upon these grounds. I tell Wang Yao's widow that I hope to write a book about the gardens that housed ideals of beauty and quietude for which so many suffered, including her husband.

"You want to see how far persecution went?" She asks me with quiet rage. Stepping outside the old, book-lined living room, she points to a cracked, stained, mold-encrusted outer wall. Getting closer, she points to a faint classical painting: A scholar on a marble bridge. "See that huge X through the face? The Red Guards did that when they came to take Wang Yao to the ox pens. It was not enough to drag him through mud. Not enough to strike his old body. They had to destroy any visible connection with the culture that once sustained him."[11]

The faded, defaced scholar is a physical link to my old teacher and to the Ming He Yuan as well. Jiao Xiong clinches the connection. He points out that Wang Yao's library/sitting room may well have been the site of one of the first buildings encountered after one entered the garden in the nineteenth century. This was a place known as the Studio for Rethinking One's Career.[12] Caught in very difficult times of war and rebellion, Prince Mianyu had created for himself a typical *zhai,* a secluded space for meditation where one traditionally abstained from meat, wine, and intimate relations before making offerings to gods and ancestors.[13]

This space of quiet, crane-like solitude did not survive the turmoil of twentieth-century China. Nothing remains today of the placard that hung in Mianyu's library. What would Wang Yao think now if he could read its message: *xi xin guan mian* (cleanse the mind, take note of wonders)? More than a century after the death of the prince who built the Singing Crane Garden, I grasp how dangerously real words can be: *xi xin* was no metaphor during the 1960s. The Cultural Revolution had made "washing the mind" a literal, daily ritual. Wang Yao had been subjected to a brutal form of *xi xin* every day of his incarceration in the ox pens. Instead of meditating in the Studio for Rethinking One's Career, highly educated intellectuals were obligated to write endless revisions of autobiographies filled with their "bourgeois crimes." Cherished days, like carefully chosen words, lost almost all meaning during the 1960s. The Cultural Revolution had attacked buildings and gardens as well as the moral value of genuine memory.

Nonetheless, the ground has managed to outwit the ravage of time. On this May walk I realize that there are enough signposts remaining for those who wish to listen once again to the "cry" of the crane. On the wall opposite the crossed-out scholar, I make out another faded painting. In this one, the scholar keeps walking on a marble bridge. Two weeping willows lean over, as if to guide and welcome the solitary guest. Despite the stains and cracks, this image testifies to another kind of link to history and to memory. It is not only violence and brutality that weaves together Wang Yao's story with that of a long-dead Manchu prince. It is also a capacity to endure, to go on, to take solace from nature's rhythms and actually breathe new life into the ashes of old culture. My history of the Singing Crane Garden cannot accomplish all that, but I can mark the places and the lives that thrived in the shadows of its history.

Back at my dormitory, after this stroll full of surprises and discoveries, I

sit down to record what I have heard and seen. I find that my own words fail
to do justice to the stories shared by Yue Shengyang, Jiao Xiong, and Wang
Yao's widow. As often before, I find myself turning to poetry, especially to the
verses of Yihuan, who managed to give voice to quietude despite the deafen-
ing din of political upheaval that surrounded him daily:

If you love pure shadows
cling to the shore where the ash tree thrives

If you ache for your lost hut
lean on stone hewn in blameless mountains

Today, a broad and straight road opens
to drum beat and cymbal music.

Enfolded by cliffs, you can still follow a serpentine path,
shunning all that is coarse

For humble dwelling, three pillars suffice,
there is no joy like leaving entanglement behind.[14]

Entitled simply "Ou cheng" (By Accident), this poem captures both the genuine emotion as well as the posturing that thrived in imperial gardens. It also
speaks to my own "accidental" discovery of an old connection to Ming He
Yuan. Prince Yihuan, like Mianyu (and even Wang Yao, during the years when
he lived safely among his books), had much more than a humble dwelling
with three pillars. These men were not Daoist hermits or Buddhist monks.
Nonetheless, each loved pure shadows in his own way. Each clung to some
lakeshore where the ash tree thrives. Each had sought a path around the highway of history, away from the drumbeat of political violence. Though unsuccessful, they left enough literary and artistic remains that I am able to piece
together a vision of refuge that still lingers on in the hamlet of Haidian.

Liquid Delight in the Shallow Sea

It was not an accident, of course, that Manchu emperors and princes were
drawn to this site. The village of Haidian lay on the outskirts of the imperial
city and was long known for its gracious gardens. Already in the Ming dynasty, scholars and imperial kin had come to find refuge here. What Haidian

had to offer was what garden builders needed the most: water. Called "liquid delight," this was the essential prerequisite for landscape design, as could be glimpsed even in the blue hues added to Yue Shengyang's map of the Ming He Yuan ruins. Without water, nothing grew. With water, it was not only trees and flowers that flourished. It was also the contemplative mind that drew sustenance here from vistas of liquid stillness. Skillfully channeled waterfalls and artfully crafted fishponds became the hallmarks of Haidian. Mighty boulders were excavated and imported from the shores of Taihu, a southern lake renowned for strange-shaped rocks that added "boniness" to the garden. Undulating hills were created artificially, by moving mounds of earth, as can be seen beneath the Yi Ran Ting today.

Called the Shallow Sea, this northwest corner of metropolitan Beijing remains well endowed with underground springs even today. This phenomenon, too, is no accident of nature. It took informed geographers and geologists to locate and preserve these source springs, especially in the Maoist years of the communist regime, when building the new was a political priority and destroying the old an ideological obligation. Few cared, or dared, to voice their concern for the waters that nourished classical gardens.

One of those who did was Hou Renzhi, who recalled with fondness the gracious setting of Yenching University before it became part of the new Beida. Even when nostalgia for pre-liberation garden design was forbidden, he found a way to argue for and record the reopening of a Qing dynasty water channel in the early 1950s. Beijing University had just been moved out of the center of the city to Yan Yuan (the garden name for Yenching University). Hou Renzhi mobilized and joined a group of students to dredge one of the rivers of Haidian:

I myself took part in the action and remember that in one afternoon when the filthy mud in the opening had all been out, a young student was so excited that he went voluntarily on all fours through the opening from the west side to the east. His passing through proved that the waterway was completely cleaned. Although he was covered all over with mud, he jumped and laughed jubilantly together with us. This little but dramatic scene of joy impressed me so much that it remains fresh in my mind. The upper part of the river has now changed direction thus enabling the water to flow into the campus.[15]

Hou Renzhi's own delight in the muddy student reflects the commitment of a historical geographer to the unique qualities of the ground beneath his feet. It was still more than three decades before his views would be consulted in the design and naming of the Sackler Museum gardens built upon the site of the old Ming He Yuan. This celebration of physical labor also took place a half a decade before the eminent scholar would be condemned as a "rightist" (in 1957) and almost a decade before his own incarceration in the niu peng.

In the early 1950s, it was still possible for intellectuals to savor connectedness to the soil. Traditional Chinese culture had long sanctioned the scholars' interest in water, in rocks, in trees, in the simple life that so attracted Yihuan when he longed to leave entanglements behind. Tuan Yi-fu, a Chinese geographer who developed his career in America, summarized this attachment to the local in terms of the character *tu*, meaning connection to locality, to hearth, to a world bounded by physical boundaries. Far from being opposed to "cosmos," this *tu* can help us "appreciate intelligently our culture and landscape."[16] Tuan, unlike Hou Renzhi, lives in an intellectual environment in which he is free to advocate the ideal of a "cosmopolitan hearth." Scholars in Mao's China—even when willing to get down into the mud to clear old water channels—were condemned for the knowledge that linked soil, culture, and tradition to the legacy of artful garden design.

In the late Ming dynasty, by contrast, when the political fate of the rulers of Beijing looked quite bleak, Ji Cheng found an opportune moment to sum up the art of gardening and its connection to local resources. His *Yuan Ye* dwells on many details about "borrowed" scenery and how it could be used to design contemplative spaces. The starting point of all garden craft, according to Ji, lay in the same element that Hou Renzhi still treasured in the 1950s—water: "Before beginning to dig one should investigate the sources and note how the water flows. Where it flows in an open channel one builds the pavilion on posts. If one throws a bridge over the water one may erect the study pavilion on the opposite bank. If one piles up stones to form a surrounding wall, it may seem as if one lived among mountains."[17]

The goal of the garden was to create a connection to the realm of nature beyond its gates. Ji Cheng, mindful of the worldly cares of his wealthy patrons, understood how they longed to live as if they were among the mountains. He did not need poems, like those that Yihuan composed in the nineteenth century, to understand the crushing burdens of politics. His *Yuan Ye* brought to life a vision of refuge alongside the realities of obligation that surrounded late Ming scholar-officials. From bamboo, which symbolized strength in the midst of adversity, to the evergreen pines that conveyed moral rectitude, the classical Chinese garden was filled with elements designed to comfort the mind's eye in times of distress.

Even such a small feature as a bracket that sustained the corner of a pavilion roof had a name that served to wake the mind. If the joint faced in one direction only, the bracket would be called *tou xin*, or "stolen heart." If the joint completed a well-balanced square under the eaves, it was called *ji xin*, or "accounted heart."[18] Since classical Chinese makes no distinction between "heart" and "mind," these brackets underneath the roof (like the garden as a whole) provided a well-informed gentleman with an opportunity to balance inner and outer worlds.

"Stolen heart," like "accounted heart," was a design element that linked garden culture to the predicament of scholars in need of spiritual and physical refuge from the din of political entanglements. Few expressed this need as artfully as Mi Wanzhong (1570–1628), the famous scholar-official who designed Shao Yuan—the most renowned garden in the hamlet Haidian. At the height of his fame, Mi reigned almost like an emperor in the realm of painting and calligraphy. A common saying paid homage to his reputation: "Dong in the south, Mi in the north." This was an appreciative statement acknowledging two unrivaled masters: Dong Qichang in Jiangsu province and Mi Wanzhong in the Beijing area. At the height of his reputation, Mi needed no retreat from politics; he had not yet turned his artistic attention to details such as "stolen heart."

This discovery came as a result of his fall from political grace. An outspoken opponent of powerful court eunuchs, Mi was removed from office in 1600. There were no ox pens in China in those days for a scholar who defied the will of the powerful. Exile to the far corners of China was the common fate of lesser luminaries. A disgraced courtier like Mi was left to nurse his wounds near the city of his former glory. The beauty of Haidian suddenly took on fresh appeal. Mi Wanzhong had more spiritual and material resources than other critics of Ming corruption. He knew the history of gardens. He was a skilled and famous painter. He knew how to entice the eye, the heart, and the mind away from disaster.

In 1612, Mi Wanzhong began the design and building of his Haidian garden. By the time it was completed two years later, its fame rivaled the admiration once garnered by his paintings and calligraphy. The name of the garden, like its design, was meant to create an alternative vision to the desiccating squabbles at court. Mindful of the importance of water in northwest Beijing, Mi decided to use it skillfully to embellish the symbolic destiny of his family line:

Because there was only a ladleful of water in the garden and because he thought that a ladle was a suitable container for the Rice (*Mi*) family, he named his new garden *Shao Yuan*—Ladle Garden. Shortly after this, Marquis Li Wei, whose family name meant Plum, established his beautiful and famous park just west of Ladle Garden . . . both parks were so beautiful that a certain Grand Secretary of the Ming Dynasty is reported to have praised their delicious flavor, saying: "the Rice garden is not tasteless nor the Plum garden sour." Long after the Ming dynasty had fallen and the Plum family's garden had become an imperial park, the Rice family still lived prosperously in their delightful Ladle Garden.[19]

Mi Wanzhong was not content to design a garden to perpetuate the family name in times of political disgrace. He was not soothed by the waters of Haidian and the opportunity to dip his "Ladle Garden" into the refreshing source springs.

Once the splendid Shao Yuan was complete, Mi Wanzhong proceeded to grace it with his painterly talent. The result is one of the most gracious, lush, detailed hand scrolls in the history of garden art. A copy of this scroll can be found in the rare book collection of the Beijing University library. One of the few scholars who had access to the fragile remnant was Hou Renzhi, the scholar who knew how to cherish the same waters, the same landscape that had inspired Mi Wanzhong at the end of the Ming dynasty.

Professor Hou has written extensively about the history of Shao Yuan and was kind enough to share with me one of the few color reproductions of the Beida hand scroll (which is no longer available for scholarly perusal). In this painting, the eye of the viewer is invited to travel slowly from the serpentine island on the left toward a central pavilion where scholars gather for the savoring of cultural arts (figure 13). An arched marble bridge is the first man-made element a guest would encounter, a concrete reminder that this is not the effete world of the imperial palace in Beijing but rather a wondrous refuge, a place where thought can take its shape at ease. As if echoing the mind's call, a boat called the Barge of Tranquility (Ding Fang) ferries guests slowly across waters named the Waters of Linguistic Refinement (Wen Shui Po).[20] This barge and these waters were meant to aid the mind in focused contemplation. Having reached the other shore, having further divested oneself of the cares of history and politics, guests could begin a slow-paced walk through a *lang*—the long, enclosed passage meant to link one vista to another, constantly surprising, constantly changing, constantly delighting. A lower, zigzagging wooden bridge finally brought visitors to the centerpiece of the garden, the stone-viewing pavilion so dear to the heart of Mi Wanzhong.

During one of our many conversations about the history of northwest Beijing, Hou Renzhi took out another, less colorful image of the Shao Yuan garden. This is an ink-and-brush sketch, most likely made by Mi Wanzhong's assistant, to convey his master's wishes concerning the architectural details of the site as it was being built (figure 14). In this garden, as in the lush painting, water predominates. Like in the rubbed-out remnant on the doorpost at Wang Yao's house,

Figure 13. Reproduction of color hand scroll painting by Mi Wanzhong toward the end of the Ming dynasty, ca. 1609. The scroll is being held in the Beijing University archives. This reproduction was made available to the author courtesy of Hou Renzhi.

scrawny willows bend into a still lake. In the very center of the sketch looms a larger, different kind of tree, perhaps a juniper. Beneath its branches, as in the hand scroll, stands Mi Wanzhong's treasure: a large, strange-shaped rock.

Figure 14. Architectural sketch of central pavilion and ornamental rock in the Shao Yuan garden, attributed to Mi Wanzhong's garden architect. Courtesy of Hou Renzhi.

Figure 15. "The Stone That Is Mi's Friend," ornamental rock currently in the courtyard of the Arthur M. Sackler Museum, identified as belonging to the collection of
Mi Wanzhong by Yang Chengyun in *Gu yuan cong heng* (Beijing, 1998), p. 15.

At the height of his fame and power, Mi had indulged a passion for collecting strange rock formations. In fact, the scholar-official was known among his friends as Mi Youshi—Mi, the Friend of Rocks. Dislodged from the center of imperial politics by misfortune, Mi embraced this love of hard stone ever more fervently. In the "bones" of the garden, he saw the kind of loyalty and truth that was sorely lacking at the court of the Ming emperor. Mi's favorite stone was called "Neither-Nor-Rock" (*fei fei shi*). A tall, boldly perforated structure anchored by a cavernous, thin wall, this rock now adorns the courtyard of the Sackler Museum of Art and Archaeology (figure 15). Ignored in the 1950s, Mi's rock was buried and thereby protected by rubble during the decade of the Cultural Revolution. Unlike residence 75, this remnant from the past was somewhat portable and thus survived relatively unscathed. Unlike the scholars on the door to Wang Yao's study, unlike the body of the aged scholar and those of his colleagues, Mi's *fei fei shi* could speak its own mind. It retained its "neither-nor" quality, its ability to challenge the powers at be. Placed in the heart of the Sackler Museum, it keeps its own counsel, labeled simply as "Mi's Friend" by the very few who know or care about the history of old gardens embedded in today's Beida.[21]

But old gardens have a way of speaking to—indeed, speaking for—those who cannot voice their own concerns. After the collapse of the Ming dynasty in 1644, the ruined Shao Yuan continued to whisper its secrets to visitors seeking solace from the new rulers of China. One Confucian scholar described the site—and indirectly, his outrage at the brutal destructiveness of the Manchu conquest—as follows.

Desolate with broken furrows and barren hills and covered with dusty crawling weeds, the place in its better days used to have verandas bright with sunshine and pavilions bathed in moonlight, cool balconies in summer days and warm houses in winter. The present dried pond, treadless paths, and snakes' and foxes' caves were once described by scholars and artists as places associated with poetry and delicate ladies and with archaic boats and cliffs in paintings. In place of the lotus flower building, the banks of pine trees, and the painted pleasure boats berthing against the houses, there are only houses with corroded beams and vast openings in the roofs. In the presence of such a miserable scene, one feels inevitably very sad. There is only one thing left behind. That is a huge stone standing as formerly in front of the courtyard and shaded by a Chinese juniper tree.[22]

The same stone that sits so proudly in the center of the Sackler courtyard today had more evocative powers in a time of violence and disarray. Set against dried ponds, it was a visual reminder that "liquid delight" flows only when scholars are well treasured. The huge stone and the juniper stand as witness to what endures when beauty has been crushed by violent events. If the stone could speak, perhaps it would give testimony. In the words of T. S. Eliot, whose "Waste Land" depicts a more modern desolation, it would cry out:

Son of man . . .
You cannot say, or guess, for you know only
A heap of broken images . . .
There is shadow under this red rock,
Come in under the shadow of this red rock,
And I will show you something . . .
I will show you fear in a handful of dust . . .[23]

Fear was more than a handful of dust on the grounds of the old Singing Crane Garden. Two centuries before Lord Elgin's troops torched the princely gardens of the Qing, violence already haunted this corner of northwest Beijing. As shadowy places of refuge became scarce, rocks were left to speak a language previously cherished by poets, scholars, and garden designers alike.

One Foot on the Island of Immortals

When the Manchus launched their plans for conquest in the 1620s, they had hoped to present themselves as Confucian pacifiers of the realm. Mindful of the political disillusionment of scholar-officials such as Mi Wanzhong, they had named their dynasty *Qing*, "purity," to connote a breath of fresh air after the supposedly "bright" *Ming* that ended up being ruled by thoroughly corrupt Chinese emperors. The Manchus even organized an army called the "Green Standard," made up of ethnically Chinese forces, so the conquest would not look like an invasion. For a while, a minority of Ming intellectuals was persuaded that the new rulers offered an opportunity to cleanse and revive the Mandate of Heaven. When news of atrocities began to filter in from central China in 1644–46, the tide quickly turned. By that time, the Manchus were determined to stay and use force to enforce the new mandate.

In Beijing, the urge to dominate both politically and culturally was manifest in the rapid transformation of the Forbidden City into the administrative nerve center of the new empire. On the outskirts of Beijing, a different kind of domination and acculturation took place. Here, the Manchu rulers sought to take advantage of natural resources to create their own space of refuge, especially for times when the court could not travel back to the ancestral hunting grounds of Manchuria. The Kangxi emperor, who reigned from 1662 to 1723, was the first Manchu ruler to commit major resources to the building of a Garden of Perfect Brightness in the hamlet of Haidian. In keeping with his vision of himself as a World Pacifier (in both Confucian and Buddhist terms) he chose to name his place Yuan Ming Yuan—as an allusion to the "round" (all encompassing) and "brilliant" (far-reaching) illumination of Buddhist wisdom. His grandson, Qianlong, expanded the grounds until they became the largest single building project of the Qing dynasty. With an almost unlimited supply of silver, gold, and wood requisitioned from commoners and scholar-officials, he completely altered the natural and cultural terrain of the hamlet once known as the Shallow Sea. The disgraced Ming dynasty scholar Mi Wanzhong had been content to take a "spoon" of water from Haidian to create his Shao Yuan. The emperor Qianlong, by contrast, had an army of designers and diggers who did not rest until they brought to life a veritable sea—the central, vast lake of Yuan Ming Yuan called Fu Hai, or "Ocean of Blessings."

The imperial will to overcome natural limitations in order to create a vast showcase for pleasure led to the incorporation of several other gardens into the enclosure of Yuan Ming Yuan. Starting with the Nine Islands of Peace (Jiuzhou Qingyan) built around a smaller lake called Back Lake (Hou Hu), Qianlong took over the Eternal Spring Garden (Changchun Yuan) in 1749 and the Variegated Spring Garden (Qichun Yuan) in 1751. Thus he expanded and created an ever more brilliant, ever more grandiose Garden of Perfect Brightness. And if the avaricious incorporation of smaller Chinese gardens into this expansive refuge was not enough, Qianlong also launched the building project of a huge European-style garden called the Palace of Balanced and Amazing Pleasures (Xieqi qu) designed by Italian and French Jesuits. The most prominent designer was Father Guiseppe Castiglione (1688–1766), who had delighted the great monarch with drawings of Italian and French palaces and fountains. With Castiglione's designs, Qianlong obtained a massive pleasure compound on the scale of Versailles—with a vigor all its own.

The Manchu ruler shared the French king's desire to use grandly designed spaces to enforce political hegemony. At the same time, the Qing ruler followed a cultural script that had its own aesthetic cadence. The geometric formality of seventeenth-century French gardens conveyed, in the words of historian Chandra Mukerji, the military ambitions of state over society. A walk in these gardens was "neither casual nor apolitical. It was an element of the geopolitics of the period . . . the *petit parc* embodied the territorial, optimistic and technical expertise on which French military geopolitical action was based."[24] The total effect of Versailles was thus quite different from the aesthetic playfulness of the Yuan Ming Yuan. The near total isolation of state from society in Qing China may account for some of the fluidity of design possible in this corner of northwest Beijing. More important, Qianlong was a genius at accumulating, digesting, and reinterpreting various aesthetic traditions ranging from the Daoist to the Confucian, from the Buddhist to the baroque. The result, according to British biologist Joseph Needman, was a landscape architecture that far from "imprisoning and constraining Nature, actually flows along with it."[25]

This "flow" was no accident. More than a space to display power, the imperial gardens functioned as a reprieve from the burdens of rule. Qianlong himself defined this ideal when he wrote: "Every emperor and ruler, when he has retired from audience, and has finished his public duties, must have a garden in which he may stroll, look around and relax his heart. If he has a suitable place for this, it will refresh his mind and regulate his emotions. But if he has not, he will become engrossed in sensual pleasures and lose his will and power."[26] Refreshing the mind was a different kind of necessity than the geopolitical calculations that occupied the heart of Versailles. Built to awe Chinese and Western visitors alike, the Yuan Ming Yuan nonetheless was large enough and meandering enough to accommodate a multiplicity of political and spiritual agendas. A center for Daoist contemplation, Buddhist sutra recitation, ancestor worship, and the Confucian arts of painting and poetry, Qianlong's Haidian palace became a vessel to accommodate many seas and continents, both metaphorical and physical.

Not satisfied with creating worlds in space, Qianlong also commissioned artists to paint forty of his favorite scenes from the Yuan Ming Yuan. Father Jean Denis Attiret was one of a large group of Western and Chinese artists assigned to immortalizing the Garden of Perfect Brightness. Each "portrait" was first assembled carefully in space, then meticulously re-evoked with brush on silk. The result was a delightful mirroring of terrain and art to the point that the aging Qianlong preferred to walk the portrait gallery of his garden rather than dislodge his body from the inner palaces of the Yuan Ming Yuan.

One of the scenes that captures Qianlong's territorial and cultural am-

Figure 16. *Ru gu han jin* (Imbibe the past; it contains the present). The eleventh painting in the series "Forty Scenes of the Yuan Ming Yuan." Courtesy of the Bibliothèque Nationale de France, Paris.

bitions is entitled *Ru gu han jin* (Imbibe the past; it contains the present) (figure 16). It depicts the emperor's private library as a double-roofed pavilion encircled by a group of other halls to encourage the perusal of old scrolls.[27] During the reign of this absolute ruler, the state had the right to confiscate any book or any work of art that Qianlong wished to add to the imperial collection. Some were requisitioned because they contained anti-Manchu sentiments, some just because the emperor fancied the writer or the artist. If the emperor chose, he could study the old. If he wanted to, he could fathom how it contained the present. The political assumption was that he defined both. Much like Mao Zedong in his later years, Qianlong imagined himself as both teacher and student. Unlike Mao, however, he never fell into a total contempt for the old. He never forced scholars to erase their attachment to Confucian tradition, to wash their minds. Qianlong never beat them to death just because they took the link between past and present to heart.

The message evoked by the title of this eighteenth-century painting is that traditional Confucian wisdom had much to contribute to the political policies of the Qing regime. This was not simply propaganda for the consumption of Chinese scholar-officials. The same dictum prevailed within the palace compound, where Chinese tutors were hired to instruct young princes in poetry and classics. These arts were meant to refine the moral personality. At the same time, Manchu kinsmen oversaw the young men's military and Buddhist education. A poet of some skill himself, Qianlong rewarded his children when they became capable of producing classical verses on appropriate themes. To inspire further literary virtuosity, he ordered a special pillar to be installed in the princes' study hall. It was marked with a tablet inscribed by the emperor himself depicting cranes alighting on pines.[28] This pillar was meant to be a visual reminder that future heirs had to soar to ever-greater heights of literary and political accomplishment.

No longer just a symbol of moral rectitude and solitude as it had been for Confucian and Daoist scholars, the crane tablet in the princes' study hall was an official reminder concerning a moral commitment to serve in the world. Previous generations of *ming he zhi shi* had cultivated rectitude in shadowy spaces apart from the bright light of political entanglement. By the end of the eighteenth century, however, Haidian had become a famed showcase for the display of literary and cultural genius. Cranes would have to learn to sing in gilded cages, or be erased from the garden landscape altogether.

No "cage" was as lavishly gilded in the late Qianlong era as that of the Gentle Spring Garden (Shu Chun Yuan), a pleasure palace belonging to an imperial favorite called He Shen. A Manchu nobleman who served as an imperial bodyguard, He Shen had attracted the eye of the aging emperor. Along with the affection of the doting Qianlong, He Shen acquired the grounds that currently surround the Unnamed Lake at Beijing University. In ironic contrast to its modest name, He Shen's garden ended up rivaling the splendor of the nearby Yuan Ming Yuan. On a smaller scale, the favorite who rose to the rank of minister used the most expensive building materials to create a sprawling complex of lakes, pavilions, and theaters.

The most ostentatious symbol of splendor was the marble boat that still

Figure 17. The marble boat from the Shu Chun Yuan owned by the Manchu favorite He Shen (with the pagoda-style water tower in the distance across Unnamed Lake). Photograph by Marc Berger.

graces the bank of Unnamed Lake today (figure 17). Like the rock in the center of the Sackler Museum, He Shen's marble boat stands as a nearly mute witness to the history that unfolded in this corner of China. In an earlier era, when Yenching University occupied this site, He Shen's garden was a sanctioned subject of study. Hou Renzhi picked up the thread from his teachers and traced the actual documents that granted this Manchu favorite a pleasure palace adjacent to Qianlong. As long as his imperial patron reigned, He Shen could build up the Gentle Spring Garden with unabashed luxury. When Qianlong, the longest reigning ruler in Chinese history, finally died in 1795, He Shen's star fell with crushing rapidity.

Jiaqing (r. 1796–1821) took over the actual reigns of power, which he had held only symbolically during the last year of his father's life. One of the new emperor's first measures was to arrest He Shen, confiscate his treasures, and execute him. According to a widely circulated list of He Shen's holdings, he had built sixty-four pavilions inside the Shu Chun Yuan. The officials who actually searched the property reported that the Manchu favorite had amassed 1,003 houses as well as 357 verandas, apart from thousands of taels of silver and gold.[29] This massive corruption case continued to shadow the gardens of Haidian well into the nineteenth century. Even after the Jiaqing emperor divided up He Shen's pleasure palace among his children, the dread of moral turpitude infected the land. Mianyu, who incorporated the largest section of the Gentle Spring Garden into his own Ming He Yuan, was especially concerned with purging its evil name.

His nephew Yihuan took another route. Especially after the violent destruction of the Singing Crane Garden, the old marble boat spoke to him about the many layers of dreams, hopes, and illusions that seeded the ravaged land. In a poem whose title is best translated as "One Foot on the Isle of Immortals," Yihuan described as follows the nineteenth-century ruins and the callous grandeur that produced them:

Lofty pavilions once reached the clouds
now topple into uncertain dust.

Towering graves dotted a winding cliff,
today they spill secrets into muddy waters.

Worn walls, cracked columns,
the trace of a timid leveret.

I cut a path through brambles
to unroll a curtain of thorns.

Imagine the minister with one foot on the isle of immortals,
sacred heaven of fleabane and bamboo.

Silk ropes fettered his body,
condemned to death three times.

Phoenix wings in aborted flight
never left this orphaned island.

Every sail leans on the wind that breaks it,
while the guest of ruins cherishes a shattered soul.[30]

Yihuan's poetic evocation of this corrupt Manchu favorite does not offer forgiveness. It does not shy away from the fact that He Shen was condemned to death three times. Yihuan has no sympathy for the lavish tastes of the man who owned the marble boat and cracked pavilions. His poem, unlike the contemporary Beida photograph, allows us to encounter the orphaned island in all its desolation. What is being mourned here is not He Shen's passing but the silencing of a landscape that once harbored so much delight. Why the landscape gets punished for the sins of its owner is a question that Yihuan asked himself over and over again, especially after the destruction of the Yuan Ming Yuan and its surrounding princely gardens.

Hall of the Seeker of Radiant Virtue

When Mianyu received a large tract of Shu Chun Yuan in 1835, he did not have to worry about the marble boat. The eastern section of He Shen's estate had already been bequeathed by the Jiaqing emperor to his daughter, Princess Changjing, in 1802. The larger, western section that became Singing Crane Garden awaited the needs and desires of the next ruler, Daoguang. In the meantime, gardens were being remodeled and renamed, with strategies similar to those used in the revision of a classical Chinese poem. The "right words" had to be found, thematic continuities maintained.

Qianlong's imprint on this revision process and on Chinese culture more generally had been huge. The He Shen scandal was merely a symbol of the grandeur that was made possible by relative peace and the massive extraction of resources in the eighteenth century. The gardens of the nineteenth century were designed in a totally different cultural and political environment. Here, war with the West, massive internal rebellions, and a waning faith in the Mandate of Heaven marked the cadence of imperial life. In this vastly different world, Qianlong's ideals endured nonetheless. The goal of combining martial and literary virtues, of blending Buddhist religion with Confucian filial piety, remained central, along with a cultured appreciation of landscaped spaces.

Mianyu grew up as an emperor's son. Like his father, Jiaqing, he studied Confucian classics in the studio where cranes were displayed. Like other highborn kin of the emperor, he was expected to embody the Manchu ideal of *mahahai erdemu*—"manly virtue." This included skill in archery, horsemanship, frugality, devotion to the ruling Aisin Gioro clan, and devotion in the service of the Son of Heaven.[31] By the time Mianyu was born in 1814, his father had the reigns of power firmly in hand. Jiaqing had already announced that he would determine the names of his own children as well as the names of "all the sons and grandsons of his brothers—all those who shared first ideograph or part of an ideograph with his own descendants' names."[32] He therefore gave much thought to his fifth son's name: the first character, *Mian*, was to be a concrete link to all his brothers and kinsmen. It meant "prolonged," "continuous," and "unbroken." Mianyu's second name was also chosen by his father with care. A personal appellation given only to him, *Yu* meant at once "joyful" and "content." This, however, was not to be taken as an invitation to pleasure. Rather, as the owner of the Singing Crane Garden demonstrated in his later years, it was to be an ideal of cultural refinement pursued with effort and determination.

The young boy's fidelity both to the unbroken traditions of his imperial clan and to Confucian traditions of self-cultivation and contentment pleased his father. After Jiaqing's death in 1820, the six-year-old was left in charge of Manchu uncles who oversaw his education. His second brother, who ruled as the Daoguang emperor, also recognized the boy's talents and virtues. By 1839 Mianyu's title had been raised to prince of the first rank. As Prince Hui (Hui Qin Wang), Mianyu was delegated to perform the Grand Sacrifices of the imperial Aisin Gioro clan. These sacrifices took place at the altars of Heaven and Earth and ensured the ceremonial legitimacy and cosmological benevolence of the Qing dynasty as a whole.[33] The first time this weighty responsibility fell upon the young price was in 1840, on the eve of war with England. A shortage of sons among imperial kin accounts partially for Mianyu's high ceremonial profile. Another likely reason is Daoguang's confidence in the young man's mahahai erdemu. "Manly virtue" would be needed more and more as the fate of the dynasty became darkened by opium wars and peasant rebellion. By 1853, when the war-weary dynasty looked like it would be toppled by the Taiping insurgency, Mianyu took on the burden of military defense. With his new title of "Worthy Military General in Charge of Sustaining the Mandate," he managed to protect the imperial capital from native rebels. By the time of his death in 1865, however, Mianyu had witnessed the invasion of Beijing by foreign troops as well as the destruction of the Summer Palace and his own beloved Ming He Yuan.

Three decades before, when he had begun work on the Singing Crane Garden, Mianyu chose a new name for himself. In keeping with the Confucian practice of a studio sobriquet, he chose an appellation that went beyond parental hopes at the time of his birth: Hall of the Seeker of Radiant Virtue (Cheng Hui Tang), a title that reveals a young man determined to erase the shadow of corruption and self-indulgence left over from the He Shen era.

Even as he proceeded to design a huge pleasure garden, Mianyu wanted to be known as the prince who overcame the cursed ground, who helped restore the moral legitimacy of the Qing. By aligning himself with the idea of Cheng Hui Tang, Mianyu displayed a skilled blending of Manchu moralism and Confucian aesthetics. His garden mirrored this self-image:

Compared to the design of other princely gardens, Singing Crane Garden was unique. It adopted features of southern gardening while preserving the special feeling coveted in the gardens of the north. Its enclosed passageways led to a back garden filled with flowering lilac. The main building here was called Cheng Bi Tang, or the Hall for Azure Purity. When the garden was flourishing, the east courtyard was used for entertainment. It was here that a room supported by five carved columns housed an indoor opera stage. . . . Beyond, toward the central section of the garden, hills ran up and down silhouetted by far reaching branches of pine. Another pavilion would then come into sight flanked by ancient rockery and a magnificent cedar that seemed to scrape the sky. Throughout the garden, willowy stones and grand buildings conveyed a sense of elegance and serenity.[34]

Lilac, cedar, and a taste for Peking opera are bits of what we now know of Mianyu's taste in gardens. A lot more comes alive from the poems of his nephew, Yihuan. The stones for mounting horses in front of Wang Yao's house provide material presence of a refuge that is no more. Jiao Xiong's skilled painting, however, brings to life the main features that adorned the grounds of the Ming He Yuan (figure 18). With this "map" one can begin to enter the garden, as Mianyu's guests might have a century and a half ago.

The main entrance to the Singing Crane Garden was in the southeast corner. Inside the first gate were a screen wall and a marble bridge across a stream. According to Hou Renzhi, this is the same stream that flows past Wang Yao's old residence.[35] Once past the entrance, Mianyu's guests would have an option to savor several main sections of the prince's garden. Straight ahead lay the eastern, more public space where entertainment took place. The central section of the Ming He Yuan, also accessible by the second gate (where residence 79 may be found today) had a different tone: Here was a more contemplative space, graced with a courtyard for cranes and for their gamekeeper. A more adventurous guest might opt to take the path to the western section of the estate, where fishponds and a unique island revealed Mianyu's more private spiritual pursuits. From the public to the personal, the garden paths conducted the visitor in a journey that traversed both physical and mental spaces. Each name in the garden, each pavilion, captured part of what the "Seeker of Radiant Virtue" was all about.

北京西郊海淀鎮北清代鳴鶴園全圖　　一九九八年十月二十二日焦雄圖

Figure 18. Painting of the Singing Crane Garden (Ming He Yuan) executed for the author by
Jiao Xiong, former archivist at the Bureau of Antiquities, in 1998. (1) Main entrance to Singing
Crane Garden—close to the entrance of residence 75, home of Wang Yao. (2) Marble bridge
leading to inner gate of Singing Crane Garden, most likely moved to the other side of the moat
in front of Residence Number 75. (3) Studio for Rethinking One's Career (Tui Sheng Zhai),
also the site of the western wall of the library/sitting room of Wang Yao. (4) Pavilion of
Winged Eaves (Yi Ran Ting) first celebrated in an eighteenth-century poem by the Qianlong
emperor, later glimpsed with longing by intellectuals imprisoned in the "ox pens" of the Cultural Revolution (1966–69). (5) Secondary entrance to the Ming He Yuan, currently the site of
residence 79, several doors down from the more elaborate entrance to the former home of
Wang Yao. (6) The Hall of Azure Purity (Cheng Bi Tang)—this was the main center for entertainment (opera, poetry recitals, musical performances with singing girls, and so on) of the
Singing Crane Garden. (7) Crane's Nest (He Chao) courtyard for housing cranes and the
gamekeeper of the Singing Crane Garden. (8) Garden of Delight in Spring (Chun Xi Yuan)—a
courtyard designed for savoring early blossoms in the Ming He Yuan. (9) Flourishing Deer Island (Fu Lu Dao)—one of the most remote corners of the Singing Crane Garden designed to
symbolize the owner's hopes for longevity and prosperity.

The centerpiece of Mianyu's garden, in the eyes of most guests, was Cheng Bi Tang. With its triple roof, this was an impressive structure that housed a well-designed stage surrounded by five magnificently carved columns. An outspoken critic of the elite's indulgence in Peking opera (and the sexual favors of theater entertainers), Mianyu nonetheless displayed the cultured taste of an educated gentleman. It was in this part of the garden that he hosted lavish banquets, family ceremonies, poetry-writing feasts attended by Manchu noblemen and Confucian scholars alike. These grand events impressed upon the guests the high social status of the man who was a favored younger brother to the Daoguang emperor. The Hall of Azure Purity was thus a morally lofty name capacious enough to house Mianyu's most physical pleasures.

A less grandiose but nonetheless important structure was situated close to Cheng Bi Tang. This was the library "For the Cherishment of New Learning," (Huai Xin Shu Wu).[36] The idea of *huai xin*—literally, "cleaving to the new"—might at first glance seem odd for a man who was a tireless advocate of traditional virtues. Living in a time of rapid change, however, Mianyu appreciated the value of innovation. He was well aware that the foundations of Confucian learning had been challenged by Western technological expertise. He grasped the limitation of classical learning and worked to keep his outlook fresh. The goal of this kind of learning (like that of the garden as a whole) was not novelty per se. It was to engage with fresh vision the master texts of a time-tested tradition. Upon this site, Beijing University developed its first archaeological exhibitions, before establishing the independent archaeology department currently housed in the Sackler Museum.

"New Learning" and "Azure Purity" were not rigid, walled-in concepts on the grounds of the Ming He Yuan. They conveyed Mianyu's fluid, earthy approach to both power and culture. Similarly, the idea of "singing cranes" was both physical and metaphorical at once. Behind the dilapidated gate to residence 79 was the Crane's Nest (He Chao), an enclosure for Mianyu's gamekeeper and several pairs of cranes. Mating season was an occasion when the garden and its name became one—blending public ceremonies with a symbolic appreciation of solitude and shadows.

Crossing northeast on yet another marble bridge, a guest would come upon three adjoining courtyards arranged around open rooms. These were the main guest suites. Each was appointed with rear rooms for servants. A peach tree was the centerpiece of this enclosure as well as a moon gate—the same one noted as a ruin in Yue Shengyang's map. When the fruit tree was in full bloom, the moon gate would transmit a gently filtered light that gave this compound its name: Chun Xi Yuan, Garden of Spring Delights. This name also recalled the eastern section of He Shen's garden that had been bequeathed to Mianyu's sister, Princess Changjing.

A discriminating guest would exit the courtyard of Spring Delights and cross yet another gracefully arched marble bridge surrounded by weeping willows to arrive at the most tranquil part of the Singing Crane Garden: "White stones stood out in relief against the blue waters, fragrant flowers and intricate rocks were reflected on the surface of the pond. A feeling of tranquility would course through the body as one's mind became fully refreshed."[37] Beyond this point, in the northeast corner of the garden, lay the most isolated spot, called Island of the Flourishing Deer (Fu Lu Dao). Set in the midst of a gourd-shaped lake, this island was Mianyu's favorite corner. He chose to grace it with a name that played upon the echo between the Chinese words for "deer" and "good fortune" (*lu* and *fu*). He even went so far as to commission a wooden bridge that would evoke the shape of a deer's antler. The bridge was painted red, the color long associated in China with good luck.

Turning south from Fu Lu Dao, a guest would come upon the part of the Singing Crane Garden most clearly designed for contemplation. It was here that the Yi Ran Ting stood out as a jewel, waiting for those willing to slow their step. Situated at the top of an artificial hill, it offered an uninterrupted view of the Western Hills and of the Fragrant Mountains beyond. The Qianlong emperor had already noted its charms. His grandson Mianyu honored that memory by making this corner of the garden particularly conducive to gazing afar. Unlike the western, socially oriented portion of the garden, the Pavilion of Winged Eaves led a visitor to look inward. Winding paths (unlike the stiff, cement steps of the promontory today) led down to the Terrace of Unblemished Flowering (Huan Qing Xie). This was yet another contemplation platform on the way to a courtyard sheltered by cypress and pine. Called Kindly Loving Spirit Clouds (Ai Ran Jing Yun), this enclosure was designed for the pleasure of gazing at flickering goldfish shaded by a canopy of verdure. Above and below, a sense of quiet amplitude prevailed.

The platform for viewing goldfish is not far from the location of Red Lake today. The most contemplative corner of the Singing Crane Garden was thus exactly the place where Maoist propaganda was displayed during the Cultural Revolution. Zhu Guanqian, glancing out of the niu peng, had caught a glimpse of kindly clouds and chose to live. Instead of suicide, he crafted for himself a future of scholarly inquiry about the philosophy of aesthetics.

The ruins of Mianyu's goldfish pond adjoin today the enclosure built by the biology department upon the land behind the Sackler Museum. In the nineteenth century, a special terrace stood here to aid the reflective visitor. It was called the Hall for Refreshed Understanding (Yu Xin Tang). On the north edge of the fishpond had stood a majestic two-storied building. This unique structure was known as the Lasting Gladness of the True (or, more literally, the Hall for Savoring Uninterrupted Consciousness, Yan Liu Zhen Shang). A decade after the destruction of the Singing Crane Garden, Yihuan recalled the name and beauty of this site with these words:

Earth cradles the old name:
Lasting Gladness of the True.

A modest soul once savored beauty here,
before the world took its revenge . . .[38]

Perhaps there is no better tribute to the life of Mianyu than the recollections of a nephew who had personally savored the beauties of the Singing Crane Garden. More than the Hall of Azure Purity, the northeast corner of the garden enabled guests to understand the spiritual outlook of their imperial host. In the western section of the garden, hierarchy prevailed. There Mianyu reigned as Prince Hui: son, brother, and uncle of emperors. Near the marble fishpond, however, a different kind intimacy was encouraged. Here, there was time to savor a refreshed understanding of old classics. Here, you were invited to watch spirit clouds float in the sky. Here, one came to understand what is most enduring in life: not titles and possessions (all of which Mianyu and Yihuan were well endowed with), but "gladness of the true." Privileged in the extreme, the owner of Singing Crane Garden managed, nonetheless, to create a space that spoke of the enduring attractions of contemplation.

Mianyu's delight in the contemplative life also shines through in his posthumously collected book of essays and poems, *Ai ri zhai ji* (Notes from the Studies of Cherished Days.) One more studio sobriquet, one more image of the self projected onto the canvass of history. In this work, as in the garden, Mianyu displayed an artful balancing act between Manchu manliness and Confucian scholarly grace. Taking his cue from the classical injunction that "a gentleman who knew his days were few served his parents with increasing dedication," the owner of the Singing Crane Garden did indeed try to make each of his days count. Wasting one's talents, like squandering one's time, was unforgivable in his eyes. Yet this is what he saw all around him in the daily conduct of younger Manchu princes. As a result, his essays and poems took on a plaintive tone. The Studio of Cherished Days ended up as a compilation of ideals rarely put into practice. The times and circumstances of Mianyu's descendants made it ever more difficult to embody his ideals. Like Mianyu's garden, the book, too, became a monument to a vanished world.

Two of Mianyu's nephews wrote prefaces for this posthumous collection. The shorter one was by Yizong, owner of Qing Hua Yuan (Garden of Flowering Purity). This was a princely retreat adjacent to the Singing Crane Garden and is the home of Qinghua University today. In his preface, Yizong recalls with melancholy how he used to sit in the study hall where his uncle customarily lectured the Manchu princes: "His gentle voice and strong moral convictions ring in my ears even today."[39] But the ring, Yizong concluded, was a pale echo of the man who had sought to remind the emperor's offspring that they had a higher calling. The longer preface is by Yihuan. This eulogy took the form of a lengthy poem full of detailed recollections about his uncle's days, gardens, and literary style. Though the sentiment was conventional, the tone of genuine gratitude remained fresh:

He achieved so much in one lifetime,
Prosperity was ever near. So many rituals,
Performed, hymns intoned when he was granted
Lordships. The Emperor ever benevolent,
Called upon him to execute justice and honor.

My brush is an inadequate tool to give voice
To the gratitude I owe him. His imperially granted garden ever
In my mind and near my own is a reminder
Of his kindness. He vowed to never stray from loyalty and duty.
All of his efforts were crowned with great success.
Each noted and rewarded by the Son of Heaven.
At home, his companions were books and music,
In the garden, he savored the pleasures of brush and ink.
The pine tree is known for its majesty and solitude,
So, too, he had the strength to withstand snow,
To thwart ambition, to scratch the clouds.

The final verdict on his towering height
Is left to posterity.[40]

Images of the pine call to mind both the garden and the man. Both aimed to convey a longing for moral rectitude. Both fell victim to times that were inimical to truth. As Yihuan noted, the emperor had rewarded Mianyu for repeated acts of loyalty and service. But the full measure of the man was not to be found in the public realm. When Yihuan wrote about the verdict of posterity, he may have been speaking as much for himself as for his uncle. Having risen even higher in his privileged access to the throne, the owner of Wei Xiu Yuan had good reason to worry about what the future held for his own offspring as well as his beloved garden.

In the Garden of Flowering Wormwood

Born in 1840, the same year that his uncle had began to perform the Grand Sacrifices for the Aisin Gioro clan, Yihuan lived to see more glory and more ravage than Mianyu. As the seventh son of the Daoguang emperor, Yihuan had little time to savor traditional education in the studio that Qianlong had adorned with cranes and pines. War broke out the year he was born; the burning of the Summer Palace took place when he was twenty. In this brief interlude, Yihuan made a great impression on his imperial kin with literacy skills as well as his devotion to family honor. When his fourth brother, Yizhu, became emperor in 1851, the young boy's star began to rise meteorically. By 1859, he had been granted his own garden and a new bride. Yihuan's wife was sister to the emperor's favorite concubine, the powerful woman who became Empress Dowager Cixi (1835–1908). In the decades after the trauma of 1860, Yihuan remained a close ally and supporter of the throne. In fact, he was so near to the seat of power that Cixi felt entitled to take his son and make him the last of her manipulable emperors. Yihuan thus had the "honor" of being the father of Guangxu (1871–1908) as well as grandfather to the last emperor of China, Puyi (1906–1967), who died during the Cultural Revolution.

This direct link from the ravaged imperial gardens of northwest Beijing to the atrocities of the Maoist era helps us see Yihuan in a fresh light. His numerous poems are more than stylized nostalgia. They are a pathway toward the historical memory that is so often left mute in China today. A visitor to Beijing University might miss altogether the brown placard with green callig-

Figure 19. Placard with the characters *Wei Xiu Yuan* (Garden of Flourishing Wormwood/ Garden of Flourishing Grace) opposite the west gate of Beijing University.

raphy (figure 19) that marks the entrance to the compound that occupies the grounds of Yihuan's Wei Xiu Yuan. Yihuan had been granted this garden in 1859. This enclosure was initially known simply as the Garden of the Seventh Prince because its owner was the seventh son of the Daoguang emperor. Highly literate, the young prince was not content to have his Haidian retreat known by such a prosaic name. Mindful of the great gardening traditions that went back to Mi Wanzhong's Shao Yuan, Yihuan asked his fourth brother, the Xianfeng emperor, for the favor of a new name. The ruler, who

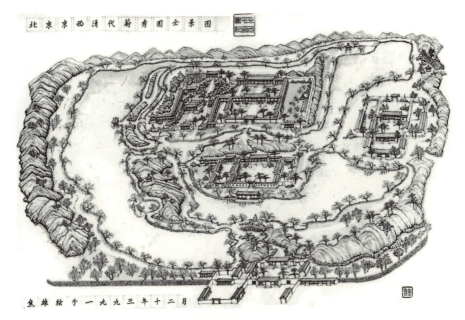

北京京西清代蔚秀園全景圖

焦雄敖于一九九三年十二月

Figure 20. Painting of the Garden of Flourishing Grace (Wei Xiu Yuan) owned by Yihuan, Prince Chun. The painting was executed for the author by Jiao Xiong in 1998.

liked to indulge this sibling, obliged. He chose Wei Xiu Yuan, which can be translated either as Garden of Flourishing Grace or Garden of Flowering Wormwood (figure 20).

Clearly, young Prince Chun wanted his garden to be a place of enduring verdancy. The first ideograph in his garden's name provided room for playful association. *Wei* means literally "wormwood," but it can also connote hard-won ethical virtues, such as a state of inner grace. At one level, Yihuan wanted his garden to be a place of relaxing contemplation. At another, he may have sensed the winds of bitter conflict swelling around the Qing dynasty. The name of the garden became even more metaphorical as the poet-prince returned to grieve after 1860. His sorrow-filled verses call to mind Ovid's lines, written during exile to the east: "wormwood . . . the bitter yield of a bitter land!"[41]

Little remains of the old Wei Xiu Yuan today. The brown wooden sign attached to a cement pillar stands at a busy intersection that marks the transition from Beijing University's west gate to the staff compound across the road. To the left of the brown placard is a crowded grocery store selling everything from Kodak film and Coca-Cola to cheap, sugary ice pops manufactured locally. To the right, behind the Wei Xiu Yuan placard, today's visitor is accosted by a coarse evocation of a "moon gate," a false door leading to the entrance of a nursery school. Built in the 1980s, this children's compound was celebrated by Hou Renzhi when he wrote his book about the history of princely gardens. In the absence of flourishing wormwood, the historical geographer suggests that the clumsily landscaped kindergarten "brings a new picture of prosperity into the old garden, a symbol of new life."[42]

To look beyond this obligatory symbol of socialist renewal one has to let the eye wander, quite literally, to the lay of the land. Wei Xiu Yuan today lingers on in the undulating mounds that border a central, algae-clogged lake. The ample, continuous flow of water discernible in Jiao Xiong's drawing has been interrupted by blocks of cement buildings. These are dormitories for junior faculty, whose homes had been taken over by campus workers during the Cultural Revolution. These squat structures with their ceramic roofs and adjoining vegetable gardens provide a small taste of the grand tranquility that must have reigned here during the time when Prince Chun had designed artful pavilions.

Nothing remains today of the tastefully sculptured gate that was the main entrance to the Wei Xiu Yuan. Nothing remains of the guest quarters set off to the east on a premonitory surrounded by water. A small path once linked this compound to the host's entertainment quarters and the garden viewing platforms beyond. In the far east corner of Yihuan's retreat stood a small pavilion, a mirror image of the Yi Ran Ting. Today, nothing remains there but a new, rather squat terrace plunked upon an artificial hill (figure 21). There is no plaque here like the one across the road reminding visitors of the origins of the Singing Crane Garden. There is nothing here to connect the single roof structure to the garden where Prince Chun once savored glimpses of the Jade Hill Pagoda. Instead, traditional-style paintings in livid turquoise depict scholars writing poetry in old-fashioned robes. Clumsy as they are, these images have been left unviolated, unlike the older, more authentic images outside the door of Wang Yao's home.

In the 1930s, Dorothy Graham was privileged to visit the ruined Wei Xiu Yuan. Befriended by Yihuan's descendants, especially his seventh son, Zaitao, this American writer walked the grounds with the voices of imperial kin in mind. Impoverished, out of power, facing a China at war (though not yet in full

Figure 21. Modern pavilion on the grounds of the former Wei Xiu Yuan (Garden of Flourishing Grace).

swing of the communist revolution), these princes bore witness to a culture that no longer flourished in northwest Beijing. Graham's description of twilight in the old Wei Xiu Yuan is poetic enough to match the spirit of Yihuan: "In the evening, a glint of gold catches the oval pool, covering it with a metallic patina. On a hillock against the setting sun, standing a pavilion with delicately uplifted eaves, a fragile silhouette in black, a one-dimensional cutting against the gold. The sun and the pool are two disks of light, with the horned pavilion standing between them."[43] For Graham, as for the more scholarly Oswald Siren a decade later, Chinese gardens were places to take note of shifting light. Whether coming through a gourd-shaped gate or around the edges of a pavilion with winged eaves, the setting sun seems to bring out the best of what was left on these sites of princely refuge.

When Yihuan walked the paths of his old garden in the 1880s, he also took note of the light. Yet, unlike Graham, Yihuan mourned the shifting light. Sunset was not simply a lyrical metaphor for this prince. It was a concrete reminder of all that he had lost:

One breath to take it in:
newly swollen waters, thicker than oil.

Twenty autumns later,
again the garden,

the archery field silent,
broken pavilions, dance halls abandoned,

a sea of shards,
new birth perhaps from rubble.

Near the terrace, a pair of pine,
call to the Western Hills,

upon a mound of charred remains
I search for the old village.

Nothing but the shadow of Jade Spring Temple,
winddriven chatter and white clouds.[44]

The passage of years accentuated Yihuan's grief for the Wei Xiu Yuan. In his uncle's garden, the din of sparrows crowded out the echo of the missing cranes. In his own retreat, oily waters, an abandoned archery field, and charred remains occupied the ground as far as the eye could see. Only temple bells retained their old power.

The very suppleness of Yihuan's poetry belies the silence of the ravaged site. If words can still be fashioned into verse, perhaps the archery field can gain another, posthumous life. This was a corner of the garden with special associations for Manchu nobility. Called Western Meadows (Xi Yuan), it had been the main cavalry parade ground during the reign of Qianlong. Its Military Review Tower still carried Qianlong's seal in the time of Yihuan. Now, wind-driven chatter enveloped the old cavalry grounds. Its very aimlessness became a form of awakened consciousness.

The master of Wei Xiu Yuan made a career of mourning the ruined gardens of northwest Beijing. The higher Yihuan rose in status, the more honors the Empress Dowager heaped on him, the darker the tone of his commemorations of the genuine grandeur that once thrived around the ruined Summer Palace. His older brother, Yixin, chose a different path. Closer to actual policy making in 1860, this Manchu prince did not have the luxury, or the inclination, for extended poetic musings. He also owned a retreat adjacent to the Singing Crane Garden and was separated from Yihuan only by a bridge. Yixin also wrote poetry. Yet he never bent so mournfully into the "wind-driven chatter" of the late Qing. The two brothers remained close after the trauma of 1860; Yihuan continued to visit his prominent, activist elder brother both in his city palace and Haidian retreat. In the privacy of Yixin's garden—Lang Run Yuan—they could share tea and regrets about the waning Mandate of Heaven.

Born in 1833, Yixin had been the sixth son of the Daoguang emperor. He was expected to play a major role in the fate of the Qing. By age nineteen, he had been given the title of Prince Gong, and a city palace as well as a garden adjoining the Ming He Yuan. These rewards were tokens of appreciation for his critical role in containing the Taiping rebellion that had taken over the city of Nanjing in 1854. Between 1854 and 1860, Yixin had ample time to develop both his city and country estates. His city compound was well documented in a 1940 study by H. S. Chen and G. N. Kates. Their essay, like Oswald Siren's photographs, is a testament to how an informed appreciation of beauty can be conveyed even in the midst of war. The images accompanying Chen and Kates's study show a palace and garden dedicated to the arts and to historical reflection. One of the most elaborate structures in Prince Gong's city palace was a multistory theater complex—not unlike the one that was the centerpiece of Mianyu's Singing Crane Garden.

Less elaborate but quite impressive, Yixin's library compound was well suited to display the sharp edges of winter light. The passageway from theater to library bore the suggestive name of Porch of the Loving Brothers (Di Hua Xuan). Yixin must have chosen this name with care. The hope for ongoing fraternal harmony was an ideal of the mid-nineteenth century, which was sorely tested in the difficult decades that followed the defeat of 1860. Loving brothers were set against one another by an increasingly avaricious dowager empress who saw benefit only where she herself could pull the strings of power and of loyalty. Her dominating reach was not as visible on the grounds of Prince Gong's country retreat, the Garden of Moonlit Fertility (Lang Run Yuan). Especially after the burning of the Summer Palace, Lang Run Yuan was left to decay. Even as Yixin was forced to sign humiliating treaties with the victorious Western forces, he was able to return to Lang Run Yuan for solace and inspiration.

Like the Wei Xiu Yuan to the west, this princely garden also had a sculptured entrance and a central island (figure 22). The courtyards appear to be fewer and more modest in scale than those of the neighboring Singing Crane Garden. Pavilions for the contemplation of the Western Hills appear to be set off more dramatically. An intentional disorder marks this garden in contrast to the owner's elaborate city palace. Dorothy Graham captured this effortless fluidity in one of the most beautiful passages of her book on Chinese gardens. Allowed to roam the site at will, she captured the wonderment of eye and mind made possible in this enclosure:

Trees fringing the lakes have their trunks obliquely set, to lead the eyes' focal point, across the water. Pools of shadow rest within pools, imparting depth and mystery. The foliage is green upon green, the darker leaves making a foil for the light. It seems that the garden has come into being without the volition of man. Yet, to realize the astuteness of the designer, one has only to look beyond its walls to where the barren steppes stretch to the whirling dust clouds raised by files of camels. From a desert, a stylized forest has been made. Within the high outer walls, a series of connecting hills was piled to shut out all sight of the world, and all sound. . . . A latticed pavilion extends over the lake so that the water beneath will soften the music of the lutes. Another is placed so that one may listen to the chirp of crickets and the dry leaves falling. There are the subtleties of sound which intensify silence—the symphonic music of the trees, the muffled soughing of the pines, the brittle staccato of the acacias, the deliberate heavy movement of the catalpas, the insidious, wistful murmur of the trailing pines. There are no flowers to fade with the changing seasons. . . . This is the perfection of the ideal: hills to stimulate the imagination, still water conducive to calm. . . . Height is balanced by depth; the stark stones are enfolded by pliant verdure. It is a place of utter loneliness. The soul escapes the ebb and flow of emotion to merge with the mystic quietude.[45]

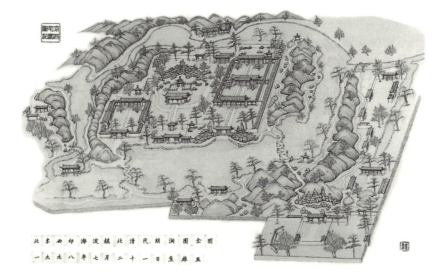

Figure 22. Painting of the Garden of Moonlit Fertility (Lang Run Yuan) owned by Yixin, Prince Gong. The painting was executed as a gift for the author by Jiao Xiong in 1998.

I quote this passage at length because it evokes the spirit of the Chinese garden with literary verve. Graham was an astute, if at times romantic, observer of the realms of imagination that Manchu princes sought to create in the northwest corner of Beijing.

Prince Gong memorialized his own garden in restrained tones. Unlike the twentieth-century American guest who let herself be carried away by subtleties of sound and silence, Yixin came to the garden burdened by political cares. His two collections of poems (one entitled *Le Dao Tang Shi Ji* [Verses from the Studio for Rejoicing in the Way] and the other *Cui Jin Yin* [A Tapestry of Incantations]) show us a Manchu nobleman, who, like his uncle Mianyu and his brother Yihuan, knew how to use Confucian allusions well. Yixin's affection for the Garden of Moonlit Fertility comes across in great detail in these poems that were compiled from the lines of previous generations of classical Chinese masters.

It is as if the distinctive solace that Prince Gong found in the hamlet of Haidian could be articulated only by borrowing from the experiences of earlier writers. In an explanatory note to a poem called "A swell of sentiment for Haidian gardens," Yixin writes: "My own garden's name is Lang Run Yuan and my younger brother's is known as Wei Xiu Yuan. Our two enclosures were separated merely by a bridge. During the reign of the Xianfeng emperor we were granted these gardens and the emperor himself penned the calligraphy that adorned our gates. Since the years of the Tongzhi reign, however, both of us were forced to live in the city due to pressing affairs at court. Neither one of us has free time to savor the grace and refuge that we once shared in Haidian. Thirty years have passed since we visited each other across the bridge and yet it seems like yesterday."[46]

These words, written around 1889, reflect the pressure of politics upon two brothers who once shared a vision of refuge in Haidian. Both Manchu princes had been drawn into court intrigue, both were charged with weighty military matters that shaped the destiny of the entire Qing. Yihuan, the younger brother, died two years after this mournful recollection of garden life. Yixin lived on to see yet another humiliating defeat at the end of the Sino-Japanese war of 1895. During the last three years of his life, Prince Gong sought again and again to find a bit of solace in the Lang Run Yuan.

No longer able to cross the bridge to the Garden of Flowering Wormwood, he chose to amble on memory's path. Like Yihuan, this Manchu prince also cherished ruins more than the lavish new summer palace built by his powerful sister-in-law, Empress Dowager Cixi. Having tried, and failed, to salvage the grandeur of the Qing, Yixin turned to Buddhist and Confucian notions of the afterlife. Here, as in the garden, he found a taste of freedom:

The next life awaiting us
is unknown,

this incarnation
almost over,

do not blame the wind
if your soul aches for the past,

autumn's light nourishes
endless thoughts—

at times, love of gardens
can be a hazard.

Now, lattice window closed
jade halls empty,

songs silenced
in deserted pavilions,

torrential rains roam
like a bird set free.[47]

Bleak, these verses fit the Confucian trope of late-life meditations. Autumn rains were a traditional symbol for the aged man disappointed by his political career. What makes this poem quite fresh is Yixin's honest reckoning with garden lore. If his Lang Run Yuan had fallen silent, it was not simply because of politics, not only because foreigners had torched Haidian. "Don't blame the wind" is a way of acknowledging his own participation, indeed complicity, in the events that brought about the ruination of the Qing. True, Manchu princes like Mianyu, Yihuan, and Yixin had loved their gardens well. Yet, like their overindulgent imperial kin who had built and cherished the Summer Palace, garden love had become "extreme." It became a force of destruction. This time, it is not wind-driven chatter but tuneless autumn rain that spells out disaster in no uncertain terms.

One Earth-Shattering Cry

Maybe the owner of the Singing Crane Garden could have foreseen this devastation. Maybe he even tried to warn that it was coming. But few of his fellow noblemen bothered to listen in the years before the burning of the Yuan Ming Yuan. Being older than Yixin and Yihuan, Prince Hui had more time to enjoy his Haidian refuge. He also had ample reason to be concerned about the corruption spreading among the Qing ruling elites. Charged with the education of young princes, Mianyu knew firsthand how crane symbolism had become empty verbiage in the palace halls. Whereas Qianlong had imagined Manchu offspring with a spirit of nobility, his grandson observed a generation all too comfortable with privilege and too reluctant to act responsibly on behalf of the state. Love of pleasure, including garden love, had indeed run amok.

In 1853, when the Ming He Yuan was at the height of its glory, Mianyu himself did not hesitate to serve the dynasty in times of danger. Eagerly, he agreed to defend the capital from Taiping rebels. He left the peace of the garden to wage war against peasant bands who attacked both Confucian values and the legitimacy of the Manchu state. While Prince Hui was busy raising an army, his nephew Yizhu ruled as the pleasure-seeking Xianfeng emperor. Infatuated by the beauty of the Yuan Ming Yuan, Yizhu spent long days out of the Forbidden City, enjoying the company of his favorite concubine—the woman thrust forward in history as Cixi. Bored by official documents bearing news of disaster, he left the defense of the state in the hands of imperial kinsmen like Prince Hui.

Mianyu's essays written in these years of national danger reflect the concerns of a Manchu prince trying to salvage and reinvigorate the Qing Mandate of Heaven. Inspired by garden metaphors, he dwells on the image of the evergreen pine that can withstand the snows of political adversity. The problem, as Mianyu saw it, was that China's soil, like the garden, was not resilient enough. Children of highborn families had become soft, rotten due to lack of moral guidance and ignorance of the world beyond the palace gate:

They deplete all the wealth of their home in quest of cheap joys like opera and theater. They do not understand history or philosophy or the correct path of moral conduct (*zheng lun*). They are easily cheated by people with evil intentions and end up losing honor as well as their inherited wealth. Others may have a smattering of classical learning but do not understand the significance of our traditions. In office, they do not care about affairs of the state. In scholarship, they show no rigor of style. They care only about food, music and entertainment. Their essays and poems do not flow from a pure source but rather from a slanted heart. . . . All these young people are my worry and I want to preach to them: Thrift is a virtue. Our holy classics are the way to become a true human being. Alas! High officials with large salaries never think of repaying those who placed trust in them! They have read books but have no understanding of genuine morality. They betray those who gave them position and the world as well.[48]

The owner of the Singing Crane Garden reveals himself in these essays as a stringent moralist at war with the culture of indulgence that was his natural milieu. Confucian precepts dominate his thoughts. He is constantly pleading obedience to the "five relationships" (*wu lun*) between father and son, ruler and minister, older brother and younger brother, husband and wife, and friends. This fifth son of the fifth emperor of the Manchu dynasty warned about the dangers of privilege divorced from self-cultivation. The same man who had walked the winding paths of the Ming He Yuan, who had entertained scholars and noblemen in his elaborate refuge in Haidian, also warned young people against the dangers of excessive self-indulgence.

Was this mere hypocrisy? His nephews insisted that it was not. In memory's eye, at least, Mianyu appears as a prince who combined privilege and responsibility. The essays and poems compiled for the posthumous *Collection from the Studio of Cherished Days* show a Manchu prince who had sought to serve the Qing with integrity. Yixin, who as a youth had studied under the tutelage of Mianyu and had been a guest in the Singing Crane Garden, wrote a preface that recalled his uncle as a fortress of moral authority. He, too, used the metaphor of the solitary pine to describe his uncle's fortitude in the face of adversity. Like Yihuan, he celebrates Mianyu's love of nature. At the same time, as a seasoned politician, Yixin dwells on times that are inimical to verdant virtue:

The pine he cultivated was once
Thin and feeble as a stalk.
After years of careful nurture, it aged.
Now resplendently green,
Like a dragon that has outgrown his skin,
It unwinds huge branches in the sky,
Rich shade prevails beneath it,
Yet not sturdy enough to be a pillar,
Untroubled by heavy snows,
Each second of its growing time
Prepares for one earth-shattering cry.[49]

Yixin's poem carries a tone of prophecy. After 1860, the dragon never roared again. None of the princes whom Mianyu educated became sturdy pillars to uphold Qing glory. After his death, the owner of the Singing Crane Garden appeared to his beloved nephews as a dragon that had outgrown its skin. During his lifetime, Mianyu had been wrapped in many titles, many honors. He shed them, along with the charred remains of the Ming He Yuan. He had witnessed many political adversities, many disappointments. Not being the emperor, he could not prop up a sinking heaven. All he could do, as Yixin painfully recalled, was to use his moral might for one more earth-shattering cry. This, too, fell on deaf ears.

In 1865, when Mianyu died at the age of fifty-one, he was granted one more title. As if Prince Hui and "General in Charge of Saving the Mandate" were not enough, he was canonized as Duan—"Fully Upright." The master of the Singing Crane Garden thus exited history wrapped in virtues that his descendants found increasingly difficult to emulate.

Chapter 2
War Invades the Garden

The cranes on Dying River rise . . .
Their bodies swift upon the sky
Describe invisible designs
And as they move their wings expound
Minute catastrophes of sound.
—Lawrence Olson, "The Cranes on Dying River"

The catastrophe that befell Singing Crane Garden after 1860 was by no means minute. The magnitude of loss can be imagined if one listens for the sound of cranes departing. This is what historian-poet Lawrence Olson did when he suggested that departing cranes expound "invisible designs."[1] In China, in the hamlet of Haidian, vanishing cranes and dying rivers were not merely a poetic metaphor. The cranes' flight coincided with the collapse of Qing imperial grandeur.

Two worldviews, two temporalities, two imperialisms collided violently in 1860 on the grounds of northwest Beijing. Singing Crane Garden with its meandering paths, fishponds, pavilions, theater, and literary guests had been designed to slow down time for Manchu princes. Lord James Elgin's armies, guns, and fleet, by contrast, were meant to speed up time for the Western powers. Garden temporality thrived on leisure and contemplation. Western diplomacy demanded prompt action, open doors—not gourd-shaped gates. The Manchu rulers of China had imagined themselves civilized monarchs of a universal empire.[2] Lord Elgin's burning of the Summer Palace and surrounding estates shattered this illusion. What constitutes barbarism, and what is genuine civilization became fiery questions in a location where cranes once presided as an unchallenged symbol of high-mindedness.

The year 1860 found forty-six-year-old Prince Mianyu retired from military affairs. He had discharged his obligations as defender of Beijing five years earlier, when he successfully rebuffed the Taiping rebels from the north. With his new title "Savior of the Mandate," he might have expected years of pleasurable retirement. Certainly, he was aware of military altercations with Western "barbarians" in south China. He was very familiar with the 1842 Treaty of Nanking, which ended the so-called first Opium War. He was also aware that in 1858, the British and the French had pushed for further concessions, especially direct trade and diplomatic representation in the imperial capital. The Manchu prince who had fought off massive hordes of Chinese rebels assumed this was no real threat. He was content to leave minor military altercations in the hands of his skilled assistant, the Mongol general Sengkelinqin. For Mianyu, garden time finally promised to unfold in peace.

The year 1860 found forty-nine-year-old Lord Elgin at the apex of his diplomatic career. Embarking upon his most challenging act of service for the British empire, he arrived in China full of determination to settle the matter of direct diplomacy once and for all. The official portrait from this mission shows a massive gentleman, decorated with signs of distinguished service, robed in furs that signaled a cold autumn in north China. His strong, direct gaze gave the barest hint of the complex calculations and seasoned sensibility that this gentleman had carried with him from his previous China mission and from his earlier experiences as governor-general in North America and in India. A fragment from his 1858 China journal suffices to convey the hesitations and the self-questioning mindset of the man charged with representing the interests of the British empire to the Chinese court: "Whose work are we engaged in, when we burst thus with hideous violence and brutal energy into these darkest and most mysterious recesses of the traditions of the past? I wish I could answer that question in a manner satisfactory to myself. At the same time there is certainly not much to regret in the old civilization, which we are thus scattering to the winds. A dense population, timorous and pauperized, such would seem to be its chief product."[3]

Here we see Elgin examining his own thoughts about British imperialism and violence. He was fully aware of the "brutal" force being applied to an older, historically anchored civilization. At the same time, he saw the legacy of the Qing imperial system to be nothing more than an impoverished, politically dispossessed society—already tottering under the challenges of Taiping rebels. When he arrived for his second China mission, James Elgin did not plan to burn the Summer Palace. He did not want to overthrow the Qing.

He demanded political concessions and became, unexpectedly, entangled in questions of vengeance and justice.

Forty-three-year-old Thomas William Bowlby, a correspondent for the *Times* of London, was part of the reason that Elgin changed his mind. This colorful, highly educated man accompanied Elgin to China in 1860. A pioneer in the risky business of war-reportage, Bowlby carried with him the values and visions of a lawyer, railway investor, captain of the royal artillery, and a generally well-traveled European. His lengthy articles from China focused on all aspects of local culture, from princely gardens to village sewage. Bowlby's focus, however, was keenly political and military. Lengthy conversations with Elgin led him to note in his diary: "Surely never was so extraordinary a war waged as this. We protect Shanghai for the Imperialists [a reference to the use of British and French troops against the Taiping rebels] and are about to attack Peking against them. We trade for tea . . . and silk . . . and everywhere the people show the greatest anxiety to deal with us. If the Ambassadors do but carry out a policy of 'thorough' and convince the Peking Mandarins that we are too strong for the Chinese, this difficulty will be settled for many a day."[4] The reference to a "thorough" policy in the summer of 1860 did not mean destruction of Chinese civilization. It did not require the burning of the Yuan Ming Yuan. Rather, T. W. Bowlby was recording Lord Elgin's determination to install Western diplomats in the imperial capital, "even if he was to walk there."[5]

On October 17, 1860, when Elgin received from the Chinese the maimed body of T. W. Bowlby, his outlook and his plans changed. Captured and tortured to death, the war correspondent changed world history. Bowlby's murder was not the primary or the only reason for the burning of the Summer Palace. But, as this chapter shows, it sharpened the conflict of views about what constitutes civilization, and what is barbarism. By the time Bowlby's obituary was published in the *London News* on December 29, 1860, the princely grounds of northwest Beijing lay covered in ash and rubble. Thomas Bowlby gazed out from the pages of the newspaper with fierce eyes and windswept hair. All of Britain's China troubles seemed to be painted on the face of this prominent victim who was "treacherously captured and imprisoned by the Tartar general San-ke-lin-sin."[6] The same trusted assistant who had helped Mianyu defend the Mandate of Heaven from the Taiping rebels was accused here of atrocities committed upon the body of a British war correspondent.

Garden culture lay quite literally in the gulf between these two disparate evaluations of imperial power. Geography, like history, condensed around the garden and invaded its previously walled-off terrain. At the height of

Qing glory, barbarians were kept far from the capital, unless they came to pay tribute to the Son of Heaven. By 1860, neither the Forbidden City nor Haidian were beyond the range of foreign armies. When Elgin's private secretary, Henry Loch, was commissioned to make a detailed map of the march to Beijing, he focused on swamps, forts, and rivers, not the Summer Palace. Yuan Ming Yuan was a distant, barely visible destination beyond the capital. As late as September 1860, the British goal was still Beijing. A political lesson was to be taught simply through the show of military force inside the imperial capital. Looting, fires, ravage came two weeks later, suddenly.

The Qing official who had to cope with this rapidly shifting situation was Mianyu's nephew, Yixin—the twenty-three-year-old Prince Gong. In a photograph taken by the Italian Felice Beato (who accompanied Elgin on his triumphal march into Beijing on October 24, 1860), the master of the Garden of Moonlit Fertility appears as a delicate youth worn down by the worries of an imperial capital abandoned by his older brother, the Xianfeng emperor. Yixin looks into the "barbarian's lens" with fear and humiliation.[7] Used to more distant gazes and more mannered spaces, the Manchu nobleman could not help betraying the grief of defeat. General Hope Grant, who had led Elgin's armies in the war against garden time, recalled:

The royal brother looked up in a state of terror, pale as death, and with his eyes turned first to Lord Elgin and then to me, expecting every moment to have his head blown off by the infernal machine opposite him—which really looked like a sort of mortar, ready to disgorge its terrible contents into his devoted body. It was explained to him that no such evil design was intended, and his anxious pale face brightened up when he was told that his portrait was being taken. The treaty was signed, and the whole business went off satisfactorily, except as regards Signor Beato's picture, which was an utter failure, owing to want of proper light.[8]

More than images of broken stone (which became emblems of the ruined Yuan Ming Yuan in subsequent decades), Beato's photograph of Prince Gong revealed a world about to end. Sepia colors, fearful eyes, Yixin's arms lost in shadowy robes, convey a spiritual defeat that mirrored the physical ruin of garden culture in the hamlet of Haidian. The Singing Crane Garden along with all of the other princely estates and the old Summer Palace had lost their power to heal political wounds. Northwest Beijing no longer offered a reprieve from clashing news of imperialism and civilization. The task of diplomacy rested on the shoulders of a young prince cut off from the delights of poetry he had once savored in Lang Run Yuan. A shrunken cultural universe required new visions of gardens and war alike.

Geng Shen: Year of the Monkey

January 1860 began a promising new year in the Chinese calendar. The agile monkey was the next zodiac symbol and with this came hopes for clever solutions to intractable problems. True, the country was still suffering from the massive Taiping rebellion. But unrest seemed to be well contained and maybe even diminishing before the armies of newly empowered Chinese generals such as Zeng Guofan. Westerners who had made additional demands in the 1858 Treaty of Tianjin were also being put off. The capital was in the hands of the war-tested Mongolian general Sengkelinqin and all seemed well. The court could revel in new year celebrations undisturbed.

Astrological calculation also assigned unique coordinates to this new year: *geng* was the sign associated with "earth," and *shen* was an omen under the influence of "wood." Furthermore, *geng* had connotations of weapons while *shen* called to mind fir and bamboo. These were, in principle, harmonious signs. As the new year dawned, no one would have imagined that earth and wood would become ravaged by the enemy element of "fire." No one in the imperial clan could have suspected that the pleasure palace of Yuan Ming Yuan would be condemned to burn for crimes against humanity.

Certainly Prince Chun, the favored younger brother of the emperor, had no inkling what heavy-hearted mourning awaited him by the late fall. He could not have imagined how the Year of the Monkey would give way to bitterness about "the shame of the *geng shen* year." This phrase became his personal acknowledgment of responsibility for the lassitude that led to the destruction of imperial gardens in the hamlet of Haidian.

In the early spring of 1860, Yihuan was still enjoying the idea of spiritual and aesthetic refuge. In a poem celebrating the new year, he describes the joys of riding out to his cousin's Qing Hua garden. These delights were more acute precisely because the twenty-year-old man had time and leisure to observe the unfolding of early spring, a season of hope that grew more verdant as he left behind the dominating architecture of the Forbidden City and public political power.

Holding the reins, I meander
once again toward Qing Hua Garden

as spring's first tendrils
arch into a cold sun.

Peach and plum, survivors
of bitter frost, refuse to bloom.

One solitary spruce keeps pace
with the harsh rhythms of nature's time.

At dawn, the nineteenth day of the new year,
I leave the court, and the dominion of Phoenix Tower.[9]

It may be too much to read a subtle critique of his sister-in-law Cixi in this relief from the dominion of "Phoenix Tower." Certainly not in this poem, nor in later works, did Yihuan actually raise his voice against the woman who held the reins of power after 1860. Instead, he dwells on the conventional symbols of peach and plum, noting as many had before him that it takes fortitude to survive bitter frost and the cold sun. The "harsh rhythms of nature's time" were still metaphorical. In ten months, the young prince himself became a survivor and had to learn, firsthand, how unprepared he was for the harshness of war and defeat.

In the capital city of Beijing, the Year of the Monkey dawned with old routines, undisturbed. The fiery danger that would consume earth, fir, bamboo (and even stone) seemed far away. A map of the imperial city reprinted in Armand Lucy's *Expédition de Chine, 1860—Lettres Intimes* revealed a gracious, well-laid-out social universe totally at peace. The enclosure of the Forbidden City occupied the center of the upper quadrant—well placed for awe and domination. Carefully planned, most rectangular neighborhoods were crisscrossed by a web of alleys that was the charm of Peking in the old days. The young Frenchman who had chronicled the military expedition of this fateful year clearly enjoyed displaying the fragile "cosmos" that Western guns and diplomacy overturned with such resounding success.

In the streets and alleys of the imperial capital daily life unfolded with its multitonal normality. Nigel Cameron, a twentieth-century historian with a learned imagination, took it upon himself to evoke the sounds and sights of Beijing in 1860. As in the carefully drawn imperial print, everything seems safely in place. Servants still take out covered bird cages every day to catch the rays of the rising sun. Cooking smoke envelops the alleys along with "ankle deep powdery dust (and mud, if it rained)." As in the visual representation, single-story houses crowd narrow passageways and florid ceremonial arches mark major intersections. Cameron's imaginary gaze brings to life even the succulent smells of street stalls:

A peddler would soon be on his rounds, bringing cooks to their doors with his cry: "Old chicken heads!"—for it was the season of water chestnuts, which resemble chicken heads in shape, "Old chicken heads, fresh from the canal!"

In the midst of this crowded and turbulent city of Peking there was embedded a second, the Imperial City, surrounded by its wall topped with yellow tiles. . . . And within this Imperial City was yet another, the Forbidden City, enclosed by its tall red walls, studded with noble gateways, with corner towers of bird-bone fineness, concealing the sacred person and appurtenances of the emperor of China.

Peking people knew little of what lay behind the rhomboid of the Gate of Heavenly Peace, had only the smallest idea of the vast courtyards, of the splendor of the pavilions, the apartments, the white translucent marble on which they stood, or of the life that went on there. But in the fine late summer of 1860, it was generally known that the emperor was not in Peking but at the summer palace outside the city, with, among others, the concubine Yi; and that he was in some apprehension for his own safety.[10]

As in the map of the imperial city, so in the popular imagination, the emperor occupied a realm apart, a world above the cares, smells, crowding of ordinary daily life. In the alleys it was "old chicken heads" that tickled taste buds. In the palaces of Xianfeng, it was turtle soup and Peking duck.

How worried was this pleasure-loving ruler in the summer of 1860? Some commoners attuned to public events had reason to be concerned about the safety of the capital and, with it, the personage of the Son of Heaven. The imperial records, however, reveal a young ruler quite content to dedicate himself fully to the pleasures of the day. On the sixth day of the sixth month of the Geng Shen year (July 23, 1860, in the Western calendar) the Xianfeng emperor celebrated his thirtieth birthday with full pomp and ceremony. The Sanqing Company (one of the great theater troupes of Beijing) was invited to perform in the Forbidden City. This was the first time that a popular troupe had been invited to the court.[11] On the grounds of Summer Palace and in the princely gardens, the summer season proved to be a balmy one. No trace here of the burdensome heat that plagued most urban dwellers. Qianlong's extravagant garden retreat continued to delight his great-grandchildren. The Great Maze (*migong*) outside of the Western-style palace provided many opportunities for amorous encounters.

Despite Mianyu's warnings about the indulgence, a joyous mood of careless optimism prevailed. Yuan Ming Yuan was a paradise of trinkets. No emperor after Qianlong bothered to learn the scientific principles that animated the rush of water upward into the sky. Chinese rulers felt no need to understand the importance of mechanization. They had no curiosity about the mathematical precision demonstrated in baroque architecture: "His Majesty had no way of knowing that the analytical geometry setting industrialization in motion would eventually make it possible for European armies to invade China and leave the Yuan Ming Yuan in ruins. In the end, the European section served no more than as another pleasant environment in which to rest, entertain, and assemble treasures of European arts. It became an appropriate casket for the emperor's *cabinet de curiosités.*"[12]

This indictment of imperial ignorance underscores the disparate worldviews that were set upon a collision course in the late summer of 1860. The Xianfeng emperor in the Summer Palace assumed that time would go on as before. He continued to pursue pleasure among his imperial kin in the restful hamlet of Haidian. Irksome state matters, never mind analytical geometry, were left in the care of uncles, cousins, and brothers—trusted intimates of the Aisin Gioro clan. There was no reason why the emperor should not have the same good fortune as previous imperial ancestors. Gardens, water fountains, and a new concubine were the main events of the day.

Close to the pleasure grounds of Yuan Ming Yuan, and very near Singing Crane Garden, was the site that would become the proximate cause of conflagration in 1860. Ji Xian Yuan—the Garden of Accumulated Virtue—was the eighteenth-century name for the prettiest part of the old Ming dynasty Spoon Garden. The culturally avaricious Qianlong emperor had taken over Ming gardens and renamed them, in keeping with his own vision of a summer palace for all seasons. "Virtue" was a Confucian value supposedly admired by all. Why not take it and assign it to a corner of Haidian that would be used to house foreign emissaries and tribute-bearing missions and thereby signal to the whole world that the Chinese emperor ruled through "accumulated" virtue alone?

Ji Xian Yuan had housed the British mission of 1793 as well as the Dutch mission two years later. Both had left enduring descriptions of this quaint enclosure near the Summer Palace. By 1860, the Garden of Accumulated Virtue lay directly adjacent to the Ming He Yuan, slightly southeast of Wei Xiu Yuan and slightly southwest of Prince Gong's garden, the Lang Ruan Yuan. Thus Mianyu, Yihuan, and Yixin were all within a stone's throw of the place where foreigner prisoners were held, and some tortured to death. What had happened, one was forced to wonder, to the idea of the garden as a place of spiritual refuge, a place to clear the mind like water in a pitcher? How did men who treasured tranquility become so deaf to the crimes committed on the doorsteps of their princely retreats? This is a question that would be forced into the open by the imperialist armies that accompanied Lord Elgin and his French ally, Baron Gros.

How did "virtue" become synonymous with atrocity? This is the same question that bothered Yue Shengyang when he described Democracy Hall on the Beijing University campus—the building that served as an entrance to the torture courtyard of the Cultural Revolution. To be sure, names, like gardens, are movable fixtures in a volatile political universe. Nonetheless, the historical trauma that began to unfold in northwest Beijing in 1860 forced Chinese and Westerners alike to wrestle with what is worth preserving and what is fatally flawed on the ground as well as in the mind.

This dual battlefield took center stage as two value systems collided in the Year of the Monkey. By September 1860, Xianfeng could not avoid looking danger in the eye. As always, he heard conflicting advice. His trusted Mongolian general urged the emperor to flee Beijing in the guise of a hunting trip to the ancestral homelands of Manchuria. High-placed Confucian advisers warned against abandoning the imperial capital at a time when common people needed heroic symbols of defiance. One minister was brave enough to call the emperor's values into question: "In what light does your Majesty regard the people? In what light the shrines of your ancestors or the altars of your tutelary gods? Will you cast away the inheritance of your ancestors like an old shoe? What would history say of Your Majesty for a thousand generations?"[13]

The Xianfeng emperor ended up taking the advice of Sengkelinqin and fled to Manchuria. But the question about the "old shoe" must have stung bitterly during the remaining year of his life. Had he given up what the British and French came to loot and burn? History and historians continue to debate culpability for the events of 1860. What remains certain is that gardens are not immune to war. Like the men who designed, owned, enjoyed, and destroyed them, gardens are embedded in a conflict-full time and language.

Nothing Could Be More Quaint than the Landscape

Across the cultural divide, Westerners were marked by their time, language, and finely hewn sense of aesthetics. It would be terribly reductionist to imagine China as civilized and the men who came on battleships and horseback as brute destroyers who cared for nothing but material benefit. One need not lapse into orientalism to do justice to the values and visions they carried across the ocean in the Year of the Monkey.

The lineage of diplomatic missions to Qing China is replete with Westerners who sought both trade benefits and an understanding of the cloistered realm they saw around them for the first time. Ji Xian Yuan, the setting of these early encounters, colored the perceptions of both eighteenth- and nineteenth-century emissaries. Lord George Macartney, the leader of the British mission to the court of Qianlong in August 1793, did not record a positive impression of the imperial guesthouse. His aides, however, were intrigued by the beauty of China's landscaped spaces. One soldier in Macartney's guard noted that the princely retreat "contained a vast variety of elegant little buildings."[14] John Borrow, the ambassador's personal secretary, was more critical of the lack of care he noted on the palace grounds. The artful disorder noted by Father Attiret a few decades earlier struck the British guests as "broken hill and dale . . . diversified with wood and lawn . . . canals, rivers and lakes are neither trimmed, nor shorn, nor sloped like a fortification . . . thrown up with immense labor in an irregular, and as it were, fortuitous manner, so as to represent the free hand of nature . . . all this fell short of the fanciful and extravagant descriptions Sir William Chambers had given of Chinese gardening."[15] These English gentlemen, it seems, had come to China ready to savor exotic beauty glimpsed from readings done at home. Educated to treasure the marvels of Greek antiquity (with their regular, geometrically comprehensible aesthetics), they found the gardens of Haidian shabby and disappointing.

The Dutch mission to the court of Qianlong came only two years after the fruitless Macartney mission. It was not much more successful in gaining diplomatic rights. This expedition, however, was lead by a man keenly attuned to the Chinese art of gardening. Isaac Titsingh (1745–1811) was a Dutch trader quite familiar with China after long years in the southern port of Canton. In Beijing, his mission was taken to the guesthouse near the Summer Palace. Here, unlike the British, the Dutch delegation performed the expected kowtow to the Chinese emperor without much protest. Furthermore, they allowed themselves to be entertained by Chinese officials eager to show off the rituals of Confucian hospitality. Titsingh's recollections of these ceremonial occasions reveal an interest in Chinese culture that went beyond the politics of diplomacy:

Never did I see a more enchanting spot either in reality or in picture. From here we were pulled across the ice to the other side in sledges with yellow ropes; there we visited five temples in beauty equaling those of Peking but far surpassing them with respect to their site, being constructed in terraces on the hillside, as well as by their natural and artificial rockeries and the free view across the water. The beautiful buildings on the other bank and the entire region furnished a picture whose beauty cannot be adequately described. From the highest temple we had a wide view on the city of Peking and this enchanting place. . . . All the picturesqueness so much admired in Chinese paintings was relished here in the highest degree. One was completely transported by the beauty.[16]

Isaac Titsingh was unusually well versed in Chinese aesthetic traditions. He had a discerning eye and was able to see the Ji Xian Yuan not in terms of Western techniques for garden design but as a site with a harmony all its own.

Nineteenth-century Western diplomats, by contrast, arrived with more urgent political demands as well as a cultural education deeply influenced by Greek and Egyptian views of beauty and eternity. James Elgin, the man who gave the order to torch the Summer Palace, was anything but a monstrous enemy of culture. In fact, he had a very finely tuned sense of aesthetics tutored by his father, Thomas, the seventh earl of Elgin. As envoy extraordinary to Constantinople (from 1799 to 1806), Thomas had ample opportunity to develop a keen interest in classical sculpture. Between 1803 and 1812, his great collection of sculptures, taken mostly from the Parthenon, was shipped to England and became the subject of violent controversy. Denounced as a rapacious vandal by Lord Byron among others, Thomas Elgin defended his actions in the name of cultural history. He ended up donating the marbles to the British Museum in 1816.[17]

Growing up in the house of Sir Thomas, young James had been surrounded by the finest relics of world civilization. Although these were mostly works of classical Western art, they nonetheless impressed the future China diplomat with their grace, as well as the controversy they generated in the public realm. Thomas saw his collection as "service to art." Others viewed it as naked looting—a charge that would come back to haunt his son on the terrain of Beijing's princely gardens. The 15,000 pounds of ancient Greek relics that Sir Thomas brought to England were seen by some critics as an ill-begotten gift that threatened public morality. Others, however, concluded that world civilization, not only Lord Elgin, benefited from this great effort. "The operations were carried on with a single-minded enthusiasm for the promotion of knowledge and art, and it is beyond question that in this direction their influence was profound."[18]

No such generous claim was ever made about the looting and burning that took place in northwest Beijing in 1860. Perhaps the objects that were

taken seemed more like trinkets than art treasures. Maybe their limited impact on the European imagination was due to the mercenary soldiers who
carried away the loot. Furthermore, Sir James, unlike his father, was not a collector of art. He saw himself, above all, as a man of peace. Ten years before
his China mission, the younger Elgin had served as governor of Canada. He
had helped settle the Franco-British conflict with relatively little bloodshed.
A faithful servant of the crown, the eighth Lord Elgin understood that complex interests were being fought out in lower Canada. Looking back over his
settlement of a rebellion in Montreal and his defense of the right to use
French as well as the English language, he had reason for satisfaction:

I have been told by Americans, "We thought you were right; but we could not understand why you did not shoot them down! I would have reduced Montreal to ashes before I would have endured half what you did." "Yes," I answered, "you would have
been justified, because your course would have been perfectly defensible; but it would
not have been the best course. Mine was a better one." And shall I tell you what was
the deep conviction on my mind, which, apart from the reluctance, which I naturally
felt to shed blood. If we had looked to bayonets instead of to reason for a triumph,
the sensibilities to the great body of which I speak would soon have carried the day
against their judgment.[19]

In Canada, James had contemplated reducing Montreal to ashes. This
turned out to be the historical dilemma that came his way later in China.
Elgin's friends had urged vengeance in Canada. Yet, the man who would
order the burning of the Summer Palace in Beijing had withstood the temptation of violence in North America. He had argued cogently for the use of
reason over bayonets. He wrote about his reluctance to shed blood with can-
dor and pride. In China, it was the same reluctance to harm ordinary people
that led Elgin to reduce priceless cultural relics to ashes. Enraged over the torture of foreign prisoners on the grounds of the Yuan Ming Yuan, he chose to
enact vengeance against stone and marble—but not the people of Beijing.

When he arrived for his first China mission in December 1857, James
Elgin saw himself again as a man of peace, not war. He was far from immune
to the beauties of the landscape that surrounded him even as his focus remained firmly political. He had come to settle the controversy that came to
be known as the Arrow War. Sparked by the seizure of a British-registered
schooner in Canton, this conflict soon grew beyond south China to encompass demands left unresolved from the first so-called Opium War. Heading
an Anglo-French military force, Elgin witnessed the capture of the Taku fort
that guarded the Beihe River leading to Beijing. He was there for the signing

of the Treaty of Tiensin (Tianjing) on June 26, 1858. These military and diplomatic accomplishments, however, did not blind him to the charms of China's countryside. Stopping off at the coastal city of Fuzhou he admired the distinctively Chinese way of combining nature and culture, a harmony that certainly challenged his boyhood appreciation for Greek statues:

I have as yet seen no place in China, which, in point of beauty of scenery, rivals Foochow. The Min river passes to the sea between two mountain ranges, which, wherever tidal torrents have not washed away every particle of earth from the surface, are cultivated by the industrious Chinese in terraces to their very summits. These mountain ranges close in upon its banks during the last part of its course: at one time confining it to a comparatively narrow channel, and at another suffering it to expand into a lake; but in the vicinity of the Pagoda Island they separate, leaving between them the plain on which Foochow stands. . . . We walked with perfect freedom, both about the town and into the surrounding country. Nothing could be more courteous than the people of the villages, or more quaint than the landscape, consisting mainly of hillocks dotted with horseshoe graves, and monuments to the honor of virtuous maidens and faithful widows, surrounded by patches of wheat and vegetables.[20]

Two years before the confrontation in Beijing, Lord Elgin could allow himself to pay close attention to agriculture and the graves of virtuous maidens. It is this affection for the common folk of China, some argued, that led him to vent his rage against the stones in the emperor's palace in Beijing.

Baron Jean Baptiste Louis Gros (1793–1870) was Elgin's cultured companion, both in 1858 and again in 1860. This highly educated French diplomat arrived in China after considerable success in settling French affairs in Japan without the aid of arms. Baron Gros, like Lord Elgin, saw himself as a man of peace who also loved classical aesthetics. An early experimenter with photography, he was famous for his images of Athens and Propylaea circulated to a wide public in 1852.[21] Again, one might imagine that a keen sensitivity to Western beauty would have left Baron Gros cold to the charms of the Chinese landscape. In fact, he was so aware of their value that he argued quite forcefully with Elgin to spare the Yuan Ming Yuan from destruction in October 1860. Both men loved historical treasures. Both men, as we shall see, were outraged by the violence inflicted on foreign prisoners by the Chinese court. Both gave their assent to looting, because they saw it as somehow "natural" for men at war. The French diplomat, at the last minute, would become an advocate for the preciousness of culture over the passions of political revenge.

The deep sympathy between Elgin and Gros may be glimpsed from a shared trip to view the Egyptian pyramids in May 1860. They had been traveling together on the S.S. *Valetta,* bound for Malta and Alexandria. From there, they journeyed by caravan to view ancient relics left from a culture that was much less familiar to them than classical Greece. Their companion on this expedition was Thomas William Bowlby, the *Times* correspondent who also saw himself as a man of European cultivation. Born in Gibraltar, educated as a legal solicitor, Bowlby preferred the company of musicians and artists. Having lived in Belgium and invested (unsuccessfully) in the railways of Smyrna, he arrived in Egypt keenly alert to the diplomatic challenges ahead and the strange beauty at hand. An entry in Lord Elgin's journal from 1860 reveals the personal bonds forged between the three men as they viewed the pyramids by the light of the moon:

We pushed on over the heaps of sand and debris, when we suddenly came in face of the most remarkable object on which my eye ever lighted. Somehow or other I had not thought of the Sphinx till I saw her before me. There she was in all her imposing magnitude. . . . The mystical light and deep shadows cast by the moon, gave to it an intensity which I cannot attempt to describe. To me it seemed a look, earnest, searching, but unsatisfied. For a long time I remained transfixed, endeavoring to read the meaning conveyed by this wonderful eye. . . . Mr. Bowlby, who was a very *sympatique* inquirer into the significance of this wonderful monument, agreed with me in thinking that the upper part of the face spoke of the intellect striving, and striving vainly, to solve the mystery. What mystery? The mystery, shall we say, of God's universe or of man's destiny? While the lower indicated a moral conviction that all must be well, and that this truth would in good time be made manifest.[22]

In Egypt, unlike in China two months later, these cultured gentlemen had time to muse about the mysteries of the universe. They were in a leisurely frame of mind that allowed them to savor a symbol of ancient civilization without demanding that it answer urgent political dilemmas. Once they arrived in Hong Kong on June 13, 1860, the mood changed rapidly. No time was lost in starting the military expedition to the north. Thomas William Bowlby, who had mused so eloquently about the enigmatic smile of the Sphinx, wrote now about the need for clear, unequivocal answers from the Chinese. In the sands of Egypt, as in the gardens of China in 1858, time had been slowed down, contemplation sanctioned, ambiguity cherished. By September 9, 1860, Bowlby's long article for the *Times* was marked by a tone of aggression: "By fear alone can China be opened to trade. Ambassadors must negotiate with arms at their side ready to act at a moment's notice. For two centuries have we traded at Canton, and we know as much about China as at the commencement of our intercourse. At length the opportunity has arrived and the ambassadors of England and France, with the troops of the two nations at their backs will, under the walls of Peking, dictate the terms of peace likely to endure."[23] Exaggerating the length of Western commerce with China, Bowlby wanted to make an important point: we know too little about the very culture we seek to engage in trade and peace. Diplomacy backed by military force was to be the way of ensuring the flow of information about China.

Bowlby's own essay was supposed to be an example of detailed observation made possible by armed conflict with the Celestial Empire. Like Elgin, the man who had found him to be so *sympatique,* this war journalist liked to notice details of the Chinese landscape. There is little in the September 9 essay to suggest the wholesale destruction of Chinese treasures that was one month away. Elgin himself had waxed eloquently about the quaint landscape around Fuzhou. Now it was Bowlby who took pains to write about gardens and women as the armies marched toward the fort of Dagu in 1860:

For upwards of six miles we passed through gardens, the produce of which supplied the garrison of the forts and the town of Taku. They were admirably cultivated. Little water wheels furnished an easy means of irrigation, and the vegetables might have put a Battersea market garden to shame. Large sweet turnips, excellent French beans, crisp radishes, lettuces, yams, and many other vegetables grew in great profusion. The fruit was magnificent. Trellised vines, whereas the ripe luscious fruit hung in mellow clusters, reminded us of Italy. Peaches, watermelons, apples—very like Newtown pippins—and pears of every description, were abundant. The road was encumbered with people returning to their homes. The women rode in a wheelbarrow fashioned after the model of an outside jaunting car. . . . I had my first good view of Chinese beauties. Flat noses, linear eyes, high cheek bones, and broad upper faces are not suggestive of Venus or Psyche, nevertheless there is an expression of sweetness about a China woman's face which redeems it from positive ugliness. Her jet black hair is combed into a turret at the top of the head, and there plastered with grease and pomatum—much after the fashion of the English dame during the days of the Regent. She is small in statue, with remarkably pretty hands, and her feet find favor in the eyes of her lord.[24]

Bowlby's observations may be too easily dismissed as imperialist arrogance. Yet for his time and place, he was a war correspondent who paid close attention to details that went far beyond the scope of military conflict. Writing about Chinese domestic gardens and produce, Bowlby acknowledged their abundance and quality even when he called to mind pippins savored at home. Chinese women, too, were scrutinized not only for how they differed from Venus or Psyche but for the way they lived with bound feet.

In September 1860, the Chinese landscape and Western political demands were moving along different axes of time. One was older, slower, nearly eternal. The other was rapid, forceful, marked by immediate demands. In his letters home, Bowlby was imagining that this was a conflict over trade, and missionary rights. He expected that the Chinese court would see the light once sufficient military might was assembled near the imperial city. The same view comes across in the letters of Armand Lucy, a young man who accompanied the French armies in their northwestern expedition. Recommended by his father to General de Montauban, Lucy imagined himself on a journey of cultural discovery—not destruction. The preface to his China letters, written in July 1861 after he had witnessed horrifying events of torture and plunder, nonetheless insists that this was a glorious expedition with no other goal than "ouvrir enfin l'empire Chinois aux peuples de l'Occident" (open finally the Chinese empire to the people of the West).[25] Young Lucy, like the more seasoned Bowlby, had viewed the Year of the Monkey as an opportunity to know China better. Of course, there was the dirty business of political treaties to be signed under military duress. But what mattered most was that the peoples of the West would finally have access to a previously shuttered realm. If young men like Lucy and Bowlby had been asked in early September what they wished to accomplish in China, they might have answered: unhindered access to gardens, cities, palaces, and peoples alike. Tearing down marble gates, torching art scrolls, stealing silks and cloisonné was far from the imagination of these cultured gentlemen. It was, however, a rapidly approaching reality for those negotiating conflicting imperialisms on the ground.

A Temporary Insanity

As James Elgin neared Chinese shores in the summer of 1860, he hoped to save, not savage, China's civilization. In his earlier negotiations with Qing authorities, he had been careful not to press the issue of legalized opium trade too far. Already in 1858, he knew that a China defeated in war would have to be brought to the diplomatic table with more universal principles than sheer force. In a letter from his first China mission, Elgin confessed: "If I were obliged to choose between the two I would rather have it written on my tombstone that I moralized trade with China rather than battered down the Great Wall."[26] This hope would not be realized. From the perspective of twentieth-century anti-imperialist critique, Elgin's musings were the froth on top of what John Wong termed "deadly dreams." No matter that Elgin said he wanted to moralize trade, he had come with armies bent upon destroying a worldview. According to Wong, this was a "global menacing entanglement, world-wide intrigue on a world scale . . . the massive destruction of lives and property with modern weaponry to satisfy the perpetrators' general covetousness and desire to make money by the misfortunes of mankind."[27] The trouble with these high-minded critiques is that they ignore the complex altercation on the ground. The covetousness and intrigue that drove the Qing court into an increasingly violent confrontation with Westerners is not fully considered here. There is no room for the ambiguous role of garden spaces in times of political terror.

According to John Wong's view, Western imperialists were purely and simply profit-driven aggressors. This view cannot possibly account for Lord Elgin's letter to his wife in the summer before the burning of the Summer Palace. "Can I do anything to prevent England from calling down on herself God's curse for brutalities committed on another feeble Oriental race?"[28] Yes, the letter is "racist;" yes, it is patronizing to "orientals." But Elgin arrived in China mindful that brutalities can and should be avoided. He had fervently hoped that his own brother, Fredric Bruce, would persuade the Chinese authorities to implement fully the 1858 Treaty of Tiansin. Bruce, a weak diplomat, waited, hoping that the advance of British and French armies would settle the question once and for all. On August 13, after another attack on the fort of Dagu, negotiations between the Westerners and the governor-general of the province of Zhili began in earnest.

It was the coming together of political representatives dedicated to very different principles. China wanted momentary relief from military threats. Westerners sought long-range diplomatic gains. The chief negotiator for Elgin and Gros was Harry Parkes, a young man known for his excellent skills in Chinese language. The Chinese governor-general Heng Fu knew no English. He used low-ranking secretaries to communicate with Westerners. His only goal was to buy time for military preparations. Born in 1828, Harry Parkes had set his sights on China at the age of thirteen. He had arrived in Macao in 1841 and managed to get himself appointed as British consul of Canton. British military victory in 1840, and again in 1858, provided Parkes with new opportunities to display his language and cultural skills. By August 1860, he presented himself to Elgin as the consummate insider—able to decode Chinese intentions, rituals, and machinations.

Behind Parkes lay the full might of British armies commanded by Major General James Hope Grant, a seasoned warrior who came to Elgin's aid from India. On the French side, the more dashing nobleman Cousin de Montauban led French troops eager for a fight and for a taste of the treasures of the unknown Chinese empire. While young men such as Armand Lucy gravitated toward Montauban's cultured airs, ordinary soldiers (British and French alike) were poised for something more immediate: loot that could be translated into money to compensate for meager pay.

Mythmaking was well in force by the time British and French military commanders brought their troops close to Beijing. In London, for example, Sir Francis Doyle, a close friend of Thomas Bowlby from the *Times*, took it upon himself to immortalize one of the British soldiers lost in the battle near Dagu. Private Moyse was presented as an ordinary British boy who had dared to fight the barbarian Chinese to the end, unlike the cowardly Sikh troops who also accompanied General Grant from India to this theater of war:

Let dusky Indians whine and kneel,
An English lad must die.
And thus with eye that would not shrink,
With knee to man unbent,
Unfaltering on its dreadful brink,
To his red grave he went . . .
So let his name through Europe ring
A man of mean estate,
Who died, as firm as Sparta's king,
Because his soul was great.[29]

Unlike Bowlby, who was close to the scene of action, Sir Francis had mixed much fancy into facts. Moyse was no Kentish lad but a tough Scotsman with an army record of insubordination. Greatness of soul was more in the eyes of distant dreamers than in the hearts of those close to the murky scene of action.

In the weeks after the Chinese defeat at Dagu, matters became more and more confused. On September 8, the Xianfeng emperor appointed his cousin Zaiyuan (Prince Yi) to serve as imperial commissioner in charge of negotiations with the British and the French. For Elgin, this was a setback and an insult. He was convinced that the Manchu rulers had seized one more opportunity to gain time. The prospect of yet another prolonged exchange of diplomatic notes was, in his eyes, nothing more than a delay intended to prevent military action. Mindful that the winter months would be inimical even for the military skills of Hope Grant's army, Elgin decided to push north, whatever the cost.

A new note of rage surfaced in his journals, accompanied by more explicit contempt for the other side. Impatient to set the Chinese "straight," Elgin launched upon a path that would make him cold to claims of cultural difference, never mind the preservation of art. Now what mattered was war, not the beauty of spaces where cranes dwelled in shadowy peace:

September 8th.—I am at war again! My idiotical Chinamen have taken to playing tricks, which give me an excellent excuse for carrying the army on to Peking. . . . We must get nearer Peking before the Government there comes to its senses. The blockheads have gone on negotiating with me just long enough to enable Grant to bring all his army up to this point. Here we are, then, with our base established in the heart of the country, in a capital climate, with abundance around us, our army in excellent health, and these stupid people give me a snub, which obliges me to break with them. No one knows whether our progress is to be a flub or an ovation, for in this country nothing can be foreseen. I think it better that the olivebranch should advance with the sword.[30]

Once Elgin's adversaries had been demoted to trick-playing idiots, there was no reason to treat them with respect. Snubbed in his strongly worded request to proceed to Beijing, the British ambassador saw no alterative but to toughen his stance against "these stupid people."

Racist as this language strikes us today, we must try to hear its meanings in its own time. September 1860 hurled several "stupidities" against one another on the increasingly vulnerable terrain of north China. Once the "peaceful march" to the imperial capital was ruled out, another kind of saber rattling began. On the Chinese side, Mongolian general Sengkelinqin had to find some way to recover his tarnished reputation after the defeat at Dagu. His former patron, Mianyu, would not be able to defend a man with a losing track record. The master of the Singing Crane Garden, far more than his nephew who sat on the throne, knew that the Mandate of Heaven was now truly in danger. On the side of the British and the French, men of war were also itching for action. Beijing, the imperial city, seemed so close, a golden prize ready for the picking. Once again, Harry Parkes was called in to use his language and diplomatic skills. On September 14, the thirty-two-year-old who viewed himself more knowledgeable than Elgin, Gros, Hope Grant, and Montauban put together, set off to negotiate with Imperial Commissioner Zaiyuan. Accompanied by twenty British subjects, including Thomas Bowlby (who loved the prospect of watching military and diplomatic confrontations firsthand) as well as thirteen French soldiers and diplomats. Parkes tried to make the case for immediate diplomatic recognition. He wanted nothing more than four hundred military guards to accompany Elgin and Gros into the imperial city. For the Qing, this was nothing less than the formal end of many centuries of the tribute system—a ritualized mode of conducting trade and diplomatic relations through ceremony and subservience.[31]

While the envoys talked, Elgin's troops kept pressing north. On September 18, Sengkelinqin did what he thought was both conventional and honorable: he ordered that Harry Parkes and his entire entourage to be seized and jailed. Putting lower-ranking representatives of disobedient tribute missions into irons was not a breach of Qing imperial regulations. To the British and the French, however, this was an insult that demanded retaliation. A proclamation was issued at once saying that "all English and French subjects were required to return to the headquarters of their respective armies. If any impediment was put in the way of their return, the city of Peking would forthwith be attacked and taken."[32] This became the point of no return.

Manchu princes had assumed their world invulnerable and their protocols immutable. Elgin was bent upon disproving their assumptions on both counts. It was not only the capital of China that was being threatened in September 1860—it was a worldview that had insisted upon the Westerners' deferential manners at the Chinese court. Subservience to the will of the Son of Heaven was an article of faith for the noblemen who had cherished nature amidst the graciously landscaped domains of Haidian. It was definitely not how Lord Elgin and Baron Gros viewed the horrifying news of mistreatment coming from the imprisoned men.

Harry Parkes was accompanied in his ill-fated diplomatic mission, not only by Elgin's *sympatique* companion from Egypt but also by Henry Loch, his personal secretary, and Colonel Walker, quarter master of the cavalry. The last report that returning soldiers had of these men was that they had been tied up in ropes and thrown upon a crate headed for the Ji Xian Yuan. Those who came to report this terrible news to Grant and Montauban may not have known the Chinese name of the Garden of Accumulated Virtue. They certainly had no knowledge of the artful musings of late eighteenth-century Western visitors to this corner of Haidian. The well-founded rumor that ran like wildfire between the British and French camps was that Western emissaries had been captured and mistreated. If there had been any reservations about the force of arms to break into the imperial city, it vanished in the days after Parkes's incarceration.

By September 29, a new prince was placed in charge of negotiations with the West. Zaiyuan was ordered to follow the imperial cortege to Manchuria. Sengkelinqin was demoted and ordered to commit suicide. The new face of diplomacy became that of Yixin, better known as Prince Gong. Five years younger than Parkes, the master of the Garden of Moonlit Fertility took charge with courage and dignity. He ordered that Parkes and Loch be taken out of bondage in the Ji Xian Yuan and moved to a temple closer to town. Eager to distance the prisoners from the terrain of the Yuan Ming Yuan (and his own garden), he tried to make amends by granting the two men certain amenities of life. Parkes and Loch were allowed to bathe for the first time in two weeks. As if this were not luxury enough, they were also served a banquet of sixteen main dishes and thirty-two minor ones. Too weak to enjoy this feast, the British prisoners understood that they were in better hands. According to Parkes: "The Chinese authorities are now treating Mr. Loch and myself well, and we are informed that this is done by direction of the Prince of Kung (Gong). We are also told that his Highness is a man of decision and great intelligence, and I trust that, under these circumstances, hostilities may be temporarily suspended to give opportunity for negotiation."[33] Even as Prince Gong ordered wine and beef to be sent to his foreign prisoners and took time each day to drink tea with Parkes and Loch from a special brew made for imperial consumption, war inevitably reached the garden gate. Upon a shirt sent to Loch, a secret message had been embroidered in Hindustani: Elgin was ready to attack. The decision to wreck vengeance against the emperor and his gardens had been finalized. The Franco-British military expedition had reached the outskirts of Haidian.

Between September 28 and October 5, twenty-eight-year-old Prince Gong kept up a steady stream of letters to Elgin and Baron Gros tying to explain the situation of the prisoners. Blaming lower-ranking officers for acting rashly in the course of a military altercation, Yixin tried to minimize the injury. He asked repeatedly that the foreign armies withdraw before any further negotiations take place. Elgin, on his side, refused to acknowledge that Parkes and the others were taken as prisoners of war in battle. He insisted on seeing them as "persons kidnapped under the most treacherous circumstances, in defiance of all international law and the customs of war."[34] In the meantime, the Franco-British military expedition kept moving north, closer to Beijing. The game of diplomacy had come to a standstill. Hope Grant's assistant, Lieutenant-Colonel G. J. Wolseley, recalled as follows Prince Gong's last communications before the gardens in Haidian were put to death:

Up to the time of marching, begging letters kept coming in daily from the Prince, sometimes two in one day: all were concocted in a half-cunning, half-frightened tone. He evidently dreaded our advancing above all things. He felt his inability to prevent it, and yet lacked moral courage enough to adopt the only course which lie could avert such a national calamity. The absolute necessity of conceding all our demands must have been evident to the dullest of the Chinese Ministers. There was a shilly-shallying about all the later dispatches, for which, in any other country under similar circumstances, it would have been impossible to account. Not so, however, in China, where an absolute monarch had left his capital to retire to such a distance from the theater of operations that all reference to him involved the loss of several days, and from whom it was impossible to obtain any more definite instructions than the vague order to keep the barbarians at a distance.[35]

According to Wolseley, Prince Gong lacked the moral will to save the nation. Accustomed to ceremonious politics, he appeared to the British as a corrupt defender of imperial grandeur. In his own eyes, however, Yixin was a defender of the Mandate of Heaven who was trying to assist his brother in yet another losing war.

Prince Gong continued to write letters that were at once pleading and threatening. By October 5, he realized that he could not avert disaster. Foreigners had reached Haidian. Yixin had no choice but to forsake the hamlet where he once found peace of mind in the garden of Lang Run Yuan. On October 6, at seven o'clock in the evening, the French troops arrived at the gates of the Yuan Ming Yuan. On this first forage, they passed the princely enclosures without heed to the gardens of leisure sequestered therein. Their goal was the emperor's own pleasure palace. One Manchu commander tried to lead security efforts in the abandoned garden. He was aided by eunuchs and lower-ranking soldiers. These guardians of Xianfeng's treasures proved no match for the Westerners' modern army. The most senior eunuch, Wenfeng, was finally left in charge of the whole place. He drowned himself in the Sea of Blessings rather than face defeat at the hands of the barbarians and humiliation in the face of his ruler.

The British arrived the next day. Hope Grant and Elgin, riding through Haidian on October 7, took note of the beautifully landscaped princely gardens, the "forty separate palaces in beautiful situations."[36] Elgin's chief interpreter (in the absence of the imprisoned Harry Parkes) was Robert Swinhoe. A man attracted to Chinese language and culture, he strolled the grounds of the Summer Palace before the armies began their looting. On his way to the now-abandoned Audience Hall, Swinhoe found two chariots that had been presented to the Qianlong emperor by the Macartney mission. For a brief moment, time stood still in the garden: "Here a solitary building would rise fairy-like from the center of a lake, reflecting its image on the limpid blue liquid in which it seemed to float, and then a sloping path would carry you into the heart of a mysterious cavern artificially formed of rockery, and leading out onto a grotto in the bosom of another lake. The variety of the picturesque was endless, and charming in the extreme; indeed, all that is most lovely in Chinese scenery, where art contrives to cheat the rude attempts of nature into the bewitching, seemed all associated in these delightful grounds."[37] On October 7, 1860, at least one foreigner managed to stand still long enough to savor the beauty that had been built up with such care in this corner of northwest Beijing.

This beauty did not affect Lord Elgin in the same way. He saw in the surroundings of Yuan Ming Yuan nothing more than a gracious park, somewhat like those he was accustomed to at home. By the evening of that first day, the beauty of Qianlong's Summer Palace was willfully shattered. Who started the looting of the abandoned pleasure grounds is still a matter of contestation. Elgin and Hope Grant blamed the French, who arrived the day before. "There was no room that I saw," Elgin recalled, "which half the things had not been taken away or broken to pieces."[38] The French pointed the finger at the more numerous British. They had, after all more horses and more carts to take away looted treasure. Together, in three short days, French and British troops emptied fourteen palaces of their varied collections. In what may have been the largest art robbery of the nineteenth century, soldiers tore apart thrones, furniture, paintings, jewelry, costumes, and statuary.

A veritable frenzy took hold of the two armies encamped in the Yuan Ming Yuan. While eunuchs kneeled and the local Haidian population hid in terror, French and British soldiers rummaged through three centuries of Manchu wealth. Still blaming the French as the instigators, Wolseley recalled in detail the naked assault that flattened the terrain around Haidian before the fires of October 18:

A mine of wealth and of everything curious in the empire lay as a prey before our French allies. Rooms filled with articles of vertu both native and European, halls containing vases and jars of immense value, and houses stored with silks, satins, and embroidery, were open to them. Indiscriminate plunder and wanton destruction of all articles too heavy for removal commenced at once. Guards were placed about in various directions; but to no purpose. When looting is once commenced by an army it is no easy matter to stop it. At such times human nature breaks down the ordinary trammels which discipline imposes, and the consequences are most demoralizing to the very best. Soldiers are nothing more than grown-up schoolboys. The wild moments of enjoyment passed in the pillage of a place lives long in a soldier's memory. Watch them approach a closed door; it is too much trouble to try the latch or handle, so Jack kicks it open. They enter, some one turns over a table, out of which tumbles perhaps some curious manuscripts. To the soldier these are simply waste paper, so he lights his pipe with them.[39]

In Wolseley's eyes, the plunder at the Summer Palace started out as school-boy's fun. For a while, it seemed "normal" to kick open doors, to finger Chinese fineries with greed. The frenzy of the French, however, shocked the veteran soldier:

If the reader will imagine some three thousand men, imbued with such principles, let loose into a city composed only of Museums, he may have some faint idea of what Yuen-ming-yuen looked like after it bad been about twenty hours in possession of the French. . . . The ground around the French camp was covered with silks and clothing of all kinds, whilst the men ran hither and thither in search of further plunder, most of them, according to the practice usual with soldiers upon such occasions, being decked out in the most ridiculous-looking costumes they could find, of which there was no lack as the well-stocked wardrobes of his Imperial Majesty abounded in curious raiment. Some had dressed themselves in the richly-embroidered gowns of women, and almost all had substituted the turned-up Mandarin hat for their ordinary forage cap. Officers and men seemed to have been seized with a temporary insanity; in body and soul they were absorbed in one pursuit, which was plunder, plunder.[40]

The French came out looking more ridiculous than the British in this retrospective justification of the despoiling of the Yuan Ming Yuan. Nonetheless, Wolseley acknowledges a common proclivity: strange beauty will wake the most destructive urges of ill-behaved schoolboys. "Temporary insanity" is an oddly contemporary plea to excuse this ravage of priceless artifacts. Wolseley was unwilling to acknowledge just how lucrative the looting was for British soldiers and officers. In fact, General Hope Grant had to set up a system for auctioning looted articles. Then, he proceeded to distribute the booty equally among the plunderers. Wolseley's recollection does not touch on this thirst for wealth nor on the strangeness of beauty that spurred on the frenzy for plunder.

Robert Swinhoe, who had stood still to savor a solitary pagoda, recalled the auction of the booty in detail. Whereas Wolseley saw in this process a discipline problem, Swinhoe recalls the delight in the huge prizes fetched by imperial treasures sold off right under the walls of the compound left behind by the Xianfeng emperor:

The British share of the plunder was all arranged for exhibition in the hall of the large Llama temple, where the Head-quarters' Staff were quartered, and a goodly display it was: white and green jade-stone ornaments of all tints, enamel-inlaid jars of antique shape, bronzes, gold and silver figures and statuettes, fine collections of furs, many of which were of much value, such as sable, sea-otter, ermine, Astracan lamb, and court costume, among which were two or three of the Emperor's state robes of rich yellow silk, worked upon with dragons in gold thread, and beautifully woven with floss-silk embroidery on the skirts, the inside being lined with silver fur or ermine and cuffed with glossy sable.[41]

The sale continued over three days. Both officers and enlisted men bid for the emperor's treasures. A mania for competition appeared to have seized all ranks. The prices realized were indeed fabulous. The most trivial article fetched two or three pounds, and one of the court robes reached one thousand. "Had the Emperor been present he would doubtless have felt flattered at the value set by the foreigners on objects solely because these had belonged to him. Imagine the sale of an emperor's effects right beneath the walls of the capital of his empire. And this, by a people he had despised as weak barbarians and talked of driving into the sea! The proceeds of the sale amounted to 32,000 dollars, and the amount of treasure secured was estimated at over 61,000 dollars. Of the total, two-thirds of 93,000 was set apart for distribution in proportionate shares to the soldiers and one-third for the officers."[42] Everyone engaged in active service on the day of the capture of the Summer Palace was in on the booty. Hope Grant very generously gave his share over to the men. As a token of respect, the officers presented him with a gold claret jug richly embossed, one of the handsomest pieces of the loot.

Swinhoe's recollections make it clear that the urge to humiliate the Chinese emperor unleashed the first ruination of the Yuan Ming Yuan. His mocking references to a ruler "doubtlessly flattered" at the value set by foreigners on his objects reveal a deepening gulf between Chinese and Western views of the plunder. Foreigners were now in charge, not only of the prices of plundered objects but the future of China as well. In early October 1860, what seemed to be at stake was silk and jade. A couple of weeks later, the calculus became more dramatic. The arrival of the coffins of men who had been imprisoned on September 18 erased lingering reservations about the destruction of Chinese beauty. The only thing left was to exact punishment for blood unjustly spilled.

"On ne venge pas sur des pierres le sang injustment versé"

The British and the French had a joint agenda in China—to force the Qing government to comply with the Treaty of Tiansin. Lord Elgin and Baron Gros were the designated leaders of this effort. Since 1858, these two noblemen had traveled together, shared meals, exchanged letters, and agreed that France and England needed to press harder if the full advantage of representation in the imperial capital was to be achieved. Although the Arrow War started out as a British altercation in Canton, the summer of 1860 found the two men allied once again in the march to Beijing. Their military officers, General Hope Grant and General Montauban, worked closely together to coordinate the assault on the capital. Although Montauban had arrived one day earlier to Yuan Ming Yuan, both officers had witnessed their soldiers turning into marauders.

By October 17, a disparity of outlook emerged between the French and British concerning vengeance in China. Baron Gros started to sound a note of caution that was not heard in the British camp. As the fate of the garden was about to be sealed, the representative of French imperial interests tried to salvage whatever remained of the beauty that was once the Garden of Perfect Brightness. What made the French ambassador more caring about garden rockery in a moment when blood was on everyone's mind we may never know. Perhaps the very look of the Western palaces in the Yuan Ming Yuan recalled the ambiance of Versailles. Maybe this visual echo made Baron Gros reluctant to partake in a ravage that even the French Revolution had managed to avoid. Maybe it was the fact that the number of French prisoners taken by the Qing was only thirteen, unlike the British, who had to deal with the incarceration of twenty-six men, including Henry Parkes and Thomas Bowlby. Of the French prisoners, seven were killed and six returned alive. Of the British captives, thirteen were killed and thirteen returned alive. The ratio was nearly the same, but sentiments about vengeance differed profoundly. Henri Cordier, one of the first scholars to study the diplomatic documents relating to the events of 1860, summarized the French point of view as follows:

Un cri d'horreur se fit entendre dans les camps alliés:
  Aspect des cadavres restitués, l'état des prisonniers survivants témoignaient de la plus brutale manière à quels abominables traitements avaient été soumises des martyrs de Pe-King et du Youen-Min-Youen. Les atrocités chinoises ne pouvaient rester impunies; aucun doute n'était permis à cet égard; quel était l'instigateur et le principal coupable de ces crimes: il fallait remonter jusqu'à la personne de l'Empereur; mais Hien-Foung avait fui à Djehol. Les Anglais, et ils avaient raison, voulaient punir personnellement ce grand coupable; le général Grant et lord Elgin crurent lui porter un coup sensible en détruisant Youen-Min-Youen; je ne pense pas que la solution fût bonne; nous donnions aux Chinois le sentiment que nous étions vraiment des Barbares— d'autre part, on ne venge pas sur des pierres le sang injustement versé. Les Français se trouvèrent en désaccord sur ce point avec leurs Alliés: pillards, mais non incendières.[43]

Cordier's conclusion was that the French were robbers but not destroyers of beauty. Baron Gros was not the one who gave the order to burn the Summer Palace. He was, at the same time, not totally opposed to Elgin's decision. The French had shared the British outrage at the mistreatment of the prisoners. Both had looked in horror at the caskets of the tortured (figure 23). Both ambassadors believed that honor was at stake in responding to this wanton disregard for human life. Both wanted to send a scorching message to the Xianfeng emperor in Manchuria. Unreachable, he could still be hurt through his passionate attachment to the ground on which the crimes had been committed.

On October 18, 1860, the French chose to imagine themselves as spectators of disaster. This self-perception comes across in the recollections of Count Maurice d'Herisson, who witnessed the plunder of October 7 as if it were a theater of the absurd. Having heard much about the evil of opium in China, he used the metaphor of the opium den to convey the madness that took place even before the large scale fires of October 18:

I was only an onlooker, a disinterested but curious onlooker, positively reveling in this strange and unforgettable spectacle, in this swarm of men of every color, every sort,

Figure 23. Identification of murdered prisoners, Beijing 1860—from the sketches of Colonel Crealock, military secretary to Lord Elgin. Henry Hope Crealock, *Chinese War: Sketches of the Allied Expedition to Pekin* (London, 1861), 2:20.

this serum of all the races of the world, as they flung themselves on the spoil, shouting hurrahs in every language on earth, hurrying, pushing, tumbling over one another, picking themselves up, cursing and swearing, and returning laden with their loot. It was like an ant-hill disturbed by the toe of a boot when the black swarms have been roused up and hurry off in all directions, one with a grub, one with a tiny egg, another with a seed in its jaws. There were soldiers with their heads in the red lacquer boxes from the Empress's chamber; others were wreathed in masses of brocade and silk; others stuffed rubies, sapphires, pearls and bits of rock-crystal into their pockets, shirts and caps, and hung their necks with pearl necklaces. Others hugged clocks and clock-cases. . . . It was like a scene from an opium dream.[44]

Like Lieutenant Wolseley's memoir, this account blames the "other." The English are named before the French. Chinese coolies are portrayed as "ravens, dogs, and jackals" for attacking everything beautiful with no feeling other than raw greed. In contrast to the British accounts of the army's misconduct, Herisson's narrative tries to sound impartial. He was, after all, a well-heeled traveler with a soft spot for Chinese antiquities.

Baron Gros, by contrast, was a diplomat in charge of deciding French policy on the spot. When the Franco-British expedition neared the gates of Beijing, Gros could not distance himself from the opium den frenzy that was engulfing both armies. Nonetheless, an appreciation for his distinctive sensitivity may be glimpsed through the letters that Prince Gong addressed this French diplomat. To Elgin, Yixin wrote mainly about the emperor's willingness to comply with the Treaty of Tiansin. The goal of that correspondence was simply to avoid war in the imperial capital. To Baron Gros, by contrast, Prince Gong wrote about the invaluable cultural loss suffered by the dynasty through the looting of the Summer Palace. In a letter sent on October 12, the owner of the Garden of Moonlit Fertility described his own reaction to the ravage of his royal brother's pleasure quarters: "Pourquoi les soldats français ont-ils pillé et brûlé le palais d'Eté de l'empereur? La France est un empire civilisé, ses soldats sont soumis à la discipline; cornment donc ont-ils, de leur propre autorité, incendié le palais de l'empereur? Ce que les généraux et Votre Excellence paraissent ignorer."[45] Yixin's tone in this letter was both haughty and humane. He assumed that his correspondence with the French diplomat (in contrast to brief and acrimonious notes exchanged with Lord Elgin) would be deemed as a Favor from Above. At the same time, Prince Gong wanted to create a common ground with the French. He hoped to cement a vision of civilized nations sharing a mutual aversion to the destruction of cultural relics.

This common ground was shattered on October 16, 1860. On this day, coffins arrived with the bodies of the men who had been detained a month earlier. Death changed the parameters of empathy in the hamlet of Haidian. When Parkes and Loch had been released on October 8, good will seemed on the rise and the possibility of war on the capital was briefly averted. News of Prince Gong's generous treatment of these high-level British representatives trickled back to the military camps. Within days, however, the mood began to change. Lower-ranking prisoners returned and declared that they were the last of the surviving prisoners. Unlike Parkes and Loch, these men had not shared tea with Prince Gong. Instead, they brought news of terrible mistreatment. Swinhoe's account describes them as "fearfully emaciated, with their arms and wrists lacerated by the tight cords that had bound them."[46] The coffins that started arriving on October 16 confirmed the worst of Elgin's fears. Some bodies were in such a state of decomposition that their features were unrecognizable. Torn garments and macerated limbs were inspected by doctors who tried to identify the remains.

The body of Thomas Bowlby was among the disfigured corpses to arrive on October 17. The passion for vengeance became more acute as survivors described the horrors they had been forced to endure. Again, it was Robert Swinhoe (the same gentleman who had enjoyed the beauty of the Summer Palace in September) who now dwelt on mutilated cadavers. His retrospective account is filled with rage:

We drew near and examined these coffins, naturally supposing that they contained the remains of our murdered countrymen. Our surmises turned out to be correct: on the head of each coffin was pasted a piece of paper, inscribed in Chinese characters, with the name of the deceased person it contained. We all agreed that the one marked "Po-ne-pe," died of disease on the 25th September, referred to Mr. Bowlby, the ill-fated correspondent of *The Times*. From the statements of the surviving sowars, we learned that after the capture of their party at Chang-chia-wan, they were led to the rear of the Chinese troops and disarmed, but were allowed to remain mounted on their horses, and so conducted along the stone road towards Peking. Before reaching that city, they were told to dismount and had to spend the night all together at a wayside temple, whence they were led to the summer palace, where they were put up in tents. About an hour after their arrival, they were called out, one by one, thrown on their faces, and their bands and feet tied together behind. The sowars were tied with single cords, but the Europeans with double ones; and not content with drawing the cords as tight round the limbs as possible, the pitiless captors wetted them with water, that they might shrink firmer together. The unfortunate sufferers were then carried into a courtyard, and exposed for three days to the sun and the cold without either food or water. In the daytime, the doors were left open, and the gaping crowds admitted to stare at them in their misery. If they spoke a word, or asked for water, they were beaten, stomped upon, and kicked about the head and when they asked for food, dirt was crammed into their mouths.[47]

Evidence of the mortification of human flesh changed the fate of Haidian forever. Other prisoners may have been tied up on these grounds in the late Ming dynasty. Even Mi Wanzhong had no doubt used and abused slaves in his retreat called Shao Yuan. Imperial bondsmen were likely tortured on the grounds of the Yuan Ming Yuan at the time of the Macartney and Titsingh missions in 1790s. Death wore an ugly face on this terrain even as Mianyu embellished the Singing Crane Garden.

The torture and death of Western prisoners, however, created a political earthquake of major proportions. Precisely because the army of General Hope Grant was poised outside the gates of Beijing, vengeance could be taken with fierce rapidity. When Elgin looked into the coffins, he saw men he knew well. He read in their disfigured bodies a confirmation of his views about a Chinese proclivity toward atrocious crimes. Later, recalling his emotions at the loss of his travel companion, Thomas Bowlby, Elgin portrayed himself as a statesman who had tried to overcome the urge to vengeance: "I deplored his loss, not only because he was a highly-accomplished and well-informed gentleman, but also because, from the conscientious and liberal spirit in which he addressed himself to the investigation of the singularly complicated problems presented by the moral, social, political, and commercial condition of China, I had conceived the hope that he would be the means of diffusing sound information on many points on which it is most important for the national interest that the British public should be correctly informed."[48] Retrospectively, the British diplomat mourned a man who might have done justice to the complex problems in China. If he had not been killed, reasoned discourse might have prevailed. Dead, however, the *Times* journalist became one more spark for vengeful fires. On October 17, Lord Elgin was not concerned with British public opinion. Bowlby's mauled body provided the final reason for an act of unprecedented punishment against the Chinese court. The emperor had sinned. No matter how often Prince Gong tried to blame the ill treatment of the prisoner upon officials already dismissed from office, Elgin insisted that the emperor was solely culpable. Having visited the Summer Palace in the heat of the looting of October 7, Elgin had glimpsed enough of its charms to know that here lay the heartstrings of China's ruler. Attachment to pleasure and beauty had to be severed so that severed bodies could rest in peace.

General Hope Grant and Lord Elgin were in perfect agreement: punishment had to be meted out to the emperor alone. They chose not to punish the innocent people of Beijing. An obvious path of action emerged: the emperor's garden had to burn. The Yuan Ming Yuan was called to the witness stand, as it were. Because it had housed the prisoners, Elgin deemed the Summer Palace guilty of being an accomplice to murder. Hope Grant took on the role of prosecuting attorney when he wrote to the Home Office:

I have the honor to state that my reasons for wishing to destroy the palace of Yuan-min-yuan are: first, because it was in that place that the prisoners were treated with such barbarity, being bound hand and foot together for three days, with nothing to eat or drink; and, secondly, because the English nation will not be satisfied unless more lasting marks of our sense of the barbarous manner in which they have violated the laws of nations be inflicted on the Chinese Government. If we were to now make peace, sign the treaty and retire, the Chinese Government would see that our countrymen can be seized and murdered with impunity. It is necessary to undeceive them on this point.[49]

Demons Glorying in Destruction

Vengeance in the hamlet of Haidian seemed to descend as if from Heaven. It was, in fact, started by well-organized men. On October 18, Hope Grant's first division under the command of Major-General Sir John Mitchell marched from the British encampment near Beijing to Yuan Ming Yuan. The men had been given a clear order: torch the palaces and gardens to the ground. Within hours of their arrival in Haidian, the sky darkened with plumes of smoke. These covered all of northwest Beijing for two whole days. The sky was filled with ashes even after the fires went out. Three centuries of garden art were leveled in a couple of days.

Never again would Haidian's waters and hills nestle the dreams of wealthy and lettered men with gentle assurance. History entered the garden with vengeance. Decades later, memory re-embroidered the grounds with longing for its previous graciousness. In the twentieth century, other conflagrations brought back an echo of the fire and terror of 1860. Slogans invented by Red Guards wreaked damage upon lives and buildings with a fury that matched Lord Elgin's vengeful heart. This later destruction lasted an entire decade, Elgin's but two days. Not surprisingly, recovery from twentieth-century terror has been slower and more difficult.

Robert Swinhoe was both witness to and participant in the destruction that took place in this corner of China in the late autumn of 1860. As the main translator for both Elgin and Hope Grant, he was close to the decision-making process. He was not immune to the beauty of the gardens about to be destroyed. Nonetheless, he recalled the day of burning as a heaven-sent event. It was as if God had dispatched General Mitchell to Haidian to teach the universe a hard lesson—evil cannot always be repaid with good:

Before sunset of the 19th, every place had been fired, and the troops were marched back to camp. We were among the last to leave, and we passed the summer palace on our return; flames and smoldering ruins deterred our passage every way, and unhappily many of the peasants' houses adjoining the contagious fire had caught, and were fast being reduced to ashes. We passed the chief entrance to the Yuen-ming-yuen, and watched with mournful pleasure the dancing flames curling into grotesque festoons and wreaths, as they twined in their last embrace around the grand portal of the Palace, while the black column of smoke that rose straight up into the sky from the already roof-fallen reception-hall, formed a deep background to this living picture of active red flame that hissed and crackled as if glorying in the destruction it spread around. "Good for evil," is a hard moral for man to learn; but however much we regretted the cruel destruction of those stately buildings, we yet could not help feeling, a secret gratification that the blow had fallen, our hapless countrymen revenged on the cruel and perfidious author and instigator of the crime.[50]

The "mournful pleasure" experienced by this civilized gentleman while passing the burning gates of the Yuan Ming Yuan is something that begs an explanation. Did fire provide a satisfaction that went beyond the butchered bodies viewed in the coffins two days earlier? The erasure of the Bamyan Buddhas in Afghanistan (just to mention a recent case of vengeance upon stone) provoked a similar rejoicing among the religiously motivated Taliban. Tearing down pre-Islamic statues and edifices was deemed necessary by men determined to purge the world of any trace of holiness before their time. Warriors who start fires and burn down statues and palaces do not see themselves as destroyers. In their own eyes, all too often, they see themselves as emissaries of God teaching mankind difficult lessons. "Crime" is a word they use for what others did, never for the ruination of life and art that they leave behind.

To Robert Swinhoe's credit, he did not write only about his side of the story. Open-eyed and clear-minded, he allowed himself to confront the hell created in northwest Beijing. Unlike the Taliban of the twentieth century, Swinhoe mourned the loss of beauty that accompanied this act of moral vengeance. In the China of the nineteenth century, British diplomats could still look at their actions with regret: "As we approached the Palace the crackling and rushing noise of fire was appalling, and the sun shining through the masses of smoke gave a sickly hue to every plant and tree, and the red flame gleaming on the faces of the troops engaged made them appear like demons glorying in the destruction of what they could not replace."[51] Seeing the Yuan Ming Yuan in ashes, Swinhoe assumed that imperial China had died. In fact, it would go on for another five decades. Its artistic treasures endured and continue to exert their spell upon the historical imagination of China, and the West.

Something did, however, perish irrevocably in October 1860: the certainty of refuge once savored in Haidian by Manchu princes and their imperial kin. The inferno set up by Mitchell's men quickly consumed the wooden buildings of the Yuan Ming Yuan. The fire licked its way around and through stones. It leaped across the enclosure of the imperial palaces and started torching the princely gardens, including that of the Singing Crane Garden. The Year of the Monkey that had started with auspicious hopes and lavish celebration ended in shame and disaster. Yihuan, the seventh brother of the emperor who had abandoned Beijing in its hour of need, was left behind to chronicle the catastrophe. Early in the Geng Shen year, he wrote about the beauties of a chilly spring. By October 1860, he was describing the ruination of the Singing Crane Garden as well as his own Wei Xiu Yuan:

Terrace and courtyard,
no human sound,

persimmon blooms blood red,
the west wind scatters

river grass, fleabane petals
choke the trampled path.

I break my stride, glance back—
ashes after fire.

Water. Tree. Stone.
Such ordinary things, why

this boundless ache as if
for lost sons and daughters?

The mind replays last year's stage,
all that flourished, shimmered,

now swallowed by red flames
a gnarled pine my sole companion,

to search for nests in barren mountains,
along dry rivers, pure futility.

The ravaged garden
is not my wound,

rather a generation born
into a misshapen world.[52]

Just how "misshapen" the world had become would be fully apparent in the days following the burning of the Summer Palace. Not only did the tribute system vanish, but a new period of ruination began at the hands of foreign and native foes alike.

On October 24, 1860, Lord Elgin's triumphant troops moved toward the heart of the forbidden city. The arched and tiled roofs of imperial architecture stood as mute witness to an utterly changed world. No foreign diplomat before Elgin had marched to the Board of Rites with four hundred infantry and one hundred cavalry and two bands playing strange music. Elgin was carried in a sedan chair. He looked more like an emperor than the frightened Xianfeng, who stayed away from the scene. In the hall of ceremonies, Prince Gong waited solemnly. He touched his hands together and bowed in keeping with Confucian ritual. Elgin returned him a proud contemptuous look and bowed slightly. The superficial inclination of the head, according to General Hope Grant, "must have made the blood run cold in poor Kung's veins."[53] In fact Yixin had no choice but to accept all the demands of the foreign victors in 1860. He had tried and failed to reduce the indemnity payments required to reimburse British and French troops for their expenses in destroying the Summer Palace. He had tried to argue for some traditional rituals in the signing of the foreign treaties, and was roundly rebuffed. All he could do was let his own deportment bear witness to Confucian values. Prince Gong waited for Elgin with bowed head and folded arms.

The next day, October 25, Yixin had to go through it all over again with Baron Gros. In the excited letter that Armand Lucy wrote to his father, this was a day that changed world history forever: "Mon bon père, 25 octobre 1860. Relis bien cette date, et souviens-t'en, car elle marquera dans l'histoire due monde. Un prestige sans exemple, la gloire d'avoir tenu en Echec pendant plusieurs siècles la civilisation de l'occident, tout cela s'est effacé sous. . . . Nous sommes entrés 2,500 environ dans Pé-King, où la paix été signé."[54] Whether there were in fact 2,500 armed Frenchmen who accompanied Gros to the Forbidden City does not seem to matter to Lucy. What rings out is the poetic bravado of "occidental civilization." All past defeats were supposedly erased in the glory of horses' hooves resounding in the courtyards of China's imperial capital.

The grief of ruins, the discipline of recollection, and the slow-paced rebirth of garden culture in Haidian was unimaginable to the prideful Armand Lucy. In the end, October 25, 1860, was less of a world-changing date than a moment in which Chinese and Western imperialisms passed one another in the dark. Both were waning. Both would leave behind enough traces of material culture to spur the imagination of less bellicose successors.

Chapter 3
Consciousness in the Dark Earth

It is terrible to survive
as consciousness buried in dark earth.
—*Louise Glück, "Wild Iris"*

Broken remains of China's past cluttered Haidian after October 1860. The gardens that were destroyed seemed condemned to an eternity of shame and silence. Yet this was not to be. Voices and visions of renewal emerged, almost literally, out of the singed ground. How could ash-covered earth have anything new to add to history's narrative? For an answer, it may help to turn to poets trained to listen to the unsaid, even the unsayable, that lies dormant in our spaces, as well as in our hearts. The American poet Louise Glück turned to vegetation when she sought to hear muted voices in her Pulitzer Prize–winning collection *Wild Iris*. By letting plants and the hours of the day speak their mind, she enables us to hear what we know darkly from our own human experience as well: that survival in the wake of disaster is not a blessing. That it might even be quite terrible to endure beyond fiery events with nothing more—or less—than consciousness of all that has been destroyed.

Chinese poets had been attuned to this predicament for many centuries before 1860. Crane metaphors were part of the poets' repertoire of expression for grief in times of historical trauma. The great birds had symbolized eternity, fidelity, and high-mindedness in the study halls of Manchu princes. Cranes were also given the burden of carrying images of historical disaster as well. Premonitions of vulnerability can be heard long before the actual crane's nest (*he zhao*) in Mianyu's garden was destroyed by Elgin's fires. Already in the period of disunity that followed the Han dynasty (200 B.C.E. to 200 C.E.), cranes were seen as fragile guardians of greatness. Writers who lived through centuries of violence wrote about the disappearances of the yellow crane mindful that it had become a symbol of unrest. A new saying emerged: *yuan ru huang he*—"leave no shadow (or trace) like the yellow crane." Later in the Tang dynasty, longing for vestiges of lost grandeur became further linked to the disappearance of the birds that once promised enduring nobility:

The yellow crane has lifted off
Never to return
The sky thick with white clouds
Remains empty for a thousand years.[1]

In Louise Glück's poems, it is dark earth that gives voice to grief. In Chinese culture, it was the very thickness of clouds that captured the sorrow of missing greatness.

The grounds of the princely gardens of Haidian bore witness to the vanishing crane. Broken marble arches, weed-infested lakes, bramble-thickened paths, and peeling pavilions were all reminders of a place that was once a cherished retreat from the cares of politics and history. Prince Yihuan, in his initial reaction to this vast ravage, imagined Haidian's beauty as lost forever, devoid of crane music for at least a thousand years. Visiting the terrain of his uncle's Ming He Yuan, he fell into great despair: Not only was the owner of the Singing Crane Garden gone from the world of the living, but it seemed as if he had taken with him all the promise of genuine nobility. Where once rare and mighty birds sang, the prince hears only common sparrows.

Gone are the cranes
though the garden remains,

distracted by the dying waves,
I seek for the enchanting scene

below the eaves of Yi Ran Ting,
hundred-year-old ponds and pavilions

have exhausted their charms,
on winding paths shaded by cypress

sparrows chatter,
nothing but noise.[2]

The Pavilion of Winged Eaves cannot bring back the cranes, or the genuinely vibrant culture of the Qing before 1860. Dying waves and choked ponds underscore the common noise echoing through spaces that once sheltered quiet thought.

The Yi Ran Ting would, however, have a second and third life in the

Figure 24. Shrine of Abundant Kindness (Ci Ji Si)—a Qing dynasty fragment renamed Temple of Flower Angels (Hua Shen Miao) when the ruined gate was moved to the campus of Yenching University in the 1920s. Photograph by Marc Berger.

century after the burning of the Summer Palace. It would become the delicately painted School Scenes Pavilion during the Yenching era, when liberal learning returned to the scorched terrain of Haidian. It even held its beauty intact in silence during the noisy years of the Cultural Revolution. No matter how feverish the sloganeering became, no matter how cruel the beatings inflicted on intellectuals, Yi Ran Ting stood near the ox pens—a silent reminder of the nobility of spirit. Even when sparrows ruled supreme, crane music was not fully silenced. In time, its muted tones would be heard again.

This rejuvenation was, in fact, facilitated by the ruined landscape itself. Pieces of the Yuan Ming Yuan and its surrounding gardens made their way into new gardens, into the refreshed imagination of subsequent generations. One fragment of the old Summer Palace tells this tale quite vividly. It is the gate of the Shrine of Abundant Kindness (Ci Ji Si) that is now one of the cherished sites on the campus of Beijing University (figure 24). It is actually a fragment whose very name has been buried for a while beneath layers of political dogmatism. If it is recalled today, it is because the climate for "crane music" has changed so dramatically in China after the death of Mao Zedong.

This temple gate was once part of Qianlong's Summer Palace, one of the many structures built and named to signal the emperor's devotion to Buddhist and Confucian ideals. When it stood whole, the structure had two spacious chambers, one facing east and another west. In fact, it was so gracious in its proportions that the emperor gifted it to his favorite minister, He Shen, along with the surrounding Shu Chun Yuan.[3] After the destruction of 1860, the gate became severed from its temple, a broken reminder that "kindness" and "helping" had lost their meaning in public life. *Ci* used to suggest the full-hearted benevolence of parents and rulers in epochs when Confucianism still mattered in both personal and public life. *Ji* connoted a merciful abundance, a showering of aid from those who were powerful enough to ordinary folks. Thus named, the temple functioned as propaganda for the Qing rulers who enjoyed the pleasures of the Summer Palace. Destroyed, it called to mind not only what has been lost in space but also what vanished in myth as well.

The severed temple gate was rescued and brought back as an ornamental landmark for the new Yenching campus built in the 1920s. Much like "borrowed scenery" used to adorn the classical gardens before 1860, so "borrowed" ruins from the older Summer Palace were used by the American architect Henry Murphy to create a more "Chinese" atmosphere for a new kind of university in Beijing. Standing guard on the banks of Unnamed Lake

(Wei Ming Hu), Qianlong's shrine was renamed as the Temple of Flower Angels (Hua Shen Miao)—an appellation that could be taken poetically in both Christian and Confucian terms. With its subtle red hues and delicately curved archway, the gate of Ci Ji Si outlasted war and revolution alike. Not only did it survive Elgin's fires and the Japanese invasion of Beijing, it was also massive enough to withstand the ravages of the Cultural Revolution. Repainted in more livid colors, it was deemed "revolutionary" enough to become a marker for the stairs leading up to the grave of Edgar Snow, Mao's personal friend—a foreigner willing to follow every twist and turn of the changing party line.

One gate, a fragment of a fragment of the sumptuous gardens destroyed in 1860, thus encapsulated the possibilities of cultural renewal despite ruination. Cherished by remembering minds, broken bits of the past can create a new kind of wholeness. In the words of Louise Glück: "For something whole, the act of giving directions is simple business, nor is any virtuosity involved in the act of hearing such news. What wholeness gives up is the dynamic, the mind's need not rush in to fill the void. . . . In the broken thing, moreover, human agency is oddly implied: breakage, whatever its causes, is the dark complement to the act of making, the one imply the other. The thing that is broken has particular authority over the act of change."[4]

A Sea of Shards

As an American poet, Glück has learned the lessons of the "broken thing" late in the twentieth century. Seeing beyond wholeness, however, has been an ideal of Western aesthetics from a long time. What is fresh is the poet's keen appreciation of breakage. Violence is not the object of cherishment here, nor the suggestive shard itself. Rather, human agents—those who wrecked stones as well as those who had to make new lives around the ravage—are moving to the center of Glück's concern. In northwest Beijing, ravage was a familiar theme as well as an ongoing predicament.

Half a century before Henry Murphy found the remains of the Shrine of Abundant Kindness, Chinese visitors to Haidian schooled themselves in the art of making sense out of ruination. Wang Kaiyun (1833–1916) was but one of many scholar-officials who made it their business to take the journey out of Beijing and walk the rubble-laden grounds of the Yuan Ming Yuan. He recorded his impressions in the following poem, which seeks to record what remained after the windswept smoke of 1860. Far from the "dynamism" celebrated by Louise Glück, Wang catalogues absence with a mournful gaze:

The buildings here all disappeared . . .
Lonesome visitors stand in the garden's solitude.
The exciting past, the sorrowful present,
Distinguished guests shall never come.
Not any more!
When I peep behind the scenes
Of the Inner Palace Gate and the Main Audience Hall,
I find a lot of broken bricks.
Cattail leaves grow wild in the lakes.
Mugwort grass rustling in the air, blocking stairways.
Some burned trees blossom anew,
But are cut and taken away for firewood.[5]

Wang Kaiyun's gloom in the inner palace suggests a distinctively Chinese way of mourning garden spaces. One would have thought there would be a tinge of pleasure, of finally penetrating the intimate spaces of the pleasure-loving Qing emperors. Instead, however, the visitor dwells on the broken bricks, the missing guests, the weed-choked lakes. Even blossoming trees, the very vegetation that had suffered along with stones and silks in Elgin's fires, is now being carted away for firewood. The orgy of destruction unleashed by Westerners is here augmented by Chinese robbers, peasants, and warlords. Wang is too honest an observer to blame outsiders alone. He is too much of a Confucian intellectual to celebrate "dynamism" in the midst of shards.

Wang Kaiyun's approach is different from the "pleasure of ruins" analyzed by Rose Macaulay. Victorian travelers of the nineteenth century sought out sites of breakage because they called to mind a stupendous past that aided the imagination to soar beyond myths and dreams. Here was the power of the living past, not simply the melancholy of moss-covered stones. In Macaulay's words, ruins provided Victorians with evidence for "the stunning impact of world history on its amazed heirs . . . it is less ruin worship than the worship of a tremendous past."[6] In China after 1860, there was little room and even less time for the worship of a glorious past. To visit the grounds of the Yuan Ming Yuan and its surrounding princely gardens was to reckon with the loss of grandeur. It was a grim reminder that Qing noblemen no longer reigned as unchallenged rulers of the Central Kingdom. China was no longer the pivot of a moral universe. Ravaged spaces signaled an increasingly brittle Mandate of Heaven.

Art historian Wu Hung has suggested that this fear of evil omens accounts for Chinese disinterest in portraying ruins in visual art. Poetry such as that of Wang Kaiyun was deemed a suitable vehicle for cultural mourning. Beyond that lay the dreadful prospect of further ruination:

Although abandoned cities or fallen palaces were lamented in poetry, their images, if painted, would imply inauspiciousness and danger. In the mid-nineteenth century, European photographers made the first serious effort to document architectural ruins in China. Beginning early in the twentieth century, some young Chinese artists studied in Europe, where they absorbed the prevailing "ruin" aesthetic and pictorial formulas for representing ruins. Upon returning to China they found similar inspiration in old temples and pagodas. Such picturesque and sentimental images never gained real life, however. A different kind of ruin image became influential and finally became part of a modern visual culture in China. Instead of inspiring melancholy and poetic lamentation, these images, including images of wars, the Cultural Revolution, and large-scale demolitions of traditional cities, evoke pain and terror. They shook their audience because they register, record, restage, or simulate destruction— destruction as violence and atrocity that left a person, a city, or a nation with a wounded body and psyche.[7]

According to Wu Hung, there was a cultural "taboo" in effect in pre-modern China that prevented intellectuals from either preserving or portraying ruined sites. When twentieth-century artists and architects began to travel to the West, there was a brief period of appreciation for ruin art. War with Japan and the Cultural Revolution, however, brought back the pain and terror glimpsed after 1860. Destruction as atrocity marked China's wounded psyche far more than the dynamic "human agency" celebrated by Louise Glück.

While Chinese visitors grieved in the presence of the missing past, Westerners captured ruination with skilled and interested eyes. One nineteenth-century photograph by Thomas Child captures this attentiveness well. Titled "West Princes Porch" (figure 25), this image from 1877 captures a terrain that seared the minds of men like Wang Kaiyun. It shows an elaborately carved marble gate (one of two that used to connect the Western and Chinese sections of the Yuan Ming Yuan). It may well have been a meeting point for Manchu noblemen such as Yihuan and Yixin when visiting their brother, the Xianfeng emperor.

All that remains of Manchu grandeur are broken stones and twisted trees. Thomas Child, an engineer who came to Beijing in 1870, was a civil servant in the British-controlled Maritime Customs Office. Having heard diplomats talk about the haunting beauty of crumpled rocks in northwest Beijing, Child took frequent trips to the same sites that had attracted Prince Chun. In

Figure 25. Thomas Child, "West Princes Porch" (1877), reproduced from Régine Thierez, *Barbarian Lens: Western Photographers of the Qianlong Emperor's European Palaces* (Amsterdam, 1998), p. 123, by permission of the author.

this image (unlike Beato's 1860 photograph of Prince Gong), the camera does not pierce the decorum of a humiliated Chinese official. Rather, the so-called barbarian lens is slow enough to record all the details of the broken steps leading to a shattered marble garland. Child's image is decidedly nostalgic. It stands as an eternal monument to a moment of lost greatness.[8]

Yihuan's poems, by contrast, pulsate with ongoing grief. Like his older brother Yixin, Prince Chun took personal responsibility for the devastation of 1860. To revisit the grounds around the Yuan Ming Yuan was to recall all that went wrong, all that might have been saved, all the terrible contingencies of human action. Even when he was forced to follow the imperial cortege, this Manchu nobleman could not tear his mind away from ravage of Haidian. In the well-furbished palace grounds of Manchuria, fall greeted Yihuan with riotous colors and tasty wines. Even while savoring delicacies that were his privilege as brother of the Son of Heaven, brother-in-law of the powerful Cixi, Prince Chun turned his mind's eye to the ruined gardens of Haidian. Unlike Thomas Child's camera, Yihuan's poems call into question the very medium he is using to catalogue the vagaries of history:

Here, fallen leaves crowd the boat,
wind streaming,

wine in hand, I swallow the end
of a song, brush the river's shore.

Bamboo shadows wave lustrous,
a sea of singular jade,

the maple forest in riotous color,
a vat of red.

There, ululation of autumn's gloom
is endless,

ravaged pavilion and terrace,
more wretched still.

Though linked in soul,
cut off by gaping space,

as time grows coarse and heavy,
who can find rest in supple verse?[9]

In this poem, the Manchu prince does not hide his idleness nor his indebtedness to traditional poetic conventions. He describes a posture of melancholy while sharpening the boundary between two settings, two moods. Written in the autumn of 1861, this poem lets us know that Yihuan's body is at ease in the imperial retreat of Jehol. On the other hand, his soul is linked to the ruined gardens of northwest Beijing. During this first autumn after the burning of the Summer Palace, Yihuan is not willing to sever himself from images of the recent past. He could have found rest in bamboo groves far from Haidian. Instead, he chooses a conversation with a historical event filled with pain. His conclusion was that there was no rest to be found in supple verse.

The poetic metaphors that surface in Yihuan's musings after 1860 are increasingly dark. They flow from a wellspring of traditional expressions for historical catastrophe. While the taboo on visual representations of ruins remained in effect, the mind's eye had plenty to draw upon while countenancing the most recent spectacle of intentional destruction. In his most famous poem circling the ruined site of Ming He Yuan, Prince Chun had written:

White mulberries swallowed by the blackest sea,
and you don't grieve?

Still seeking miracles? A rescuing dragon?
Nothing but bitter dreams.[10]

Addressed to his ninth brother, this was an invitation to sit under the eaves of the Yi Ran Ting and give voice to the missing past. At the heart of the wordless grief lay the well-worn phrase "dark sea mulberry fields." Each of these words evokes the distinct geography of the east China coast. Unlike photographs, these words draw upon a long tradition of loss and grief that goes back to Daoist and Buddhist concerns with the fragility of human existence. As early as the second century, the philosopher-poet Ge Hong (183–243 C.E.) used these four characters to write about earth-shattering events: "How rapidly mulberry fields turn into water. . . . Will the black sea ever give back the soil and hills again?"[11] Condensed into four characters, *cong hai sang tian,* Ge Hong's question endured for centuries. Whenever learned men faced ruined landscapes, his words came to mind. Yihuan used them to warn his younger brother against placing too much hope upon a "rescuing dragon." He had much less success in arguing the case for enduring grief at court.

On May 9, 1874, Prince Chun led a delegation of family members to try to convince his nephew, the young Tongzhi emperor, not to rebuild the ruined

Yuan Ming Yuan. After the death of his brother in 1861, this sickly boy was left in charge of the Mandate of Heaven. Manipulated by Cixi, Tongzhi had used Confucian values such as filial piety to requisition huge amounts of silver and timber from an impoverished nation to re-create the pleasure palace destroyed by Western armies. Yihuan understood only too well the foolishness of this effort. He had trained himself to mourn with words a landscape that could never be brought back in space. Accompanied by Prince Gong, he argued against further requisitions of funds and materials. The meeting was a complete failure. Prince Gong was demoted, Prince Chun silenced.[12] To make matters worse, when the Tongzhi emperor died suddenly in January 1875, Empress Dowager Cixi picked Yihuan's son Zaitian (1871–1908) to be the next ruler of China. Yihuan could do nothing but retreat from palace politics. With fewer voices to criticize her grandiose plans, Cixi became free to build an entirely new summer palace—the garden enclosure beyond Beijing University called the Joyfully Harmonious Garden (Yi He Yuan).

Prince Chun's son grew up to become the Guangxu emperor. In 1898, Guangxu tried to change the fate of the Qing dynasty. His "Hundred Days of Reform" were intended to transform China on the model of Japan's Meiji Restoration. When the empress dowager staged a coup against Zaitian, nothing remained of this visionary program but the skeletal foundations of Da Xue Tang, an institution that became the predecessor of Beijing University. Overruled by his powerful aunt, Guangxu spent his remaining years under house arrest. Yihuan's other sons also held high positions in the last decade of the Qing: Zaixun became head of the new navy while the youngest son, Zaitao, became head of the imperial army. Carrying on their father's fruitless efforts to save Manchu honor and Confucian values, these men rallied around imperial kin toward the end of Qing rule. Zaifeng, the next Prince Chun after Yihuan's death in 1891, rose to the position of prince regent. It was his son, Puyi, who became the last, ill-fated Qing emperor. Demoted to a gardener in the imperial compound and tortured by Red Guards, Yihuan's grandson completed the circle from art to atrocity in northwest Beijing.

The empress dowager had tried to both bribe and silence advocates of historical memory. During his lifetime, Yihuan was rewarded with more and more lavish titles, and forced to accept funds for the renovation of Wei Xiu Yuan. He refused most of the titles and made few repairs on the grounds of the Garden of Flourishing Grace. In private, away from palace intrigue, he continued to write poems of lament. Again and again, he turned to the missing past. Sparse words carried the burden of historical witnessing. Even decades after the burning of the Summer Palace, he could do no more than record ongoing devastation. Returning to Wei Xiu Yuan in 1881, Yihuan wrote:

Twenty autumns later,
again the garden,

the archery field silent,
broken pavilions, dance halls abandoned,

a sea of shards,
new birth perhaps from rubble . . .[13]

The metaphor of a sea of shards links this poem to mulberry fields swallowed by a black ocean. Yihuan used this poem to mark a moment in time. Twenty autumns after 1860, the old village of Haidian retained its attraction to a prince in search of mourning. In the distance, the Jade Hill Pagoda provided accompaniment for loss with the winddriven chatter of its abandoned chimes.

Idle temple bells, like common sparrows, underscore the dominion of an ignoble present over a once-glorious past. One might be tempted to go as far as Goethe—who saw in ruins nothing more than the willingness of history to relinquish its stranglehold upon the living. The past, he claimed, had nothing to bequeath but mortality. Historian Didier Maleuvre expands Goethe's idea to suggest that the past is good for nothing but "compost" for the modern: "To bequeath mortality is to offer the gift of the past's obsolescence to the present time. Through the image of the ruin, the past shows itself as the place where the dead, keeping to themselves, bow out of the present. That explains why, in the romantic tomb, history proves itself to be one with the wisdom of natural cycles: the ruin reconciles human history with the cosmic forces that confine the dead to their tombs. There they are recycled back into nature."[14] According to Maleuvre and Goethe, the gift of history is found in its willingness to pass out of the present. In China, however, the past was assumed to have moral priority over the present. The dead, far from bowing out, called to their descendants from places where ruins reigned.

A High Price for the Lesson We Received

To study the history of ravage and rebuilding in northwest Beijing is to explore a different kind of modernity from the one suggested by Didier Maleuvre.

Nothing in China's history of landscaped spaces suggested that the past could just "bow out." It was physically and spiritually embedded in the very soil that moderns trod. New and old found ways of coexisting, of inspiring each other here even when political authorities were inimical to influences from the past. Red Guards could smash old marble gates. They could, and did, imprison professors who knew the history of Qing gardens. Nonetheless, as this study shows, there were simply too many ruins, too many poems, too much ardor invested in historical memory to turn Haidian into a blank slate for Maoist visions.

It is the tenacity of recollection that enabled spatial markers such as the Shrine of Abundant Kindness to become meaningfully incorporated into new landscapes. Far from consigning the dead to a distant realm, advocates of China's modernization sought out the light of the past. In the decades that followed the burning of the Summer Palace, this quest took many forms. Yihuan himself had tried to build a strong army to defend north China. The funds collected ended up being siphoned off for the building of Cixi's new summer palace. Here, a lavishly sculptured marble boat mocked the aspirations of Prince Chun. Further away from the reach of palace intrigue, however, Chinese scholar-officials were considerably more outspoken about the need to take to heart the "lessons" of 1860. By 1895, the Chinese ambassador to London, far from blaming foreigners alone for the ravage, argued that destruction could be used to pave the way for new vision: "By the light of the burning palaces which had been the delight of her Emperors, [China] commenced to see that she had been asleep while all the world was up and doing. . . . The Summer Palace, with all its wealth of art, was a high price to pay for the lesson we received, but not too high, if it has taught us to repair and truly fortify our armor—and it has done so."[15]

For a very brief period at the end of the nineteenth century, it seemed as if Qing officials were willing to "see" by the light of this burning event. The radical measures inaugurated in 1898 by the Guangxu emperor revealed a young man bent upon learning from the scorching past. As the son of Yihuan, Zaitian knew that it took more than new arsenals to save China. The rescue mission required new languages and new sciences as well. Inspired by Confucian officials, he tried to pioneer a constitutional monarchy based on the Japanese example. His aunt, the empress dowager, however, would have none of this. She crushed the Hundred Days of Reform and became a staunch enemy of Chinese nationalism. When the dynasty collapsed in 1911, Cixi's Manchu pride collapsed as well.

After the antidynastic revolution of 1911, the ruined landscape of Beijing continued to inspire nationalist aspirations as well as the hope that China's

past may yet be used to build a more vibrant modern society. Chinese intellectuals looked at the sea of shards in Haidian as a place to refresh their vision. Gathering around broken stones and withered trees was not just a
pastime of the idle. Dressed in long silk robes, modern thinkers continued to
circle the terrain once inhabited by Manchu princes (figure 26). European-
style broken arches did not compel their interest. The politics of "national
humiliation" did. Recalling the burning of the Summer Palace, they could fan
the flames of rage against both imperial autocracy and foreign aggression.
They gained new strength from old shards.

This urge to gaze into the ruination of Haidian for political lessons was not
limited to Chinese reformers and revolutionaries. Westerners also circled this
terrain to illustrate their own visions of what modernity meant in the wake of
Elgin's fires. Victor Hugo was one of the first European intellectuals to seek out
this site in order to condemn Western aggression. Hugo had never looked into
the coffins to see the mangled bodies of the dead. Far from the theater of war,
Hugo could afford to sound high-minded. In an open letter dated November 28,
1861, the great man of French letters declared that the burning of the Summer
Palace in Beijing was a crime against humanity. He did not hesitate to blame the
French and British alike: "We call ourselves civilized and them barbarians: here

Figure 26. Yuan Ming Yuan Western-style palace in ruins, 1922. Photograph by
Oswald Siren.

is what Civilization has done to Barbarity."[16] By the end of the 1870s, Europeans shuddered as they wrote about the "rape of the Summer Palace." This sexual metaphor would continue to be used whenever a seemingly weak China became prey to outside aggression. The "rape" of the Yuan Ming Yuan became a precursor for twentieth-century rage against the "rape of Nanking"—a series of events in the winter of 1937 that left thousands dead and nationalist sentiments fired up against Japanese atrocities. The number of dead is not what mattered. It was China's perceived impotence that outraged witnesses and historians alike. Beneath the rhetoric of humiliation and rape lay an old assumption: If this ancient civilization had not been so female—so delicate somehow—she may not have been subjected to forcible ravage again and again.

It was this assumption that was challenged and redefined around the broken stones that littered Haidian. Here, the ravaged past revealed a hardened, more enduring visage. In time, shards of marble combined with historical memory could be used to create a more resilient vision of the future as well. While Chinese intellectuals circled the ruined princely gardens with words, Westerners traveling in China used the camera to capture the vistas on platinum prints. Thomas Child was not alone in his use of new technology to capture the beauty of ruins for hungry audiences at home. John Thomson (1837–1921) was a fellow Englishman who traveled across China with the express purpose of producing an illustrated record of the landscape that Lord Elgin had traveled through in military haste. The goal was knowledge and accuracy. What the Frenchman Lucy thought could be had only by force of arms was now revealed through black-and-white pictures. Thomson described his own goals as follows: "My design in the accompanying work is to present a series of pictures of China and its people, such as shall convey an accurate impression of the country I traversed as well as of its arts, usages, and manners which prevail in different provinces of the Empire. With this intention I made the camera the constant companion of my wanderings, and to it I am indebted for the faithful reproduction of the scenes I visited, and of the types of race with which I came into contact."[17] As an early example of professional photography, Thomson's illustrated book sold quite well. The insatiable interest in travel literature was no longer limited to cultured gentlemen, nor to such classical sites as the Greek Pantheon or the Egyptian pyramids. After 1860, Westerners wanted more and more images of the once-sequestered Central Kingdom. Thomson's first volume went on sale in May 1873 and sold over six hundred copies. The second volume sold even more and received positive reviews in both British and continental journals.

It was not only the faces and the land of China that fascinated Western-ers. It was the ruination of a nation as well. The longer Western visitors stayed in China, the more they grasped the distinctive attractions of the layered terrain around Haidian. Oswald Siren was but one of the many twentieth-century travelers who sought out the former imperial gardens of northwest Beijing. Here the march of time could be measured, and portrayed in a more evocative fashion than other parts of the war-burdened country. Close to the ground, talk of "rape" made less and less sense. Instead, as Siren's 1922 image of the Yuan Ming Yuan shows, there was an increasing interest in witnessing the enduring beauty of the past. There was something artful, inviting, spa-cious in the broken stones that had not been apparent in Haidian when Qing indulgence reigned supreme. Here, we can actually see how brokenness cre-ates a sense of cultured resilience. For Oswald Siren, as for Louise Glück, mute stones spoke volumes about a complex past. The camera's eye, like the poet's words, excavated meanings slowly, leaving plenty of room for reflec-tion. In the presence of material remains, there was an opportunity for re-birth. When Yenching University took over these rubbled grounds, Henry K. Murphy was able to create a totally new kind of garden—a garden for liberal learning.

Figure 27. Qing period marble columns, originally from the An You Palace (the ancestral shrine) of the Yuan Ming Yuan.

Figure 28. Stone carved unicorn from the ruined Yuan Ming Yuan that graces the entrance to the administration building of Beijing University today. Photograph by Marc Berger.

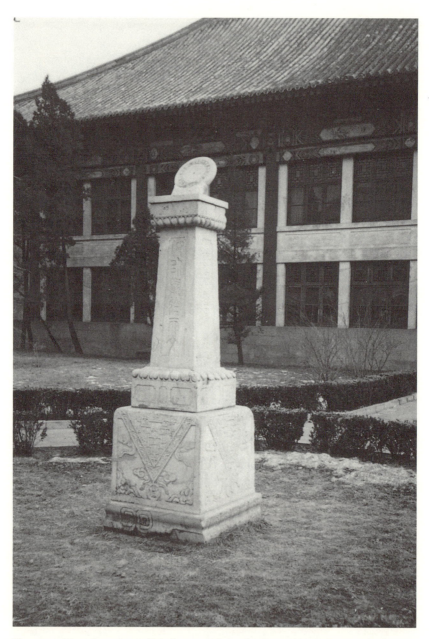

Figure 29. Qing dynasty sundial, fragment from the Yuan Ming Yuan, currently decorating the courtyard in front of the Arthur M. Sackler Museum of Art and Archaeology at Beijing University.

On the campus of Beijing University today, Qing remains continue to speak their tale both loudly and sotto voce. It takes a tutored eye to learn what lies behind fragments of monumental stone. Two huge carved pillars, for example, greet the visitor at the entrance of Beida's west gate. On each pillar intertwined dragons reach up to the sky, where a mythic animal reigns supreme. A cloud of white marble gives the impression of stone floating into timeless grace (figure 27). These remains from the Yuan Ming Yuan Imperial Ancestor Hall (the An You Palace) have been reproduced in various-sized crystals at the Beijing University History Museum shop. These imperial columns have become both commodity and memory. Much like the guardian unicorns that adorn the administration building and the Qing dynasty sundial that graces the entrance to the Sackler Museum, these are explicit reminders of enduring grandeur (figures 28 and 29). In bold, romanticized color, these remnants argue for optimism about the socialist future of China's premier university. They also testify to the passions of foreigners who appreciated the complexity of traditional Chinese garden architecture. These well-schooled men knew the ruinous history of the nineteenth century. They also knew how to bargain, cajole, and bribe various officials to obtain fragments from the Yuan Ming Yuan for a new educational institution designed on the grounds of the old Singing Crane Garden.

Rehabilitating a Garden Is More Difficult than Revising a Poem

To conduct an authentic dialogue with the past has been a challenge in this corner of Beijing. When Prince Gong and Prince Chun argued against the rebuilding of the Yuan Ming Yuan, they pointed out to the Tongzhi emperor that the replicated past would be but a costly sham. When Henry Murphy went out to Haidian, he knew that the past could not speak its language without some translation into the idiom of the present. Too much had been burned, looted, and buried to replicate history as it once was. Instead, something new had to be designed that would capture the spirit of traditional aesthetics while conveying it forward in time.

Chinese garden historian Chen Congzhou likened the challenge of "rehabilitating" the garden to the difficulties of revising a classical poem.[18] The word choice here is no accident. A survivor of the Cultural Revolution, Chen has reassumed his garden studies with great difficulty. After many decades during which both classical poems and traditional gardens had been objects of scorn, he has linked them in a path-breaking study of Chinese aesthetics. To revise a poem requires familiarity with tens of thousands of characters and their historically conditioned connotations. To "rehabilitate" a garden requires prolonged listening to its muted terrain as well as the skill to breathe new life into its withered bones. Many Chinese intellectuals were "rehabilitated" after the Cultural Revolution without the breath of life ever infusing their remaining years. Those like Chen Congzhou and Hou Renzhi, who went on to make significant new contributions to scholarship, had an inner connection to the past that withstood the scorn and violence of Maoism.

The ideal of combining past and present has a long history in Beijing. In 1870, when a group of American Methodist missionaries started a one-room school house in Beijing, this vision was but a distant dream. In the heady atmosphere that accompanied the Hundred Days of Reform of 1898, Yenching's forerunners started plans for a "Confluence of Cultures College." At the official Imperial University, Manchu and Chinese reformers also experimented with Western-style pedagogy. Their goal was primarily to strengthen China's military defenses. American missionaries, by contrast, envisioned an institution where Chinese students could learn about their own culture as well as Western science, technology, medicine, industry—and of course, Christian theology was to be part of this mix too.[19] Both dreams failed in the waning years of the nineteenth century. After China's defeat by Japan in 1895 and the collapse of the Qing in 1911, the ideal of new education lingered in increasingly dire circumstances. In Haidian, various warlords used the ruined princely gardens to enrich their own pleasure palaces. Uninterested in pedagogical innovation, they sent soldiers to cart away precious Taihu rocks, large timber, and movable pieces of marble. Disconnected from the surroundings that had lent them grace, Qing fragments became meaningless metaphors for fallen grandeur. Impoverished Manchu kinsmen, such as Yihuan's sons and grandsons, had fewer and fewer resources with which to resist this large-scale robbery.

In the fall of 1923, the president of the republic, Cao Yunxiang, formally asked the royal family to yield some of their lands in Haidian to build Qinghua College, a missionary-inspired institution that preceded Yenching in this corner of Beijing. Faced with reluctance, Cao went as far as to offer special scholarships for Manchu students at the new college. In the end, little came of this proposal until a more visionary—and more lucrative—offer was developed by the American trustees of Yenching. They were able to bring together a uniquely inspired college president, an unusually talented architect, and the funds necessary to create an entirely new "garden" on the grounds where cranes once roamed and ruins reigned. This garden, fondly called Yan Yuan by Yenching faculty and alumni, was truly a re-vision of the old princely retreats. Taking the poem analogy a step further, Yan Yuan was not a "translation" of Chinese aesthetics into the American missionary vernacular. Rather, it may be conceived as a "rendition"—an encapsulation of something essential about the harmonious landscapes of Haidian before 1860 in the form of a new garden that would provide a moral compass for a country hurtling toward war and revolution.

Challenging as it had been to combine *dong* and *jing* (motion and contemplation) in the old Singing Crane Garden, this blending became even more difficult on the terrain of Yenching. How to maintain affection for old traditions in an environment that made it obligatory to praise the new was a question that haunted many Chinese intellectuals. Educated men and women felt torn between conflicting alliances. Garden "poems" were thus revised, preserved, and handed on in the midst of a history that was marked by nationalism and liberalism alike. John Leighton Stuart (1876–1962) knew these conflicting passions well. Born in China to idealistic Presbyterian missionaries, Stuart was uniquely well suited to lead a new educational institution in Beijing. In 1919, when several Christian colleges wanted to create a consortium, Stuart was chosen precisely because he was "a man exceptional in the Chinese language and [knew] the Chinese point of view."[20] His mandate was to find a new home for an enlarged institution that was to be known as Yenching (so as to distinguish it from the former imperial institution that now also called itself Peking University in English).

John Leighton Stuart began the project with adequate financial support and a strong commitment to building a unique institution for liberal, Christian learning. From his first exploration of the terrain outside of the city gates during the summer of 1920, he was drawn to the natural beauty and garden traditions of Haidian. Stuart was especially attracted to one of the old princely retreats that had become known as the Korean Garden because a Korean dairyman was renting it from one of the Manchu descendants of Mianyu. The Singing Crane Garden seemed to have vanished from memory while Chinese warlords, impoverished imperial relatives, and prosperous farmers negotiated with the Americans to get the best price for the ruined terrain. On October 13 a deal seemed at hand: $60,000 in Chinese currency was to be paid for a parcel of land that occupied about half of the ground previously enclosed in the Singing Crane Garden and in He Shen's Shu Chun

Yuan.[21] These negotiations, however, were frustrated by the complex claims upon the land that was held jointly by General Chen Shufan and Yihuan's sixth son, Zaixun—known as Prince Rui.

Forty thousand more dollars and Stuart's persistence finally led to the acquisition of the Rui Wang Summer Garden for Yenching. The land, surveyed shortly upon acquisition by an American engineer, looked promising enough: "The property fronts on the east side of the main highway, rolling back to the west, so that the elevation at the east boundary is about sixty feet above the highway—the entire property contains artificial hills, waterways and islands, being watered by streams running in from the west from the same source which supplies the Jade Fountain and the Summer Palace. Large Chinese fir and pine trees, artificial grottoes and caves enhance the natural beauty of the place, while from the highest points of the property a wonderful panorama of the surrounding country can be viewed."[22] The fact that this princely retreat lay but a few hundred feet south of the old Yuan Ming Yuan was known to Stuart and to his committee. They knew the history of the war that had led the French and British soldiers to ravage Haidian in 1860. They had read about the cruel treatment of Western prisoners. Awareness of that dark hour may have made the idea of building a new institution for Chinese learning here even more attractive. If the past could be reshaped with grace, a genuinely new beginning for Chinese thought could perhaps be fashioned here as well.

Two years before the land deal in Haidian was clenched, Stuart had already engaged the firm of Henry Murphy to design the new university. In this Yale graduate, Stuart found a kindred spirit: they both admired traditional Chinese architecture and were on guard against overly "American" statements on the Chinese terrain. The goal was to create a new educational institution that Chinese students would find inspiring—and also familiar. As Stuart later recalled: "We had determined from the outset to use an adaptation of Chinese architecture for the academic buildings. Graceful curves and gorgeous coloring were designed for the exteriors while the main structures were to be constructed throughout of reinforced concrete and equipped with modern lighting, heating and plumbing. Thus the buildings were in themselves symbolic of our educational purpose in preserving all that was most valuable in China's cultural heritage."[23] This commitment to China's cultural heritage distinguished Yenching University from its inception. Stuart, as well as the trustees and fund raisers for the new institution (especially Henry Luce), knew that money would be easier to find if the site and the vision of

Yenching were truly unique. At the same time, they wanted the Chineseness of the design to go beyond a fund-raising ploy. They advocated a genuine conversation with the Chinese past. It was this dialogue that shaped the buildings that came to house Yenching's liberal, Christian mission.

The partnership of Stuart and Murphy was not a matter of convenience only. It brought together two men who shared an informed appreciation for Chinese history, culture, and aesthetics. Stuart's anchoring in Chinese language gave him a keener, deeper sense of what the Yale-trained architect had glimpsed in a few brief visits before obtaining the Yenching commission. China-born, John Leighton Stuart ended his distinguished career by serving as American ambassador from 1946 to 1948. In contrast, for Henry Murphy, China provided a concrete opportunity to explore emerging ideas about "adaptive architecture." Without necessarily knowing or understanding the garden-poem analogy, Murphy threw himself into building Chinese-style missionary colleges with his own distinctive verve.

Strolling in Haidian half a century after the burning of the Summer Palace, and four decades before the ox pens, Henry Murphy had the luxury of an open-ended conversation without the past. Not being Chinese, he did not feel compelled to choose native aesthetics for nationalistic reasons. He could savor what the grounds offered without the burden of responsibility for the ruination of imperial splendor. Moved by the endurance of shards, he was determined to build around them an educational institution that would breathe new life into withered bones:

In miniature the Chinese Garden—"the Ideal, realized in Nature"—symbolizes the kind of world in which its builder would best like to have lived: artificial lakes, carefully placed with a view to the most pleasing reflections, cunningly curved to give apparent distance and gracefully spanned at their narrow points by the "tiger-back" bridges; steep little hills built up, when the lake was dug, around the far sides of the garden, to shut off the outer world; trees of widely varied size and shape, among which wind alluring paths to lead the wanderer on; and, best loved of all, the little pavilion that so continually lends its charm to Chinese imaginative literature:

> "Out in the artificial lake
> there is a pavilion of green and white porcelain;
> it is reached by a bridge of jade
> arched like the back of a tiger."[24]

Murphy knew enough about Chinese poetry to hear its echoes in Haidian. His goal was not to revise the poem, or the past. Rather, he sought a dialogue with it. On the occasion of his first visit to the site acquired by Stuart and the Yenching trustees, he stood on one of the artificial hills that remained from the old Singing Crane Garden. His gaze fell upon the Jade Hill Pagoda in the distance, and he exclaimed: "Here is the point we are looking for. The main line of our axis will be directed to the pagoda of the Jade Mountain hill."[25] Like emperors and princes before him who had stood under the wings of the Yi Ran Ting, Henry Murphy understood the majesty of the wellsprings that provided water for all of Haidian. When he came to design the water tower of the new university, it was to be the most explicitly Chinese part of the Yenching University campus.

Henry Murphy celebrated the experiment undertaken in northwest Beijing by playing with the motto of "old wine in new bottles." Having designed many of the buildings at Qinghua University and at Peking Union Medical College as well, he was not a novice to garden terrains. Nonetheless, the Yenching project allowed him to converse most exuberantly with the voices of the Chinese past. In an essay written in 1926, as the new project in Haidian was nearing its completion, he wrote:

"Old Wine in New Bottles"—a clever caption, strikingly bringing out one aspect of what we are accomplishing at Yenching University by the use of the new reinforced concrete construction for buildings in the old Chinese style of architecture. But in another aspect this might be called "New Wine in Old Bottles"—for I like to think of adaptations of Chinese architecture as furnishing an old setting for the new education offered to China by such institutions as Yenching. The more deeply I get into the beauty, richness and dignity of the best of the old buildings that have come down to us from the great Chinese builders of the past, the more certain I am that it is worth all the time and trouble and expense we are putting into our efforts to translate this wonderful art from mere archaeology into the living architecture of today, and so to preserve to the Chinese, and to the world, their splendid heritage.[26]

This commitment to the preservation of the Chinese heritage would be restated on the same grounds fifty years later by Arthur Sackler, as he pleaded with the authorities of Beijing University to allow him to establish a museum of art and archaeology. Unlike Sackler, however, Henry Murphy was a builder commissioned to create a new framework for learning on the terrain of the princely gardens. The idea of refurnishing an old setting for a modern educational institution was almost unheard of in China at that time. Perhaps it was foreign funding and the political vulnerability of China in the 1920s that enabled Murphy to succeed on a larger scale than Sackler in the 1980s.

Henry Murphy also did not have to fight the same battles that reform-minded Chinese intellectuals had waged at National Beijing University during the New Culture Movement. They had tried to shake off the stranglehold of Confucian tradition by turning to Western thinkers such as Henrik Ibsen, Bertrand Russell, and Karl Marx. Unlike these cultural radicals smitten by the idea of the "new," Murphy was not embarrassed by his avid interest in the Chinese past. The editors and writers of *New Youth* magazine had to fight against their own educational traditions to develop a critical attitude toward the values of their parents and grandparents. The American architect of Yenching, by contrast, was both arrogant and well funded. Murphy was free to adopt a posture of "listening" to the voices of old buildings and ruined gardens. The result was truly new wine in old bottles.

The first structure erected on the site of the old Shu Chun Yuan was Ninde Hall, Yenching University's School of Religion. It was originally situated in a complex that adjoined the same courtyard where the Sackler Museum stands today. Beyond the Ninde Hall stretched the main axis of a campus carefully aligned with the Jade Hill Pagoda that Murphy had glimpsed on his first visit to Haidian. Dormitories for men and women framed a central space that guided visitors toward the Wei Ming Hu (Unnamed Lake) and the marble boat that remained from the era of He Shen. The library, separate gymnasiums for men and women, the Sage Chapel, and various instructional buildings named after former teachers and current donors followed. Bashford, Gamble, and Miner were just three of the most graceful of the two-story buildings that shimmered in their bright colors below gracefully arching roofs.

Friendly Shadows

Winged eaves, an old marble boat, the rechristened Hua Shen Miao were just some of the physical "threads" that wove the new Yan Yuan into the fabric of the old princely gardens. There were, however, many other aspects of the Murphy design that enabled Yenching to become a modern space for old-fashioned reflectiveness. The goal, in the end, was not merely exportable Christianity, not merely a site where Chinese youth could sing hymns and nationalist songs at the same time. Embedded in Stuart's vision was a university that made meaningful overtures to past and present alike. Prince Yihuan had sought to convey a similar message to his younger kin in the shadow of the Yi Ran Ting. He had done this in the midst of ruins and grief. The rehabilitation of garden architecture in Haidian in the 1920s afforded China a brief, more optimistic encounter with its own past. For one decade before the war with Japan broke out in 1937, a corner of northwest Beijing managed to harbor history in a "friendly" fashion.

Alice Frame, dean of the Women's College at Yenching, glimpsed this harmony with the past during the first night she spent in Gamble Hall. Here was a female administrative officer overseeing the development of a radical new vision for women's education in republican China. At the same time as she was fostering an utterly new idea about women's learning, Frame also found solace and inspiration in the traditional aesthetics that had been brought to life in Yan Yuan:

I shall never forget that first night, when at dusk I walked into the graceful, square Chinese building with its big button top that is the new Dean's residence. There was a lump in my throat as I shut the door and hung up my hat and went upstairs to my room. There was no electricity then, and the rooms of the beautiful new home were full of soft shadows—friendly shadows. I leaned out of one of the windows. Sage loomed dark and stately against the starlit sky on one side, our big science building farther on the other; close beside me was the lovely twin building of the Dean's Residence and Administration Building.[27]

This tribute to friendly shadows echoes Dorothy Graham's appreciation of the Lang Run Yuan in the 1930s. Both American women had enough background in the history of Chinese aesthetics to hear what the garden setting had to tell them. Graham, in conversation with Manchu princes, dwelt on the history of the Yuan Ming Yuan. Alice Frame, a new kind of educator seeking to sink roots in China, looked out upon the campus designed by Henry Murphy and knew it to be a genuinely fresh start for both Christianity and liberal learning.

Seven decades later, in the fall of 2006, the China-born architect I. M. Pei returned to his old hometown of Suzhou to design a modern museum that also sought to pay homage to consciousness buried in the ground. In the wake of Maoist attacks upon the past and contemporary preference for cheap, flashy modernities, Pei created an innovative structure that combines traditional gray colors, wood, and the garden spirit. Perhaps more than any other architect since Henry Murphy, this American-educated architect understood the inseparability of the present from the friendly shadows of the past. Looking over row upon row of shabby real-estate projects in Suzhou, I. M. Pei conceded: "Terrible things are happening. I can't stop it. I can't stop progress. But I hope it will be temporary. . . . In China, the architecture and the garden are one. . . . A Western building is a building and a garden is a garden. They are related in spirit. But they are one in China."[28]

The "terrible things" Pei spoke about encompass far more than cheap real-estate projects in today's Suzhou. They call to mind a long history of war with the past, war with the idea of the garden, war with the reflectiveness it promotes and protects. Younger Chinese intellectuals who remained on the mainland, who lived through endless series of brutal political campaigns, are only now beginning to recover the Yenching experience of "friendly shadows." They are turning to garden history and to the history of missionary institutions to learn how liberal learning can foster a more harmonious view of past and present alike. One such young scholar, Tang Keyang, unearthed new materials about Henry Murphy and linked them to the idea of a "garden for education." Distinguishing between the garden as a site and "gardening as a cultural practice," Tang portrays Yenching as a place that made room for the past in a meaningful fashion. It was not only marble bits from the ruined Yuan Ming Yuan and Shu Chun Yuan that found a new home in the rehabilitated Yan Yuan. The Chinese garden motif itself created the idea of a campus as an "undisturbed spiritual place for education."[29]

Far from being an open space where only modern, Western ideas could thrive, Murphy's plan and Stuart's pedagogical vision created a space for connectedness to tradition. The central lake, Wei Ming Hu, enabled students to try out alternative views of love, of country, of truth, and of beauty. In a university-sponsored newsreel from the early 1930s, there was an image of ice skating where a Chinese master who was believed to have performed for the Manchu royal family took center stage. In this newsreel, it did not matter if Manchu princes such as Mianyu or Yihuan really savored ice skating. What was emphasized instead was the idea of a space that connected Yenching to the imperial past not only in terms of location but through the ideal of leisure for the sake of cultural introspection. Private passions of Qing noblemen became public possibilities in the new "garden of education." *Xiao yuan*, the twentieth-century term for "campus," is nothing more, nor less, than a "learning garden." At Yenching, according to Tang Keyang, architecture and pedagogy combined to create a "consciousness of community, of public participation."[30] What enabled Yenching students, faculty, and alumni to become prominent in all aspects of public life was their very rootedness in history. Not compelled to choose between Western ideas and Chinese values, they were inspired to become bridge builders between the old and the new.

Unfortunately, China as a whole was not ready for the garden experiment.

War and revolution curbed, and eventually defeated, the spirit of Yenching. Before the vanquishing of the liberal vision in 1949, however, Yenching professors such as William Hung left a careful recording of the university's embeddedness in Chinese history. Their students, Hou Renzhi foremost among them, continued to document Yenching's history and its connection to imperial gardens. As soon as the Maoist grip on public life loosened a bit, Hou Renzhi took up the thread of research again. In fact, he was one of the main consultants on garden history when university authorities started to rehabilitate the site around the Sackler Museum. A "garden for education" seeded in the mind thus endured long after it was ravaged by dogmatic Red Guards.

Hou Renzhi's teacher William Hung had been one of the most distinguished historians hired by Stuart for the new Yenching. A Chinese convert to Christianity, Hung was a scrupulous researcher and an admirer of Confucian philosophy.[31] While architects designed the new campus to enliven the wellspring of learning, this scholar roamed the terrain and lingered in the archives. The result of William Hung's research was a comprehensive history of Shao Yuan—the old Ladle Garden designed and cherished by Mi Wanzhong. Not content to investigate the Ming dynasty origins of the Yenching University campus, William Hung proceeded to piece together the story of other Haidian gardens as well. In a modestly titled essay, "Ho Shen and Shu Ch'un Yuan—An Episode in the Past of the Yenching Campus," this American-educated Chinese gentleman evokes the fullness of a past that vanished with the arrest of Qianlong's corrupt minister. Far from being a romantic evocation of former days of pleasure, Hung's work focused upon the material and literary remains surrounding an educational institution in which he himself sought to teach the methodology of critical history. Starting with the marble boat anchored in Unnamed Lake, Hung confronted the bitterness and loss that marks this corner of northwest Beijing. Although he looked forward to the bright future to be created by the collective intelligence of Yenching graduates, Hung's essay on He Shen also gazed directly into the dark mirror of the past. His conclusion about eighteenth-century China may be read as a parable for events that unfolded two hundred years later: "Everything has a sorrowful tale, if one has the heart to listen."[32]

The art of cultivating a listening heart is what Williams Hung aimed to convey to his students in history. No matter how sorrowful, or even shame-filled, the tale, it had to be excavated, told, documented. Prince Yihuan, too, had roamed the grounds of the old Shu Chun Yuan mindful of He Shen's shadow. He did not shy away from the corruption scandal that racked the

Qing at the end of the eighteenth century, nor from the ashes and ruins that enveloped He Shen's garden after 1860. Yihuan had stood his ground in poems that mourned the shadow-laden spaces of northwest Beijing. William Hung paid homage to this tradition through critical historical investigation. Launching the *Yenching Journal of Chinese Studies* in 1927, the new chairman of the history department urged his students to study the ground beneath their own garden of liberal learning. Hung's own essays on the princely gardens, including one on Yihuan's Wei Xiu Yuan, provided a firm foundation for Hou Renzhi's later evocations of these spaces.[33]

Garden history thus managed somehow to outwit the politically mandated forgetfulness that shrouded Yenching after the communist conquest in 1949. Even after the grounds were taken over by the newly socialist Beijing University, recollections of its spirit endured, quite literally under the winged roofs designed by Henry Murphy. The old Yenching buildings were not destroyed in the 1950s, they were just pushed aside by large, Russian-inspired dormitories and a new library. The carefully constructed garden axis was compromised, but historical memory remained in place. What became most unspeakable in the Maoist era was not garden history, but the unique garden of education that Stuart had created inside the Murphy campus. It was not only Christian hymns that became outlawed on the territory once occupied by the School of Religion, but liberal learning as well. The Chinese poet Li Yong-lee gave voice to this silence in one of his own poems about missionary-sponsored education. Li was born not in China but rather in Indonesia. There, his parents were persecuted because they were not Muslims. The fact that Li's family was both Chinese and Christian made them especially odious to their neighbors. As a boy, Li tried to forget. Later, he recalled as follows the pressure to negate one's cultural past:

And since you
don't recall the missionary
bells chiming the hour, or these words whose sound
alone exhaust the heart—*garden
heaven, amen*—I'll mention none of it.[34]

This poem, while acknowledging forgetfulness, names the objects erased: the heart, the garden, the soul that might have said "amen." In confronting amnesia, the poem becomes a monument to memory. The missionary bells ring on because the poet in exile chose to break the code of silence. In China, by contrast, silence endured because of fear and persecution. During the 1950s and 1960s the "garden" of liberal learning died because intellectuals were not allowed to speak its name. The "friendly shadows" glimpsed by Alice Frame in 1926 began to turn into menacing voices as early as the winter of 1948–49.

We Were "Liberated"

When the chill of revolution invaded the grounds of the former princely gardens, liberal intellectuals were unprepared for the frost. The campus itself, the *xiao yuan*, had maintained a visual connection with Singing Crane Garden and Murphy's revision of the garden-poem. Underneath the ground, however, were also other echoes: the sounds of violence and torture had poisoned the air of Haidian in 1860. They would, again, in the 1960s. "Garden memory"—if one may speak of such a concept at all—thus includes not only beauty but terror as well. At least this has been the experience of educated men and women in one corner of China.

When Prince Yihuan visited the deserted grounds of Ming He Yuan, he had captured its desolation by dwelling on the absent cries of cranes. Where cranes once mated, Yihuan took note of the din of sparrows. Numerous and noisy, these common birds were nothing like the solitary birds that had preferred to dwell in shadows. Sparrows were emblematic of a crowd mentality that was overtaking the ground of Haidian and Qing society by the end of the nineteenth century. This contrast between cranes and sparrows grew more acute in the 1950s and 1960s. Chinese colloquial language mirrored this rapid change while coining a special phrase for the cultured gentleman: *he li ji qun*—a crane that stands out amid a flock of chickens. Even in common parlance, an educated mind was a vulnerable treasure among the clucking hens. This residual respect for the possibility that an individual might stand apart from a conformist crowd came under attack during the long era of Mao Zedong.

Yenching University, too, had nurtured the spirit of the crane. Although it was Christian motifs such as "truth shall set you free" that were inscribed in stone in Ninde Hall, classical Chinese allusions had their place of distinction as well.[35] One place where *grus japonisis* had a place of honor was on the ceiling of the School Scenes Pavilion. The old Yi Ran Ting had become a jewel of Stuart's garden of liberal learning. Its winged eaves sheltered images of the very buildings that Murphy had designed with such care as well as the key Qing "ruins" incorporated into campus life and architecture. Pride of place on the ceiling was reserved for cranes. Their soaring wings and proud necks were supposed to inspire students and faculty to look upward, to soar above petty ambition, to incorporate the ideal of community service for which Yenching's *xiao yuan* was well known. Not unlike the cranes in the study hall designed by Qianlong for princes, these images were meant to suggest distinctiveness and nobility of spirit.

These values became a source of political and personal vulnerability with the advent of communist victory in the winter of 1948–49. Students and faculty who had taken to heart the Yenching message found themselves trembling with fear at news of the approaching red armies. They were not afraid of taking risks for China's betterment. After all, Yenching students had been in the forefront of demonstrations against warlord atrocities, as well as against Japanese aggression. Several had lost their lives in patriotic struggles and in the defense of genuine democracy. Stuart, serving as American ambassador, made it seem as if there was room in public life for Yenching values. Mao Zedong's bitter essay "Farewell Leighton Stuart," however, made it clear that new China would not look kindly upon advocates of liberal learning.[36] By December 1948, fear had reached the gates of Yenching itself. Being patriotic was not enough, defending human rights was not enough. Political conformity was now the order of the day as promoted by the advancing troops of Mao's armies. Grace Boyton, one of the most distinguished members of the Yenching faculty at this time, recorded her impressions of China on the eve of "liberation" in the following words:

The day [Monday, December 13, 1948] was dull and overcast. . . . Our gates were guarded by both students and members of the faculty, but they were still open, and a steady stream of refugees tugging bundles was coming in. . . . Late on Wednesday, we learned that Communist troops were outside our gates and so we knew the changeover had taken place. . . . [The next day] Lucius Porter [a fellow faculty member] was on twenty-four-hour duty at the Yenching West Gate where he was in telephone communication with all parts of the campus. . . . He ordered the gate unbarred and found a very young political cadre accompanied by two soldiers. The cadre was unarmed, but the guards were fairly draped with weapons. The first question asked was most disarming. "Has Yenching been hit during the fighting?" No. Then "Does Yenching need anything?"

Chancellor [Lu Zhiwei] spoke to us on the Thursday saying we were "liberated." He warned us that we are now making a much greater change than has been made by revolutions or by falling dynasties in China's history. . . . Then there was the meeting in Bashford on December 17 when our "liberators" sent a member of their political team of cadres to address the assembled University community. The auditorium was crammed, for there were servants, and work people like gatemen and janitors, as well as students and us teachers. . . . It was obvious that the speaker (a former student at the American Board's Middle School in Paotingfu) was ill at ease. He had probably never completed the work in our Middle School, and here he was talking to learned university students and their tremendously learned professors! So he was sweating profusely and began rather stumblingly. But he soon recovered his self-confidence and gave us a glowing picture of our future, along with a proper pep talk about the virtues of our new masters. He was received with cordial applause, but the audience was not as thrilled as he had expected us to be. The young man bowed, and went away followed by the two guards.[37]

After this tense encounter, hope for a bright future endured. Subsequent persecution campaigns, however, taught Yenching faculty and students another lesson: there was to be no pride in liberal learning, no reward for attachment to the past—be that Chinese or Christian.

In 1948, terror was only a very distant premonition in Haidian. The enthusiastic applause described by Grace Boyton was just one sign of the eagerness with which Yenching students and faculty welcomed the "patriotic" revolution. When the Communist Party came to power, most Chinese intellectuals believed that it represented the best interests of the nation as a whole. The Nationalist Party fleeing to Taiwan under the leadership of Jiang Kaishek had abandoned the cause of patriotism. When Mao Zedong stood up in Tiananmen Square on October 1, 1949, he declared, "China has stood up!" Not the party, not the army, but China as a whole.

The Chinese people, including liberal-minded graduates of Yenching University, wanted very much to believe him. Chancellor Lu Zhiwei was but one of thousands who argued that communist "liberation" was going to bring a greater, deeper liberation to all of China. With a Ph.D. in psychology from Columbia University, Yenching's Chinese president was a Christian and a patriot. In the words of his friend William Hung, Lu Zhiwei was a man "who detested evil as if it were his personal enemy."[38] By 1951, Lu was in danger of being defined as a "devil" in Chinese public life. Mao Zedong had strengthened his control over Chinese cities. His animosity toward liberal institutions such as Yenching became ever more clear. John Leighton Stuart had left China as the officially "hated" American ambassador. Mao himself demanded that China spit him out. Stuart's followers could not be allowed to imagine themselves as leaders of the new China.

Initially, Lu Zhiwei had hoped to deflect Mao's ire by simply denouncing Stuart in print, and thereby sparing the rest of his faculty and students. This tactic did not work. Mao Zedong wanted a bigger, noisier denunciation of everything that missionary bells and princely gardens had stood for. In a January 1952 directive to communist cadres, he ordered them to make Lu their main target and to "put on a big show with flags and drums, as sudden and severe as thunder, as all pervading as wind."[39] In 1952, these words were still somewhat metaphorical. A decade and a half later they would become literal, and deadly. Flags and drums were taken up, at first just for show. Lu was denounced initially with words alone. Yet even in the 1950s, the words carried connotations of demonology. Lu Zhiwei was blamed not for what he did. Rather, he was attacked for what he supposedly stood for. In a terrible foreshadowing of the Cultural Revolution, Lu's daughter, Lu Yaohua, a graduate student in biology at Yenching, attacked him as the embodiment of "evil missionary designs."[40]

With the winds of the Korean War gaining strength in the background, the daughter accused her father of infusing in her a fear of America rather than the will to fight the imperialists' might. Lu's academic colleagues such as Hou Renzhi were not even allowed to remain silent. Everyone had to speak out against Lu, against Stuart, against the Yenching legacy. The campaign against Lu Zhiwei dragged in everyone who had once known the succor of an institution dedicated to liberal learning in a gracious garden setting.

Memory, like experience, had to be erased and replaced with ideological ardor. William Hung, who had left China in 1948, received news of these attacks with a grieving heart. Refusing to go back to China even after the death of Mao, he could only mourn from afar when he heard that Lu Zhiwei had been beaten senselessness in 1968 during the height of the Cultural Revolution: "Confused and shocked, he was locked up in a room where he lived amid his own excrement for more than half a year. After he was released, he came gravely ill and no attempt was made to give him medical attention; death resulted."[41]

The tragic fate of the man who had believed so fervently in liberation in 1948 mirrored the lives of countless Yenching graduates. By the time the "show" of violence became real, Henry Murphy's campus had been transformed by the ox pens. The grounds of the old Shao Yuan and of the Singing Crane Garden now echoed with loud chants and criminal accusations. Where William Hung once roamed documenting the history of Yihuan's Garden of Flourishing Grace, hatred of highly educated intellectuals prevailed. The terrain that once housed cranes and Manchu princes now witnessed earth-shaking devastation. During the Cultural Revolution, it was not enough to take vengeance on stones and on long-departed leaders of liberal education. All who had drunk from the wellsprings of foreign and traditional learning had been condemned as monsters and ghosts. The "logical" outcome of demonization was incarceration and death.

Red Guards deemed the idea of difference to be tantamount to original sin. They had grown up believing that the bright new order needed no nuance, no cranes. Uniqueness of outlook, like shadowy spaces, implied ideological insubordination. During the Cultural Revolution, Haidian was stripped of all its friendly shadows. No corner of the old gardens was left untouched. Demons reigned all over. The contrast with the times of Mianyu grew more acute each day. During the heyday of the Singing Crane Garden, Buddhist and Lamaist temples had been erected to deal with the threat of a vicious underworld. Manchu noblemen who retreated to this corner of China did believe in the existence of a ghost-ridden hell. However, hell was otherworldly. They had fixed times for sacrificial offerings to tame the underworld and to deal with fear of the afterlife. In Maoist China, temples had to be torn down. Christian institutions that once fostered prayer for the salvation of the soul were likewise held in contempt as extensions of imperialist propaganda. Shut out of temples and churches, demons became the scourge of public life. Attacks on educated men and women took the form of hysterical hallucination.

In 1958, eight years before the ox pens, the Communist Party's campaign for atheism seemed to have reached some kind of a truce with the underworld. Slogans such as "Thoughts are Emancipated, Ghosts Have Retreated" promised respite from mutual incrimination. In fact, however, the ground was being seeded for a wide-scale assault upon those who had dared to think for themselves. Former "cranes" came to be seen as living monsters. Chinese demonology had a rich vocabulary readily available for the political campaigns of the 1960s: *mo gui* (devils), *gui gui* (demons), and *xie gui* (vampires) were some of the underground beings used to fuel public hate during the Cultural Revolution. Eventually, the expression that embraced all intellectuals came to be known as *niu gui she shen*—ox ghosts and snake spirits. Derived from the mythology of folk Buddhism, these guardians of Hell had been depicted as monsters with bullheads, horses' faces, and the slithering bodies of snakes. The Tang dynasty poet Du Mu (803–852) had used the expression *niu gui she shen* to describe phantasmagoric beings that lived in hell.[42] For Mao Zedong, by contrast, monsters were no poetical metaphor. They stood for ideas and for persons he deemed to be dangerous and detestable.

In the heyday of Yan Yuan, when a garden of education had taken root in Haidian, metaphors, shadows, and ruins were accommodated and incorporated into personal life as well as into public scholarship. Yenching's architects could take the old Shrine of Abundant Kindness and rename it Hua Shen Miao. Diminished in size from its Qing grandeur, the finely carved marble gate adorned the vistas of Wei Ming Hu. Its muted colors invited reflection about past and present alike. For Qianlong, the shrine had been a symbol of his ancestral glory. For Leighton Stuart's students and faculty, it became a temple to celebrate the Christian spirit advocated at Yenching. Its tolerance for multilayered words became flattened during the Cultural Revolution. In 1860, it was Elgin's armies who set fire to princely retreats. In the 1960s, it was Maoist youths who declared the garden, and its spiritual heirs, to be nothing but *niu gui she shen*. Neither shrine nor temple could shelter liberal intellectuals. Their evil had to be expunged by incarceration and murder.

Chapter 4

Red Terror on the Site of Ming He Yuan

> *Voices mute forever, or since yesterday or just stilled;*
> *If you listen hard, you can still catch the echo.*
> *Hoarse voices of those who can no longer speak . . .*
> —Primo Levi, "Voices"

The terror of the 1960s silenced the Yenching legacy, and the crane music of Ming He Yuan as well. Intellectuals labeled as monsters were forced to attack each other and the cultural traditions that had nurtured the garden aesthetic. Courtyards remained, but were renamed for the sake of Mao's revolution. Stones remained, though many were smashed, gashed with knives in this outpouring of rage against history. Human minds and bodies, more vulnerable, were deemed most evil. These had to be destroyed, or at least incarcerated. Thus the niu peng were born—holding pens and torture chambers where Red Guards could settle scores with teachers and parents they had once honored and cherished.

How Mao's ideological dogmatism came to uproot centuries of Confucian respect for the aged and for historical records is a question still pondered in China today. What concerns us most directly here is how one corner of northwest Beijing weathered the red terror, how the legacy of both beauty and atrocity dating back to the Singing Crane Garden and to Yenching University came to color the Cultural Revolution unleashed over the country as a whole. By decoding the layers of violence and enforced amnesia at Beijing University, we may understand better how gardens, nations, and individuals outlast, and perhaps outwit, the forces of destruction all too common in twentieth-century history. As Primo Levi, a survivor of Nazi concentration camps, noted in his poem entitled "Voices," terror does not create total muteness.[1] There is always a trace of hoarseness left. If we listen hard—a daunting task in a landscape subjected to repeated ruination—we may in fact hear the hoarse voices of those who can no longer speak. We may even go as far as Yihuan counseled in the nineteenth century: we may succeed in "giving voice to what is gone."

My own attentiveness to the hidden strata of tragedy at Beijing University was aided by a simple, hasty sketch produced by Yue Shengyang during our walk around the ruins of the Singing Crane Garden on May 10, 1998. I already carried in hand Dr. Yue's carefully penned map of the Ming He Yuan and its remnants visible today. Walking along the perimeter of the old garden brought up memories of more recent terror and grief, including the incarceration of Dr. Yue's parents in the "ox pens" of Beida. As he began to recall his boyhood trips to the niu peng to deliver food and clothes, Yue

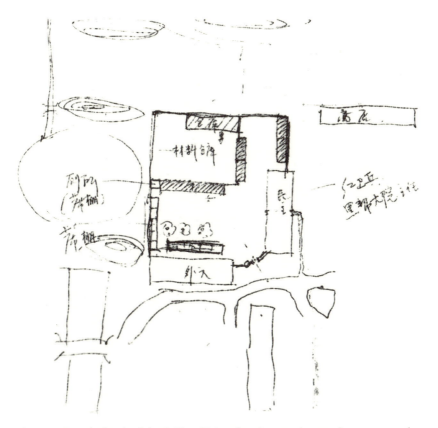

Figure 30. Rough sketch of the Beijing University niu peng (ox pens) area executed for the author by Yue Shengyang in May 1998.

Shengyang took out a pencil to sketch the buildings and some trees that had surrounded the torture grounds inside China's foremost university (figure 30). He recalled the fear and humiliation of his parents, distinguished alumni of Yenching, who had done nothing more than use their high level of education in the service of socialist society. He also noted the painful irony of delivering paltry, daily objects for imprisoned intellectuals at the gate of the *niu peng*—a coarsely drawn line between two buildings: Democracy Hall and the Foreign Languages Hall. Terror, it seems, made itself most at home in the

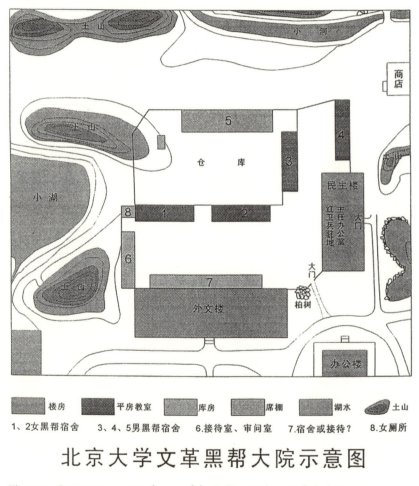

北京大学文革黑帮大院示意图

Figure 31. Computer-generated map of the Beijing University "Black Gang Courtyard," produced for the author by Yue Shengyang in May 1999.

very corner of the university that carried the name of the thoroughly smashed ideals of genuinely participatory politics.

A year later when I returned to Beida for the eightieth anniversary of the May Fourth Movement of 1919, "democracy" was much talked about, though it was still quite mute in China's public life. Hoarseness and fear lingered from the crackdown of the student movement in 1989. The recent past could not be talked about. Instead, Yue Shengyang presented me with a fuller, clear map of the Beijing University's incarceration compound of the 1960s (figure 31). Here, the professionally trained geographer noted topological details such as water and hills. He marked clearly the main entrance to the ox pens, right next to the large, historical pine tree that still stands there today. Labeled a botanical treasure, the aged fir is carefully propped up by massive supporting logs. Old and broken, the tree is thus venerated while the men and women who suffered nearby have no monument, no acknowledgment of injustice, no support but the fragile fabric of memory itself.

Yue Shengyang's map is labeled clearly: "Beijing daxue wenge heibang dayuan shiyitu" (sketch map of Beijing University compound for black elements). Without immersion in the language of demonology that was unleashed in this garden setting in the 1960s one might imagine an almost ordinary universe. Female "black elements" were housed in dormitories marked 1 and 2, their more numerous male cohorts in dormitories 3, 4, 5. Structure 7 is marked with a question mark by the scrupulous historical geographer who, as a boy, was not sure if it was used to house inmates or as a reception hall. The women's bathroom is clearly marked as hut number 8. Building 6 is labeled as "reception hall" and "interrogation chamber." This suggests a place where Beida's Red Guards questioned and beat their professors, often in plain sight of visiting delegations from other institutions, sent to "learn" from techniques championed here.

For a sense of how brutal life was within this carefully mapped compound, one has to turn to the seasoned voices of survivors from the "ox pens." Ji Xianlin, the eminent Sanskrit expert, is one of those who had literary skills, moral courage, and political support to actually write a memoir of his time in the Beida niu peng. In Ji's account, there is no room left for doubt abut the hellish nightmare that unfolded in the courtyard bordered by the historical pine, Democracy Hall, and the Foreign Languages Hall:

Niu peng is a rather clear term but no one seems to know if it is a legitimate expression or not. Nowadays, we seem to legalize all new concepts. But how can one legalize the "niu peng"? The expression itself is against the law. This term wasn't very wide spread at Beida. We called it "Garden for Labor Reform" or more familiarly as the "House of the Black Gang." . . . I used to do some research on the subject of religion. What interested me most were various traditions of popular superstition, especially descriptions of hell. Whoever hears stories of these hells has his hair stand on end. After researching the comparative history of hell for dozens of years, I found out that the underworld described in Western religions is too simple, childish, boring and unimaginative. In these matters, Eastern culture is more profound. I have great admiration for the imagination of the common Chinese people and their descriptions of hell. I used to think that their descriptions were the most superior, until I was lucky enough to become an inmate of the ox pens. Now I realize that the niu peng—built in open daylight with elaborate iron rules and fear-ridden atmosphere was much worse than any folk belief. It was a new kind of hell.[2]

Ji Xianlin's ironic tone mutes somewhat the terror being recalled here. Like Primo Levi, Ji is skilled in hard listening as well as in speaking softly about a subject that is still shrouded by enforced silence in China. The armament of comparative religion is simply used to suggest that Red Guards were especially creative in developing torture methods unfathomed even in the Buddhist hells.

The lyrical-sounding name, Garden for Thought Reform (Lao Gai Yuan), did not hide the harsher truth known to all inmates. This was no labor camp. One could not work off a bad reputation, an unsavory link to "bourgeois," "imperialist," "feudal" history—all three being merged together to blacken the reputations of highly educated intellectuals. The only "reform" that took place in this "garden" was repeated confessions of one's sins during public beatings, or in the numerous autobiographies demanded—and dictated—by the Red Guards.

The terrible irony of this confessional terror becomes fully real when we juxtapose Yue Shengyang's sketch of the niu peng with Henry Murphy's plans for Yenching University. Surviving records from the early 1920s leave no doubt that Yenching's School of Religion (Ninde Hall) was located on exactly the same site as the Beida ox pens. Four decades after the erection of a building dedicated to the study of human faith, the chanting of psalms, the exploration of liturgy, the same garden setting was used to chant slogans and confess the ideological sins of ox-monsters and snake spirits.

How could the garden bear this transformation? As with the Garden of Accumulated Virtue in 1860, one is left to ponder, how did the ground not cry out in accusation against the abuse of mind and body taking place in a setting designed for slow-paced reflection? Ji Xianlin chalks it up to Eastern "creativity"—the protean imagination that invents better and better ways to torture. There is much bitterness in Ji's tribute, as well as an ironic echo of Lord Elgin's rage at the torture of Western prisoners in nineteenth-century Haidian. Elgin had imagined brutality to be the unique trait of imperial officials. Ji Xianlin suggests that it was an "art" shared by communist youths as well.

Upon closer examination, however, it becomes clear that repeated atrocities in northwest Beijing were caused neither by "art" nor by anything unique to Chinese character. It was, as Primo Levi understood so well, the demonization of the enemy that made it possible to treat persons as if they were less than human. Nazis did this on a horrifically large scale, the Qing in a much smaller setting. The Red Guards smeared all of China in their contempt for niu gui she shen. If the garden stood mute, it was because language itself had been dispossessed. Where labels and dogmatism ruled, poetry and garden talk had nothing to add. In fact, the enforced amnesia about the Confucian tradition and the Yenching legacy made this violent event possible in the first place. Denuded of historical memory, the landscape—like China's youth—was ready for the dreadful visions invented by the aged tyrant Mao Zedong.

A Dehydrated Kernel

The ravage unleashed in China between 1966 and 1976 left no mind, no body, no stone untouched. The Beida campus offers ample testimony to the scale of this devastation, as well as to the reluctance to face its implications directly. A gashed stele stashed in the far west corner of the old Singing Crane Garden bears testimony to the ravage enacted here (figure 32). When I first came upon this fragment of Qing marble in 1991, it was covered by dirt and lay abandoned near the shacks used by day laborers at Beida. Each time I returned to the university in the following decade, I tried to inquire about the provenance of this stone. Each time I was met with disinterested silence. Finally, one Chinese friend accompanied me to the stele and informed me that the classical Chinese characters may come from an old ode to the rising moon. The carved ideographs, however, are unreadable today. What greets the eye most obviously are gashes that crisscross the stone. Inflicted by rough knives during the Cultural Revolution, these fierce scars mirror the scratched-out scholars on the entrance to the home of Professor Wang Yao.[3]

Figure 32. Qing dynasty stele defaced by gashes during the Cultural Revolution.

Thus, both the former gate to Mianyu's Singing Crane Garden as well as the northwest corner of this estate retain a maimed connection to the labor gardens designed by Maoist Red Guards. A tapestry of wounds and silenced terror ties together these grounds and the intellectuals who suffered in the ox pens.

Today, as China seeks to promote narratives of socialist politics and a capitalist economic boom, memories of red terror linger on. At times subterranean, at times vividly expressed in art and literature, visions of violence endure as a "dehydrated kernel." This is the metaphor developed by Feng Jicai in his memoir, entitled *Ten Years of Madness*.[4] A well-known artist who survived the ox pens, Feng does not put all the blame on the Red Guards and Mao Zedong. Instead, he takes it upon himself to explore the internal despair and the many-layered amnesia that led intellectuals to become not only victims, but also accomplices of cultural ruination in the late 1960s. A dehydrated kernel, however, is not a rotten, dead seed. Watered by memory, it can nourish an invigorating vision of history.

And this is exactly what is taking place at Beijing University and many other sites of ravage. Not only are there new buildings—such as the Sackler Museum—but there is a slow, painful coming to terms with what led to destruction in the first place. After the burning of the Summer Palace in 1860, Yihuan had argued against hasty rebuilding precisely because he wanted his kinsmen to grapple with the causes of the loss of Qing grandeur. The Manchu prince failed dramatically. Yihuan's intellectual heirs, however, have more time, more varied voices with which to keep the history of ravage in mind. Young researchers (such as Xu Youyu, a former Red Guard), have spent many years collecting documents as well as the oral history of the Cultural Revolution.[5] Regardless of government approval, they are detailing the complex processes that led Mao Zedong to find such willing accomplices for the destruction unleashed in 1966.

The ravage, they point out, began long before the violent attacks on steles and professors. It began with the simplistic condemnation of traditional culture and values in the May Fourth Movement of 1919. At the very time when John Leighton Stuart and Henry Murphy began envisaging a garden for liberal learning where new and old could coexist in a setting of graceful reflexivity, revolutionary Chinese intellectuals had already began to champion a vision of nationalism that required the jettisoning of Confucian civilization and the classical language of poetry. Advocates of plain, vernacular literature (*baihua*) decried the aesthetics of men like Yihuan as effete, corrupt, useless.[6]

What mattered was the culture of the "masses." Intellectuals began to attack their own cultural inheritance and to adopt the sloganeering of social revolution even before Mao Zedong came to power in 1949. In the decades that followed, he merely fleshed out with authoritarian power and military weapons the vision of "proletarian culture" advocated by radical intellectuals themselves.

The terrible irony of the Cultural Revolution was that some of the same intellectuals who had jettisoned Confucian traditions and language became the victims of Mao's final mass movement. Those most eager to become "red" were decried as members of the "black gang." The concept of *hei bang* grew to encompass anyone who disagreed with Chairman Mao. Originally used to attack racketeers who carried on illegal trade, "black gang" came to refer to the leaders of the educational institutions such as Yenching and the newly consolidated Beijing University. In the 1950s, it was Stuart's protégé Lu Zhiwei who became one of the first to be painted with this dark brush. By 1966, the president of Beida, Lu Ping (a party-appointed official), was demoted because he supposedly belonged to "an anti-Party, anti-socialst *hei bang.*"[7] After Red Guards attacked China's foremost educational institutions, no intellectual could feel truly safe again. Courtyards once carefully designed for liberal learning now were identified as nests for breeding "vermin."

To understand how rapidly "red" became "black" in the 1960s, it is important to map the shrinking ground between metaphorical and actual violence. The garden setting, which once thrived on a nuanced respect for allusion, now had to contain a mass movement dedicated to the erasure of the reflective mind. On the peeling wood outside of Wang Yao's home, a fading "X" stands as a concrete reminder of Red Guards who became enemies of classical grace. The "black" legacy of the Singing Crane Garden was attacked along with the body and mind of the formerly "red" professor who had distinguished himself through studies of left-wing literature before the Mao era. During the Cultural Revolution, neither crane-like scholars nor left-wing intellectuals were to be tolerated. The same violent "X" was applied to both.

Scholars and party leaders identified as monsters had to be cast out from the rank of the masses. In a few short months, they became so dehumanized as to be defaced without regret. They were deemed to be nothing more than life-contaminating vermin. One Cultural Revolution issue of the Shanghai-based journal *Za Lan* (Mash and Pulp) reveled in the violence embodied in the life-denying "X": The cover showed a crossed-out intellectual-artist quivering under the weight of a "proletarian brush."[8] The inside flap used the pen as a sword to skewer frightened party officials. The lead article condemned the historian Wu Han to the eighteenth level of hell, while the rest of the magazine proudly displayed famous works of art defaced by an ever-sprawling "X." In one of first large-scale attacks on cultural memory during the Cultural Revolution, Mao had accused Beijing University historian Wu Han of spewing venom and "filling the nation with evil of the *niu gui she shen*."[9] There was no room in the Chinese Revolution for anyone who disagreed with Mao's views. The chairman alone became the arbitrator of war and peace. War with demons, Mao Zedong warned, was never over.

Figure 33. Defaced painting of a classical landscape published in *Za Lan* (Mash and Pulp) (August 1967). This journal was made available to me courtesy of Shelley Drake Hawks.

"After the enemies with guns have been wiped out, there will be enemies without guns; and they are bound to struggle desperately against us and we must never regard these enemies lightly."[10] During the Cultural Revolution, monsters had to be sequestered in order to show that the enemy was not dealt with "lightly." There was to be no room for human empathy.

Inside *Mash and Pulp* the agenda of the Cultural Revolution became even clearer: it was not only historians who had to be destroyed but historical memory as well. Classically inspired landscapes had to be crossed out (figure 33). Scholars on a bridge by the garden wall had to be erased. A gentleman alone on a rock in contemplation had to be stamped out. Standing still, any appreciation of natural harmonies (all the arts of *jing* and *dong* that garden culture had fostered) were to be eliminated, condemned, spat upon. It was not only "red" intellectuals who became "black"—the entirety of traditional culture was tarred, quite literally, with the same brush.

If it had been only a brush, we would not see gashes in marble steles. If it had been just words that Red Guards bandied about, there would not have been any ox pens. Much like the Nazis before them, Red Guards attacked both art and its producers as pernicious enemies. In Europe, atrocities had reached their incomprehensible scale through the technical inventions of mass destruction. In China, it was armed Red Guards who carried out Mao's will, often with their own fists, hammers, and bullets. On the cover of *Za Lan*, the brush was portrayed as a weapon of attack. On the streets of Beijing, in the courtyards of Beida, Red Guards wielded actual guns. Gazing into the eyes of these very young students, one can imagine how little it took to attack professors and old works of art. Children born after 1949, they knew little of the classical language of Yihuan's poems. The ideology fed to them in elementary and middle schools did not teach the history of Yenching, or of the courtyards in Mianyu's gardens. All that they knew was how to show ardor for Mao and fierce hatred for his "enemies." In pictures, it was a pen that speared cowering intellectuals. In real life it was bayonets, flag poles, sticks, and stones that rained down upon any person isolated by the mob as Mao's enemy. In those days of terror, it was enough to have been educated in American-sponsored missionary institutions such as Yenching to earn one's place at the feet of crazed and murderous Red Guards.

This kind of terror did not begin suddenly during the Cultural Revolution. It started, oddly enough, with a manifesto from a young instructor in the philosophy department at Beijing University. On May 25, 1966, Nie Yuanzi, a female teacher and party member, put up the first Big Character

Poster of the Cultural Revolution. It was entitled "What the hell are Sung Shuo, Lu Ping, and Peng Peiyuan doing in the Cultural Revolution?"[11] Individuals were named. Venom poured out in red ink to destroy the lives of intellectuals who had made a career out of building a new China. Lord Elgin had been infuriated by the coffins of prisoners. Nie Yuanzi was infuriated not by corpses but by the supposed privileges of high party officials. The president of the university stood indicted for how many beds he owned, for his daughter's expensive summer vacation, as well as for his views about the importance of research at a communist university. "What the hell" was just one of the many coarse expressions that made its way onto manifestos posted in the university dining hall.

Within days, hell became a living reality on the campus of Beijing University. On June 1, 1966, the *People's Daily* published its editorial on the front page: "Sweep away all freaks, ox-monsters, and snake spirits."[12] The demons hinted at two weeks earlier were now seen as a national danger. Mao Zedong himself had sanctioned this editorial. The young female instructor had not fired her ammunition in vain. Nieh Yuanzi had been coached, urged, and armed with all the venomous details needed to make many others into culpable monsters and snakes. On June 2, the *People's Daily* published verbatim the accusations that had seemed so bizarre in the courtyard compounds of old Yenching. Given a national forum, Beida's monsters became the embodiment of a broad national threat. All possibility of self-explanation was drowned out by a crescendo of criminal accusations. By early July, Liu Shaoqi, China's premier, was also depicted as a fanged supporter of the Confucian-imperialist idea of "education for its own sake." One of Liu's essays written before 1966 had stated: "You must study with quiet minds. . . . You may ask what is happening in the outside world, but don't be interrupted by it."[13] This was, in retrospect, a distillation of the garden idea fostered by Manchu princes and developed by the pedagogical visionaries of Yenching. Now, the idea of a quiet mind itself was considered criminal. There was to be no respite in Haidian from the outside world, no meditation on anything but the Thought of Mao Zedong.

Once Chairman Mao labeled highly placed intellectuals as "ox-monsters and snake spirits," his followers knew they could be subjected to violence at will. At Beijing University alone, 206 professors and party leaders were incarcerated in the niu peng. More than a thousand were accused of being "traitors, spies, or counter-revolutionaries." Of these, more than fifty committed suicide and twenty-three were put to death.[14] This carnage and degradation of human

life surpassed the worst tortures that the Singing Crane Garden witnessed before the burning of the Summer Palace in 1860. One hundred and six years earlier (almost to the day), Lord Elgin and Baron Gros received news of the
imprisonment of thirty-nine emissaries, including Henry Parkes. The cruel
imprisonment of these foreigners resulted in eighteen deaths, including that of
Elgin's friend, Thomas Bowlby from the *Times*. The prisoners who came back
brought details of inhumane treatment suffered by those who had died. They
described what it was like to be carted around like chattel, deprived of water,
chained by hand and foot. Survivors came to think of their Chinese captors as
barbarians in need of a lesson. In Mao Zedong's torture chambers, by contrast,
both victims and victimizers were Chinese. The tortures of the ox pens could
not be dismissed as inflicted by "barbarians." Most tragically, the dehumaniza-
tion of the Cultural Revolution was so pervasive that even those labeled as "ox-
monsters and snake spirits" came to believe that they had committed a crime.
The imprisonment of these victims lasted longer and left more enduring scars
than the imprisonment of Westerners in 1860.

We Built the Ox Pens Ourselves

In the nineteenth century, as in the twentieth, one corner of northwest Beijing
became the focus of national (and international) politics. A quiet hamlet was
roused by cries of terror, by the roar of guns, by fierce soot and dust from
smashed stones. In Qing China, it was the imperial garden of Haidian that attracted the vengeance of history. In Maoist times, Beijing University evoked the
same kind of fierce ire. One young woman could pen a big character poster at
Beida, and within a month, it became the opening salvo of the Cultural Revolution. Beida students and faculty had a privileged place in public discourse
unrivaled by any other educational institutions in China. Perhaps it was the
legacy of the old Imperial University that endowed Beida with its unique importance, as well as its tragic history. Perhaps it was the concentration of academic talent from the Yenching era that led Mao to believe that this situation
could not be left alone. Beida had to become a model for revolutionary fervor.
The place where cultural knowledge could have sunk its deepest roots became
the place to pull up all traces of reflective individuality.

Enforced historical amnesia had to start with Beijing University students. In August 1966, Beida students were the first Red Guards to arrive in
Tian An Men Square to show that they took Mao's message to heart. The

main avenue in front of the Forbidden City, known as the Road of Lasting Peace (Chang An Jie), was renamed by the students as the Avenue of the Revolution (Geming Da Jie). No more peace, only mass mobilization. No more scholars, no more landscapes for contemplation. Beida Red Guards declared that new street names were to mirror new minds: only those willing to keep up with the breathless pace of history qualified as loyal followers of Chairman Mao. Anyone who walked slowly, thought in nonofficial terms, was suspect, and subject to being crossed out.

Less than one month after Nie Yuanzi's poster went up on the walls of Beida, mutual incrimination made its entrance inside the university itself. On June 18, 1966, Red Guards took over Building 38—part of the new Beida developed on the model of Yenching after the two institutions merged in 1952. Outside the building, Nie Yuanzi's followers set up "a platform for struggling with devils." Ox-monsters and spirit snakes were no longer phrases spewed onto posters. They became attached to sixty victims rounded up from all across the university campus.[15] Some were forcibly marched through the streets. Some had their faces smeared with ink, some made to kneel, some punched, others kicked. Villains identified on paper two weeks earlier became publicly labeled as germs infecting the body politic. Students roamed faculty compounds looking for *niu gui she shen*. Anyone they disliked could now be tarred and feathered. Yang Jiang, one of China's foremost translator of Western literature, describes her own transformation in the eyes of her students from scholar to monster:

On one particularly rainy day a Red Guard appeared out of nowhere to summon all those who had been "hauled in" to a meeting in the hut. We were herded onto the stage and "put on show." Everyone had to wear a dunce's cap made out of newspaper. The Masses showered us with angry abuse, and it was then that I learned that we were all Cow Monsters and Snake Demons. I stole a glance at what was written on the others' hats: there were Blackguards, Kuomintang Agents, Soviet Revisionist Spies, Reactionary Scholastic Authorities, Bourgeois Scholastic Authorities, and so on. I tried to guess what I had been labeled. After the meeting I was pushed and shoved off the dais, but I had already managed to take off my cap and have a look. Bourgeois Scholar! I was pleased to have been given such a low rank. Everyone now had to hand in their caps so that the classifications could be adjusted. I was subsequently promoted to Bourgeois Scholastic Authority.[16]

An intellectual had to reach for the dunce cap on her head (or the placard hanging by metal wire on the neck) to learn the full extent of her own monstrosity. For a while these "enemies of the people" were hauled out from their homes during the day and returned to their families at night. Eventually, that became inconvenient. The urge to herd them into one place grew stronger with time.

By August 15, 1966, the Beida campus was deemed too small to accommodate the large crowds eager to unmask devils and snakes. Larger lessons needed to be taught in larger spaces. The Beijing Workers' Stadium was the only facility that could accommodate 100,000 people. It became the site for a mass criticism session of university president Lu Ping. The former educational leader now faced his accusers in a novel posture of enforced submission: the "airplane position." Lu Ping had to hold his hands behind his back and bend low in humiliation for hours on end. This tactic for torture and humiliation became widely used throughout China during the Cultural Revolution.

By March 1967, the war within Beijing University expanded in scope. Voices previously silenced now joined the fray. In the previous year, sloganeering had been limited to the Red Guards. Now, even former victims of the thought-reform movements of the 1950s started to scream out loud. Factional struggle broke out among various groups claiming to defend the Thought of Chairman Mao. One day, a new poster appeared on campus: "New Beida must rectify incorrect work styles, starting with Nie Yuanzi. . . . Rectify the Leftist factional troops, mobilize the broad masses and rise to new heights during the Cultural Revolution."[17] Nie Yuanzi was no longer the sole commander of the ideological struggle. Other, more timid souls discovered their own capacity for shrill counterattacks. The overused expression "mobilize the masses" was now embraced by the professors themselves.

"Cranes" started to fight against the "sparrows." Ji Xianlin, the soft-spoken Sanskritist who had witnessed the dangers of mass hysteria in Nazi Germany, joined the struggle. His contribution was a placard hung outside of Building 28 calling Nie Yuanzi an old-fashioned *poxie*. In English, the two characters can be translated innocuously enough as "broken shoes." But in the charged atmosphere of foul curses at Beida, all knew that *poxie* meant "prostitute."[18] It took guts to call Mao's favorite representative at Beida by this old insult. The Cultural Revolution had succeeded—even victims shouted as coarsely as their accusers.

On April 4, 1967, Nie Yuanzi's faction, the Campus Cultural Revolution Group, struck back. They convened a meeting with more than 10,000 Red Guards at which Lu Ping, Jian Bozan, chairman of the history department, and Zhu Guanqian, from the philosophy department, were seized and beaten. Zhu was publicly identified as a prominent monster. The philosopher who had been content to write about beauty and truth now faced his accusers stripped of all dignity. His home in the old Yenching courtyard called South Swallow Garden was searched and ransacked. His precious books were burned. Personal letters and journals were confiscated to be used in further criticism sessions. The septuagenarian was forced to stand for hours in the "airplane position." Students slapped and kicked him again and again. By April 26, 1968, war had broken out between different factions contesting the occupancy of Building 36. The campus that Murphy had imagined as a sacred grove for learning became rattled by gunfire. Young students now stood on the front lines. They had automatic weapons (stolen from a nearby armory) as well as an increasing repertoire of slogans: "Attack in defense of Chairman Mao's revolutionary line. The brave do not fear death! Those who fear death are cowards!"[19] The violence of April 26 lasted five hours. More than two hundred were slain or wounded.

The murderous revolution unfolding on the campus of Beijing University was mirrored in news coming from all corners of China. On other campuses, in other cities, youth had also taken to the streets to support Mao's sacred cause. The chairman, the holy helmsman of a ship of state denuded of all authority, had declared that "it is right to rebel." How far that "right" would carry became obvious when the Red Guards began to set fire to books and papers confiscated from professors and party officials. On August 5, the principal of a prestigious Beijing middle school was the first to die from physical abuse. Thousands followed. A century before this murder, Elgin's ire had been directed against wood and stone. Now, hammers were taken up to physically destroy all remnants of traditional architecture that dotted the public landscape. Street names had to be changed. Traffic signals were adjusted so that red became the color for "go."

Just how far vengeance against the past was carried out in northwest Beijing became apparent with the smashing of the gates at Qinghua University. A neighbor of Yenching with many buildings designed by Henry Murphy, this campus, too, had been a treasured garden site in the nineteenth century. In fact, its main entrance was made of marble pieces salvaged from the ruins of the Yuan Ming Yuan. At the height of the Cultural Revolution, Red Guards set up a scaffold so as to be able to hammer out the old-fashioned calligraphy that once graced the entrance to a liberal arts university. Young men wielded instruments of destruction with vigor. Children looked on with claps of joy. A delight in vandalism took hold of China after 1966 as "history" itself became a mark of criminality. To show any caring for the past was deemed a political sin. To remember what came before the Cultural Revolution was to have an alternative value system that endangered the ethics sanctioned by the ever-changing line of Mao Zedong Thought. Professors had to be reeducated. Scholars had to be spat upon.

Broken gates and renamed streets set the stage for the establishment of the niu peng. Since no one cared to remember the history of Qing gardens, since no one was allowed to lay open claim to Yenching's liberal legacy, Red Guards were freed to think up new solutions for persecution upon a silenced landscape. During the first twelve months of the Cultural Revolution, professors and party leaders who had been labeled as enemies of Mao Zedong Thought had been attacked at various locations on the campus, sometimes in a large gymnasium, sometimes in front of the official guest house of the university. The biology department, for example, was deemed large enough to accommodate "devils" from other departments as well. University president Lu Ping, for example, had been interrogated for hours in the biology department while suspended from the rafters with bound hands.

Any corner of the campus could be turned into a "garden for thought reform" (*lao gai yuan*). Roaming terror characterized this stage of the struggle: A faculty member could wake up at home yet end his night in some rancid bathroom, forced to clean toilets for the Red Guards. By October 1968, the Campus Cultural Revolution Office sent a special notice to various Red Guard factions alerting them to the fact that chaotic violence was not effective enough. Something more was needed in order to "augment supervision over sinister gangs."[20] The war was no longer one of youth against isolated criminals. Seen as a collective threat, intellectuals had to be cut off from the community at large.

What better place than the rubble-covered ground behind the unused Foreign Languages Hall? No one had bothered to teach or learn any English or Sanskrit or French there for over a year. Perhaps the Qing unicorns nearby fed the Red Guard's sense of historical might. Maybe it was plain ignorance that led them to the former courtyards of the Singing Crane Garden. The nearby shadow of the Yi Ran Ting did not offer any guidance, any challenge. It could be left alone while aged professors were forced to build the shacks of their own imprisonment.

Ji Xianlin's memoir captures poignantly the reflections of an aged professor "invited" to dwell in the newly established niu peng. While Red Guards still talked as if all they wanted was to "reform" their teachers, Ji had learned firsthand that this was a subterfuge for torture. Good will, common sense had vanished from the Beida campus along with the historical memory of gardens and art. In a denuded physical and spiritual landscape, willful humiliation could reign unchecked:

We built the ox pens ourselves. Then, we were "invited" to live there. Yes, there was life in the ox pens. Didn't some writer say, "there is life everywhere"? I will start with my theory of torture: The purpose of all activities undertaken by the Red Guards centered on one idea: to torture inmates, anytime, anywhere. Although they claimed that this was for the sake of revolution, the truth is they tried every means simply to inflict pain. These hard-working youths learned from each other all kinds of advanced torture. When something new was invented it spread with lightening speed. . . . What was the ultimate purpose of this torture? The revolutionary guards who now recall those days will never reveal the darkness in their own hearts. They cling to the euphemisms of "labor reform." This kind of reform was directed not only at our bodies, but our souls as well.[21]

Darkness of the heart and soul-shaking terror were routine in the ox pens. Yet few have been willing to talk about it as openly as Ji Xianlin. The shame of victims and victimizers alike has deepened reticence about the torture inflicted at Beida on the ground now occupied by the Sackler Museum. One former Red Guard was honest enough to recall, years later: "We are always criticizing the Japanese for altering history, yet, when it is our turn, we don't dare face it either. Most Chinese people shy away from the subject of suffering. The Cultural Revolution is a nightmare that they do not want to think about."[22] Ji Xianlin, by contrast, rakes over this shame as if he were an archaeologist of suffering. His own experience is part of the layers to be laid bare so that posterity may build another kind of edifice on the niu peng terrain at Beida.

No aspect of the daily torture is overlooked in Ji's memoir. He is careful to detail the morning interrogations in which aged prisoners had to write and rewrite their "crimes" again and again. Red Guard overseers had insisted that inmates recite a full passage from the works of Chairman Mao. If a professor-devil stuttered or failed, he or she would be beaten. If the test was passed, the inmate would be "free" to carry bricks and sand all day for the expansion of the ox pen huts. "Evening scolding" was a ritual unto itself:

We gathered in the ox-pens after dinner to listen to the guard criticize us. The content of this criticism session changed each day. Sometimes it was about our daily mistakes, more often about errors in our daily reports dealing with our previous crimes. We tried our best to make perfect self-incrimination reports. But there was always one unlucky person. . . . Whoever was picked by the guard was beaten until he was black and blue. . . . One night I went to the bathroom and one of my pen mates was standing in the darkness. He just stood there hugging a tree. I did not know how long he had been there or how much longer he would have to stand.[23]

Today, the old trees near the Sackler Museum are honored with Latin preservation plaques. None of them mention the terror witnessed here.

Nazi Milk

In the time of Prince Yihuan, the muteness of grief could be overcome with poetry. After the fires of 1860, it was still possible to revisit the ruined terrain of the garden with the mind's eye. Memory could amble along paths that no longer existed in space. During the Cultural Revolution, however, terror was too pervasive to inspire poetry. What the Red Guards deemed most evil was the attachment of intellectuals to cultural recollection, their proclivity for rambling off the high road of Mao Zedong Thought. Narrowing the vista of imagination was integral to the mission of the ox pens.

Even Zhu Guanqian, the eminent philosopher of aesthetics who had drawn succor from a glimpse of the Yi Ran Ting, experienced this constriction of vision. Short of stature, in poor health before his incarceration, he was ill prepared for the degradation and depravation of the niu peng. One of his pen mates, the political scientist Zhao Baoxu, recalls how famished the aged philosopher became during the long intervals between skimpy meals. The man who once wrote so gracefully about theories of tragedy in Goethe was reduced to painful ditties when dealing with his own hunger:

I stand at the end of the line waiting for food.
I am so hungry my stomach hurts.
Why are you so eager to gobble some tomatoes and eggs?
Why do you push to the front of the line?[24]

This image of highly educated intellectuals shoving each other to satisfy the brutal cry of hunger calls to mind daily life in the concentration camps of Europe. To be sure, the terrors endured on the grounds of the old Singing Crane Garden never reached the diabolic forms developed in the extermination chambers of Auschwitz. But the will to dehumanize the "enemy" was as much in force in the ox pens of Beida as in the dread-filled universe of Birkenau. Zhao Baoxu recalled later: "The ox pens were worse than Hitler's camps.

Hitler killed you once. In the niu peng, they killed you again and again, each day."[25] Reduced to vermin, men and women were forced to fight each other for crumbs, while overseers watched and became more convinced that their charges were indeed subhuman.

Ji Xianlin's recollections dwell on all the techniques that Red Guards developed to dehumanize inmates. "Regulations" included: "Don't look up while working (so we became more familiar with the shoes of our guards than their faces). Don't cross your legs while sitting, especially when interrogated by the masses."[26] Looking at the torturers' shoes all day, Ji recalls, was not that bad. Not crossing one's legs, however, was much more burdensome. Especially if one was old and tired. The temptation to cross one's legs grew unbearably strong at night after a full day of interrogations and back-breaking labor. If caught, the beatings would begin anew. The ox pens were never a stable hell. It kept changing its face, its name, the depths of its terrors. One night, a biology student named Zhang Guoxiang (who "excelled above other guards") was in charge. He came riding one of the bicycles commandeered from the home of niu peng inmates. Sitting under the trees, Zhang was free to scratch his toes. He was also an expert interrogator. He had been one of the chief inquisitors to decide on the torture of university president Lu Ping. This night, he turned his attention to Ji Xianlin:

"How come you have connections with Western, capitalist spy organizations?"
"No, I do not."
"How many wives do you have?"
"Not many."
The next night, around the same time, I heard my name called again. I ran fast only to find Mr. Zhang shouting angrily: "Why did it take you so long to get here? Are you deaf or what?"
Before I had time to figure out what was going on, a bicycle chain hit my head. It kept on ringing blows. My head hummed, my eyes went black, but I did not dare run away. It hurt at first, but then I lost consciousness. My nose, mouth, ears were all burning. All I remember is the chain waving in front of me like lightning.[27]

Hou Renzhi, a fellow inmate of the ox pens, recalls Ji Xianlin stumbling back to the crowded room, which they all shared at night. Blood was dripping on his face. Ji's student, Yue Daiyun, also recalls Ji's brutal treatment on the grounds of the Ming He Yuan. Returning one evening from her own forced labor march, she heard the sounds of drums and slogans. Two "reactionary gang members" were being paraded on the grounds of the ox pens: Zhou Yiliang and Ji Xianlin. Both of them had signs hanging on their chests and were hauling iron pots on their backs. Thin metal strings around their necks left bloody marks. The Red Guards kept shoving them, screaming loud "instructions" (quotations from Chairman Mao): "Small temples are infected by horrendous devils, shallow ponds birth many turtles."[28] These folk sayings were intended to remind victims and torturers alike that no mercy was to be shown to members of the Black Gang.

Zhou Yiliang, the historian who had been forced to march alongside Ji Xianlin on that bloody walk around the ox pen, also recalled those days of madness. Zhou's incarceration was due to the fact that he had joined the Cultural Revolution faction opposed to Nie Yuanzi. That, however, was not enough of a "crime." Guardians of the niu peng needed daily fodder for tortures that could not be attributed to power struggle alone. The ox-monster must have been guilty of something more. Hence, Red Guard students kept coming back for more comprehensive house searches. Relatives of the niu gui she shen had to open their homes to the inquisitive hands of various committees, often composed of young students or illiterate workers from other cities. From the house of Zhou Yiliang, Red Guard groups confiscated valuable materials such as paintings and ancient books and also something that looked like a manuscript: "This was in fact a two-volume diary by the Chinese ambassador to Italy during the Nationalist period of the 1930s. . . . Unable to read it, the Red Guards assumed it was my own diary, that I had been a representative of the Nationalist Party. . . . I was also accused of 'drinking Nazi milk' simply because I had been nursed by the wife of a German missionary shortly after my mother died in 1914."[29] Armed with this new "information" the Red Guards plastered the walls of Zhou Yiliang's home with new slogans about the crimes of this prominent member of the Black Gang. A courtyard in the eastern corner of the old Yenching campus (the lot that had stretched quite literally into the back wall of the Singing Crane Garden) became a "museum" for the invented crimes of a professor who languished in the ox pens.

Zhou's neighbor in this Yenching courtyard was biology professor Chen Yuezeng. This eminent scientist also became an inmate of the niu peng. A decade and a half after the nightmare, Professor Chen still remembered the words upon which his fate hung in those dark years. One night when he was singled out for special "attention" by one of the biology graduate students, they forced him to write out repeatedly some quotations by Chairman Mao. Tired and dispirited, Chen Yuezeng made a mistake: "Or maybe the Red Guard himself changed what I had wrote. But what appeared on all the walls the next day was a phrase attributed to me. Instead of the commonly used phrase about the Great and Venerable Chairman Mao, they said that I wrote 'Disobey Chairman Mao.' One stroke made all the difference. To the Red Guards, this proved that I had always been opposed to the leadership of Chairman Mao. I received the most severe beating after this incident."[30]

The two neighbors who became inmates learned the same lesson inside the ox pens: Words cannot be trusted. They had too many meanings in the mouths of the accusers. Any moment, a character or a book could assume a new life as invented history. Words had the power to leave bloody marks on the body and on the mind. Philosopher Feng Youlan shared this sentiment when he recalled: "all our writings were a mark of criminality."[31] Never sequestered in the squalor of the ox pen, Feng nonetheless paid dearly for his connection to words. Suffering from an infected bladder during the Cultural Revolution, he was kicked out of a Beijing hospital during surgery, since no doctor would dare to have a public connection to such a notorious member of the Black Gang at Beida. Inside the niu peng, depravation forced intellectuals to beg for the simple necessities for daily living. Not unlike the Western prisoners mistreated on the grounds of Singing Crane Garden in 1860, they were deprived of comfort, aid, and clothes.

Professor Wang Yao, one of the "ghost spirits" taken into the compound at this time, wrote a letter to his wife, Du Xiu, requesting some winter supplies. The scanty words that survived the torturous winter of 1968–69 reflect the shrunken spirits of intellectuals held without hope beyond the gates of "Democracy Hall":

Xiu,
   The Reform Supervision Group wouldn't let me go home. The following is a list of things that I'm in need of right now. Please manage to send them over.
   1) Woolen pants or thick sweat pants.
   2) Cotton jerseys and pants.
   3) The quilt cover is too thin. If you send a cotton-padded mattress over, I can use the blanket as the quilt cover. Otherwise, one more blanket is also fine.
   4) My woolen socks are worn out, please do a bit of patching and send me one pair.
   5) The soap is almost used up.
   6) Sweaters.
   7) Blue windbreaker.
   If you can manage to patch that pair of worn woolen pants that I wore the winter before last, it would actually be quite suitable to wear for the work here. However, this is not urgent. Right now, woolen or sweat pants will do.
   I have received my allowance. When you send those things over, you can ask to see

me so that I can give you my allowance to bring back home. I will tell you the rest when we see each other.[32]

By the time Wang Yao wrote this letter, he had been under attack for a full year. His books had been burned, his teeth broken during various interrogations. Fellow inmate Zhao Baoxu recalls Professor Wang fleeing from the Red Guards in charge of the compound, slapping himself along the way.

The degradation of terror is something that few of us can fully fathom today. Wang Yao survived because he managed to beg for and received the basic necessities for survival. The companionship and loyalty of his wife also carried him through the darkest hours. Zhu Guanqian received some solace from glancing at the winged eaves of the Yi Ran Ting. Ji Xianlin promised himself not to forget the details of the nightmare that called to mind his years in Germany. Though they endured, none of them was above the pull of despair that led so many of their fellow intellectuals to commit suicide. Inside the ox pens it was nearly impossible to take one's life. Constant supervision and interrogation afforded few opportunities for ending one's misery. By contrast, some high officials who fell out of favor with Mao were "lucky" enough to be able to end their suffering in peace. Cui Xiongkun, for example, the former party secretary of the university, managed to get away on the night of October 17, 1968, to seek eternal refuge in one of the small lakes left over from Mianyu's Singing Crane Garden. One month before the full establishment of the niu peng he drowned himself near the Island of Blessings. Because of his powerful position, Cui had been subject to many severe interrogations. On this night, he escaped from Building 28 and made his way to the most hidden parts of the old Yenching campus. Here, he found Red Lake—the artificial pond built out of the lakes that once graced the Ming He Yuan. Cui Xiongkun had not come here to swim. While Red Guards were busy torturing other "monsters," he found his moment and his space. He drowned himself in Red Lake. His accusers became even more furious. The official conclusion posted on Big Character posters left no room for ambiguity: "He had besmirched the red water and the good name of our revolutionary hospital."[33] In the eyes of the Red Guards, suicide was an aggressive gesture against the revolution. Cui's death had "polluted" the cause and the landscape as well. Lakes were for the "people," not for ox-spirits and snake-monsters.

The most gallant "pollution" of revolutionary ardor came two months later with the spectacular double suicide by Professor Jian Bozan (1898–1968) and his wife. A personal friend of Mao, Jian had been the official chronicler of the Chinese revolution. A widely published scholar and prominent member of the Communist Party, this sixty-year-old intellectual held the prestigious position of chairman of Beida's history department. Since historical memory was one of the main targets of attack during the Cultural Revolution, Jian Bozan's fate was sealed as well. What was most striking, however, was the delay in his incarceration in the ox pens. This gave him and his wife enough time to use death as a retort to a revolution gone awry. In the first year of violent confrontation between Red Guards and faculty, Jian had been a frequent target of mass interrogation. Most of the time, the aged historian had to bend his whole upper body in the abject position of an "ox-monster." On some occasions he had to bend over a bench shoved into his groin while one of his own graduate students chronicled his crimes "against the people." One time, when he was cornered in a courtyard of the history department (designed as dormitories for female students by Henry Murphy), young women and their male cohorts take turns berating the communist historian who had sought to justify the revolution led by Mao Zedong in 1949.[34] All surviving images of Jian Bozan from this period are marked with the deadly "X." There was no doubt that the Red Guards intended to defame Jian Bozan to the point that he would become subject to execution.

A recently published memoir of Jian Bozan's persecution details the daily interrogations that led the aged historian to final despair. It was not enough to parade and berate him in front of huge crowds. In the privacy of his own home, too, Jian Bozan was forced to acknowledge that he hated Mao. This he refused to do. A particular brutal interrogator called Wu Jian did not give up:

On the third day, Wu came again. Hearing that Jian was still "unable to remember" he shouted: "Confess or die!" . . . On December 10 in the morning, Wu came again. After Jian said he still could not remember, Wu suddenly took out a handgun and threw it on the table: "Confess today or I'll shoot you!" Jian's face turned white. Wu went up to Jian, pointed the gun at his face and yelled: "Say it! Say it or I will kill you!" Jian was petrified by this sudden act. He trembled. Still he was unwilling to lie. All the rest of the afternoon and night, Jian and his wife sat up, face to face, silent and unable to sleep. December 18, Jian took out his pen to write a note. He wanted to write something but the pen was out of ink. He sighed, murmuring: "No ink in my pen, my death is near."[35]

When the bodies of Jian Bozan and his wife were found on the morning of December 20, their bed was perfectly made. The couple rested on top of their marriage quilt in repose. Both were dressed in the dark woolen suits reserved for high cadres of the Communist Party. In Jian's pocket was a simple note: "Long live Chairman Mao." Zhou Yiliang (Jian's colleague in the history department), recalling this detail, commented: "It sums up the whole tragedy of the Cultural Revolution. To remain a loyal official of an emperor who has nothing but contempt for you is the essence of the intellectuals' predicament in modern China."[36]

During the late Mao era, as in previous dynasties, scholars had hoped to bring their moral perspective to bear on the political fate of the public realm. Mianyu and Yixin had made this effort from within the imperial family. They also failed. Jian Bozan inadvertently became their soulmate. Simply because he was chair of the history department in 1966, he was cast among the vermin. Unable to withstand the sullying of his reputation, he managed to commit suicide. Zhou Yiliang did not have the same resources available to him. Incarcerated in the ox pens with Ji Xianlin and Chen Yuezeng, Zhou was beaten for his opposition to Nieh Yuanzi as well as for being too much of a scholar. After the Cultural Revolution, Zhou chose a new pen name: "Shusheng," or "Offspring of Books." Having outlived Mao Zedong, Zhou Yiliang returned to historical scholarship grateful for the company of books once forbidden. By the end of his life, Zhou could profess loyalty both to history and to the party. He seemed to have become both "crane" and "sparrow," at least in his own eyes.

A different reading of Jian Bozan's suicide appears in his students' writings. They use the tragedy of this prominent intellectual as a moral indictment of Mao Zedong. Literary scholar Yue Daiyun, for example, in her memoir *To the Storm*, describes how she used to pass Jian's house on her way to forced labor. When she heard rumors that the old scholar and his wife had died with clothes neatly arranged, their faces peaceful and in an attitude of repose, she felt both envy and awe. Unlike older party members, Yue was not riveted by the subservient note in Jian's pocket. Instead she recalls the aged historian's spiritual kinship with the *ming he shi*—the "singing crane scholars" of ancient times— who had nurtured moral righteousness on the margins of political life:

A famous story, for example, relates the defiance of an ancient Shang dynasty prince who, when the empire was destroyed, went into the mountains to eat wild ferns, weeds, and seeds, living as a recluse rather than accept the favors of the conquering rulers. This principle, known as "the refusal of food from an immoral government," has been a precedent respected by intellectuals for centuries. Jian must have felt so deeply offended by the implication that from then on he would simply be kept alive, being fed by the state, that he had to make the strongest protest conceivable.[37]

This vision of Jian Bozan as a virtuous "prince" who refused the nourishment of a corrupt ruler fits well into Yue's narrative of the Cultural Revolution as moral tragedy. In Zhou Yiliang's remembrance, by contrast, Jian Bozan had become so diminished that he could do nothing but die for his loyalty to Mao Zedong. Yue Daiyun's goal was to lift the former chair of the history department to heights of moral indignation that bring back the glory of ancient times.

Moral indignation, however, is not the same as historical memory. It does not make a full accounting of senseless accusations such as drinking "Nazi milk." It paints the Cultural Revolution with a broad brush. In the end, it is details that matter. Like the shards from the Yuan Ming Yuan, so too fragments of the red terror at Beida are being pieced together today for the sake of a new generation of students. The official chronology of Beida produced for its centenary celebrations managed to include two full pages about the ten years of the Cultural Revolution. For the first time since Mao's death, exact details about the nightmare that unfolded in this garden setting were given. Shards of memory were finally assembled and labeled. In addition to the exact date for Cui Xiongkun's suicide, this official chronology provided an overview of the two months that led up to the completion of the niu peng on the ground currently occupied by the Sackler Museum:

October 1968: fifteen people died from suicide or by being pushed out of windows at Beida. The highest toll in one month. Perhaps this was the reason to speed up the building of the ox pens. Under the watchful eyes of their guardians, ox-monsters would find it more difficult to take their own lives.

October 16, 1968: Physics professor Rao Yutai hangs himself in his home on the grounds of Yan Nan Yuan. Other colleagues took a similar path: Fu Yin from Chemistry, Chen Tongdu from Biology, Shen Keqi from Philosophy, and Cao Richang from Psychology.

October 18, 1968: Professor Dong Tiebao of the Education Department committed suicide. No longer able to endure the reeducation campaigns in progress, this expert teacher took matters into his own hand.

December 18, 1968: Professor Jian Bozan, former chairman of the History Department, and his wife enacted a double suicide with the aid of sleeping pills.[38]

The official version of the history of the history department at Beijing University published five years earlier dwells simply on "ninety years of glorious scholarship and social activism."[39] No mention here of the circumstances that led Jian Bozan to take his own life. No mention here of Xiang Dai, an instructor who died of injuries sustained during a criticism session attacking him for having in his possession an image of Mao Zedong with teeth bared. No mention here of Wang Qian, a student of the Cantonese historian Chen Yinque, who also suffered endless beatings during the Cultural Revolution. Wang had been doing research on righteous officials who had dared to oppose the dictatorial authority of emperors before the Qing. No mention of Yang Rengeng, the specialist on Africa who was already in his sixties when he was knocked down a hill while laboring in the ox pens. Yang had refused to acknowledge his "mistakes" and died while being beaten.[40]

The list of Cultural Revolution victims at Beida is longer and more difficult to come to terms with than the number of coffins delivered to Elgin in 1860. Torture in the nineteenth century took place in the context of a culture conflict between China and the West. The atrocities that took place on the same terrain in the twentieth century pitted Chinese against each other. Students attacked and murdered teachers. Highly educated men and women who had been leaders of the party had to grovel before crazed youths who knew only how to shout slogans and brandish guns. Details about this thoroughly native nightmare have been slow to be assembled, slow to be publicized. When the Beijing University Museum finally opened in 2002, several courtyards away from the Sackler Museum and the grounds of the niu peng, the Cultural Revolution remained a muted event. The inaugural exhibit focused on two hundred and fifty famous teachers who had been connected to Beida from its earliest days as the Imperial College of 1898. Among the faces skillfully mounted on Plexiglas were twenty-one scholars who had died during the Cultural Revolution. Other than the date of death—somewhere between 1966 and 1970—there was no mention of the circumstances of their torture or suicide. Among the distinguished scholars featured in the University Museum who lost their lives because of the Cultural Revolution were:

Yu Hongzhen (1897–1966)—Professor of chemistry who focused his research on soil conditions of northwestern China.

Fan Wenlan (1893–1969)—Professor of history who had begun his career with research on ancient China and ended up an innovator in Marxist theories of modern history.

Bi Huade (1891–1966)—Professor of medicine and editor of the *Encyclopedia of Ophthalmology*.

Chen Yinluo (1890–1969)—Historian who began his career at Tsinghua University and ended up at Zhongshan University in Canton with a research specialty in Sui-Tang history, Mongolian studies, and Buddhism.

Zheng Shaolun (1899–1966)—Professor of chemistry and dean of Beijing University who also served as president of China's Chemistry Association and did research focusing on organic compounds and molecular structure.

Xu Baolu (1910–1970)—Professor of mathematics who specialized in probability theory and statistics.

Xiong Shili (1884–1968)—Professor of philosophy who specialized in research about Buddhism, Neo Confucianism, and worked to develop a new cognitive theory.

Zhao Jiuzhang (1907–1968)—Meteorologist who went on to make significant contributions to the study of space science and was awarded, posthumously, with the Medal for Achievement in Nuclear and Space Science.

Ai Siqi (1910–1966)—Philosopher who taught at Beijing University while also serving as the nation's most renowned scholar of Marxism and Mao Zedong Thought.

Jiang Longji (1905–1966)—Beijing University graduate who served as vice president of the university from 1952 to 1958, with research interests in higher education.

Xie Jiaorong (1898–1966)—Professor of geology and chairman of the geology department who pioneered the study of economic geology and directed the discovery of mines in many parts of China.

Rao Yutai (1891–1968)—Professor of physics and provost of Beijing University whose research focused on the atomic and molecular spectrum.

Jian Bozan (1898–1968)—Professor of history and chairman of the history department who started out his research in ancient Chinese history and emerged as the main Marxist historian of the modern period.

Wu Han (1909–1969)—Historian who taught at Qinghua University with a research focus on the Ming dynasty and who went on to write the historical drama *Hai Rui Dismissed from Office*. He was also the author of a collection of essays entitled *San Jia Cun* for which he was tortured to death during the Cultural Revolution.[41]

This last biographical snippet in Plexiglas was the only one in the well-lit gallery to speak directly about the atrocities of the Cultural Revolution. The other displays offered only a reticent testament to the many prominent scholars born at the turn of the century who lost their lives in the years of terror. Those aged intellectuals had made extensive contributions in all fields of knowledge ranging from physics to Marxist theory. What the photomontage does not mention is that contribution to knowledge itself constituted the greatest "crime" committed by all these "ox-ghosts and snake-spirits."

On the lower level of the new museum there is a small display about the Cultural Revolution period. Some newspapers of the time are framed to show the centrality of Beida in the events that unfolded. Here, too, references to violence are muted by a generic condemnation of "leftist extremism." The exhibition emphasizes not the ox pens of Beida but rather the transfer of incarcerated intellectuals to the countryside for "reeducation." Neither the upper-level photographs nor the basement documents point the finger to Beida's role in China's national tragedy. They do not dwell on humiliation, on suicide, or on garden sites transformed into torture chambers. Beida's history museum is meant to celebrate past glories so as to provide a solid foundation for socialist accomplishments of the future. For an inner narrative of the "Garden of Labor Reform," one needs to look beyond Plexiglas. Artists and intellectuals who went through the Cultural Revolution did manage to leave behind some snippets that can help us hear their hoarse voices even today. Mao Zedong's Red Guards had used and abused the idea of the yuan as a protected space for reflection. Survivors of atrocity, on the other hand, held on to and even deepened the meaning of garden spaces during the years that were meant to erase all traces of historical memory.

The Orchid Is Fragrant, the Plum Makes the Snow Red

Shi Lu (1919–1982), one of the most prominent artist-victims of the Cultural Revolution, embodies this quest for the garden ideal most poignantly. One of Mao's official painters, Shi Lu had made his reputation with a large-scale image of the chairman painted in 1959. Like Jian Bozan at Beida, so too this well-known professor at the Xi'an Academy of Art had every expectation of living out his years in peace with the communist revolution. When the red terror broke out in 1966, however, all such dreams were shattered. As a result, Shi Lu went "mad"—using his incarceration in the niu peng to paint, probe, and celebrate his own spiritual garden.

While aged intellectuals at Beida were forced to shove each other for a bit of gruel with tomatoes, Shi Lu was locked up in a shed designed for refuse. In this cage of stench, the artist managed to create a "scholar's studio." Using pen and paper issued for daily confession, the prisoner began to compose new poetry and art. The more he was attacked and beaten, the richer the soil of the imagination became within. Outside his shed, Red Guards catalogued Shi Lu's crimes against the revolution and against Chairman Mao. Inside the niu peng, Shi Lu made a different kind of reckoning. In a poem entitled "Counting on Heaven's Abacus," written between 1974 and 1975, two kinds of accounting are given voice:

No breeze stirs against sky's door.
Counting on Heaven's abacus,
My life, similarly weightless.
Long ago I was good at doing somersaults.
My teacher punished me by making me kneel on bricks.
So I filled his teapot with urine.
Really, I don't dare eat people.
But my character from birth has despised bad people.
The bamboo is lofty and pure.
The orchid is fragrant.
The plum makes the snow red.
The bird chirps.
Within Nature so many different aspects reside.
Those who dare to oppose nature will be cursed with no offspring . . .[42]

A life rendered weightless by fabrications of monstrosity is recovered here by turning to bamboo, orchid, and plum. Against a generation that single-handedly "capsized the boat" of the state and of public civility, the artist had no weapons but his inner gaze. As another poem by Shi Lu makes clear, crazy monkeys had besmirched the world. All he could do now was to seek out butterflies and yellow flowers.

Shi Lu's effort to talk back at the Red Guards did not stop with poems. He went on to actually build himself an alternative space out of pen and paper where he imagined the peace of mind denied him during daily torture. One of his sketches in ink that survived the years of atrocity appears simple but its solace is complex (figure 34). Shi Lu's son, who saved this Cultural Revolution journal entry, calls it an imaginary spiritual garden (*jing shen de zhuang yuan*) that helped his father survive. At first glance, the enclosure appears, troubled, agitated. Nervous strokes mirror the anxiety endured by the artist in prison. Upon closer inspection however, the dense details reveal a mental universe where one could retreat for meditation. Just as it was once possible to meander the paths of the Singing Crane Garden, so too, Shi Lu allowed himself in this drawing to ramble through the gardens of his youth.

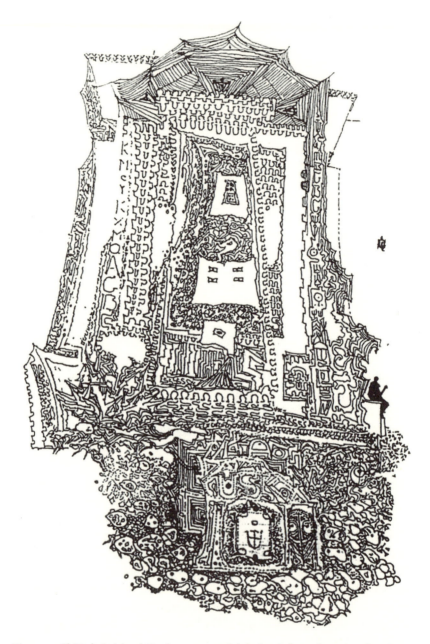

Figure 34. Shi Lu's *Spiritual Garden*—pen-and-ink sketch from the painter's private diary, ca. 1973–74. This image was made available to me courtesy of Shelley Drake Hawks.

Forced to disown all connection to a world he had cherished, Shi Lu brought it back to life through intricate brushwork.

Most important, the artist himself is back in the picture. In the center of the garden built out of the mortar of calligraphy, Shi Lu appears in a blank white space behind the walls. Small renditions of his name, as well as Western alphabetic letters, create a maze along the garden's walls. On the left side, a pure white orchid bursts from a crevice in the architecture. In another self-reference, a small turtle can be discerned on the grounds just outside the garden. A terraced roof at the far end of the structure, apparently made of spider webs, may denote the concrete space of the ox pens from which this garden emerged. The total effect in this sketch is that of a particularly dense surrogate reality. Unlike nineteenth-century scholar-officials who had the luxury of actual seclusion, the painter in Xi'an preserved his mind by taking refuge in madness. Shi Lu's childhood home had included an impressive garden on the grounds of the family compound. From this reservoir of beauty and peace, Shi Lu fashioned his own distinctive edifice. Its walled parameters and the artistry of its interior mirror the painter's own struggle. This spiritual garden contains a vision of self that is far more endangered than the repose cultivated by Mianyu and Yihuan. These Manchu princes had built privileged gardens in hamlets of Haidian at a time when it was inconceivable for scholars and artists to be totally cannibalized by politics. To be sure, they too, had witnessed corruption and destruction in Beijing. As their family and dynasty became more vulnerable, the challenge of remaining "mentally alive" became acute even for these noblemen. Yihuan cultivated an alternative vision each time he returned to the ruined Ming He Yuan, and to his beloved Wei Xiu Yuan. For Shi Lu and other inmates of the ox pens, a physical return to ruined gardens was not possible. They had to make do with darker symbolism.

The miniature turtle in the mental garden is a symbol for endurance. Like the yuan itself, this plodding animal teaches Chinese artists how to preserve spiritual resources for the long struggle ahead. In another sketch from his niu peng days Shi Lu made the turtle even bigger and added to it the symbol of the crane—a most readily recognized emblem for inner freedom. The drawing with the crane takes the form of a stele. Unlike the marble stele with deep gashes, at Beida, Shi Lu's imaginary rock is dedicated to the preservation of language. As in the garden sketch, the artist puts himself in the picture—this time as a scholar paying homage at the altar of poetry. He stands with shoes removed and a column of alphabetic letters bearing down on his head—a silent witness to the moral degradation of a disintegrating universe. This self-portrait shows the length to which one had to go to reimagine connectedness to the past in times of cultural amnesia. Shi Lu took many risks to place himself back into the garden of poetry. At one point he even escaped from his niu peng in Xi'an to wander in the wilderness of Siquan. Captured and tortured again, he sank deeper into mental illness. Whether this predicament was real or a ruse remains unclear. What we do know is that Shi Lu emerged from the Cultural Revolution a changed man. Looking like a disheveled peasant, he lived out his remaining years going in and out of asylums, receiving various treatments for schizophrenia. While mind and body ached, he continued to turn out dramatic works of monumental calligraphy. Shi Lu finally received critical appreciation in China and abroad after his death in 1982.

Other artists and intellectuals did not have the fortitude—or the luck—to run away from their imprisonment in the ox pens. Remaining at the beck and call of the "little generals," they had to recite their "crimes" daily. Without a spiritual garden, many became what the Red Guards accused them of: beasts of burden without consciousness or hope. Self-doubts about their contributions to the revolution increased under the pressure of interrogation. Many had supported communism out of nationalism. They saw Mao Zedong as a valiant patriot who made China strong and respectable in the world. Patriotism, however, proved to be too thin a veneer. Yenching graduates discovered this early in the 1950s. Others intuited it even earlier. Zhu Guanqian, for example, began confessing his "sins" long before he was imprisoned and beaten in the Beida niu peng. As early as November 1949, Zhu had published a self-confession in the pages of the *People's Daily*. Before communist officials had the power to demand conformity with their version of the past, Zhu showed himself willing to indict his own previous attachment to beauty and to academic pursuits. Recalling his research on the philosophy of tragedy in Europe, Zhu Guanqian blamed aesthetics for leading him to turn away from politics.[43]

By the late 1950s, Zhu had turned self-blame into an art. He did all he could to uproot the garden of his own mind. He became a scrupulous student of Marxist theory who condemned all his previous works on the philosophy of aesthetics as useless. Nothing that Zhu had thought or written before the victory of the Communist Party seemed worthy of preservation. Yet this self-incrimination did not suffice during the 1960s. In the niu peng Zhu's accusers used even harsher techniques. Under their assault, the old philosopher's vulnerable backbone grew stronger. If not in body, at least in spirit, he managed to access sources of strength he had willfully ignored before. The same "feudal past" that he cursed in the 1950s now greeted him at the window of his prison in the form of the Yi Ran Ting. This glimpse of beauty, combined with the covert practice of *tai ji quan*, enabled the octogenarian scholar to withstand the temptation of suicide.

Unlike Jian Bozan, Zhu did not end his life during the Cultural Revolution. He survived to see the death of Mao and even the repudiation of the excesses of the 1960s. More important, he lived long enough to begin a new, important intellectual project: the translation of Vico's *New Science*. Like the painter Shi Lu, the philosopher of aesthetics went on to write works that justified his insights before the Mao era. By the end of his life, Zhu Guanqian had circled back to his first book on the psychology of tragedy. Having lived through atrocity, he understood even more deeply that the essence of tragedy lies just in the fact that it is different from the terrible. "The truly tragic, because of its nobility and grandeur, can awaken thereby what is our own soul. It presses, as it were, and lights up a hidden divine spark."[44]

A contemporary of Zhu Guanqian, the flower painter Pan Tianshou (1897–1971), also managed to hold on to this ideal of nobility and grandeur. Not daring to descend into madness like Shi Lu, Pan continued to paint in the traditional style even after the Red Guards had accused him of being a spy for the Nationalist Party. Depicted by his torturers as an evil vulture feeding off the carcass of the masses, Pan Tianshou refused to give in. Pressured to paint human figures, he remained faithful to his flowering plums, making their blossoms ever more fragile under the light of a cold winter moon. Unlike Zhu Guanqian, who had accused himself of mistakes repeatedly before the Red Guards, Pan remained determined to avoid the "brambles" and the "abyss" of politics. In a poem written in 1969 on a train carrying him to a particularly humiliating struggle session in his hometown, Pan Tianshou wrote:

The cage is narrow,
but I will not complain—

My mind is as broad
as Heaven and Earth.

From ancient times,
gross injustices have filled the world . . .[45]

For this painter of winter plum, imprisonment in the ox pens became a window into his own mind. Despite the narrow cage, Pan managed to look at himself and at China's history with fresh eyes. Like Shi Lu with his heavenly abacus and Zhu Guanqian with his glimpse of the Yi Ran Ting, Pan availed himself of a depth of vision unavailable before the violence of the Cultural Revolution. With vision came a renewed sense of purpose, meaning. However deeply buried, art managed to outwit atrocity.

The willful myopia inflicted by the Red Guards did not last. Yenching's old motto—"Freedom Through Truth for Service" (*Yi zhenli de ziyou er fuwu*)—had been rubbed out of stone. Yet it retained its hold in the mind.[46] Independence of thought was never fully erased in northwest Beijing because its roots ran deep. A dehydrated kernel, it came to life again after the death of Mao. Amid the ruins of the old Ming He Yuan, a thirst for reflection endured. The idea of the yuan outlasted all its destroyers. Neither Elgin's fire nor the Red Guards' ire managed to dismantle all traces of crying cranes.

When Arthur Sackler arrived in the 1970s looking for a space to build a new museum dedicated to the arts of cultural preservation, the yuan was ready to be reseeded. Silenced and vandalized, it had not been totally destroyed. Without the garden space, there may not have been a museum of art. Without Sackler's vision, the garden legacy of Yenching as well as the name of Ming He Yuan might have vanished from public consciousness through a combination of neglect and ignorance. As it turned out, garden and museum reinforced each other beyond Sackler's boldest dreams.

Chapter 5
Spaciousness Regained in the Museum

Those odds and ends of memory are the only wealth
That the rush of time leaves us.
We are our memory,
We are the chimerical museum of shifting forms,
This heap of broken mirrors.

—Jorge Luis Borges, "Cambridge"

How does healing start on ravaged ground? By a slow-paced cherishment of broken remains. This was the process that began at Beijing University with the founding of the Arthur M. Sackler Museum of Art and Archaeology. Arthur Sackler, like the Argentinean poet Jorge Luis Borges, treasured the odds and ends of history. A psychiatrist by training, he understood that "we are our memory," that a museum cannot fix forever the meanings of shifting forms. Dedicated to the preservation of archaeological relics and to the teaching of museology, Dr. Sackler's institution at Beida sought to create a space for reflection on the site formerly occupied by Mianyu's Singing Crane Garden. Joined, the garden and museum represented a forceful retort to historical amnesia in northwest Beijing (figure 35).

The coming together of curatorial and landscaped spaces, of course, is not a new phenomenon in China—or in the European context, for that matter. A long-standing symbiosis between culture and nature accounts for the fact that most often museums have been embedded in a garden context. In China, traditional *hua yuan* were meant to guide the knowing eye through calligraphy, paintings, sculptured rocks, and artfully fashioned furnishings every bit as much as through bamboo, chrysanthemum, goldfish, and artificial hills. In Europe, early models of the "cabinet of curiosities" were similarly housed in garden settings. As John Dixon Hunt has pointed out in

Figure 35. The Arthur M. Sackler Museum of Art and Archaeology at Beijing University, southwest view from the newly landscaped garden, with the Ming He Yuan boulder and Qing dynasty sundial visible in the back.

his essay "Curiosities to Adorn Cabinets and Gardens," the history of land-scaped spaces is intimately tied up with the birth of modern museum-build-ing.[1] Both underwent significant changes in the wake of scientific and nationalist revolutions, while retaining the ideal of the garden as a privileged concentration of both natural and cultural elements.

On the campus of Beijing University, all ideas of privilege had been fiercely attacked during the Cultural Revolution. The Sackler Museum of Art and Archaeology not only revived the name of the Singing Crane Garden, it also created a building and a landscape that sanctioned the possibility of slow-paced reflection upon nature and culture alike. Today, three decades after the Cultural Revolution, a sense of spaciousness, of safe interiority is once again returning to the Beida campus. The museum and its surrounding gardens are bringing back some of the grace that had characterized the Singing Crane Garden as well as the Yenching gardens before the terror of the *niu peng*. The well-maintained paths around the Sackler Museum provide refuge from the busy pace of study for practitioners of *tai ji quan*. One can

Figure 36. Artificial waterfall in the newly landscaped lake behind the Arthur M. Sackler Museum.

stop here and listen to the sound of water, almost as if one had stepped back in time to Mianyu's fishponds (figure 36). Seven decades after the burning of the princely gardens, Chinese undergraduates can once again savor what the French philosopher Gaston Bachelard called the "great immensity within ourselves."[2]

This appreciation of personal and cultural immensities is the result of a conscious reconnection to the history of garden spaces on the Beida campus. It was Sackler's specially chosen architect, Lo Yi Chan, who brought back the courtyard idea from its ox-pen connotations to an earlier vision of refuge and contemplation. During the crucial year that preceded Sackler's sudden death in 1987, this Harvard-trained architect made sure that a conversation with the history of landscaped spaces went beyond the formalism initially suggested by Beijing University officials. Once the grounds for the new museum were allocated (without any mention of their use during the Cultural Revolution) the assumption was that the new museum would somehow fit into the Yenching style that dominated the northwest corner of the Beida campus. Lo Yi Chan, however, did a lot more. He demanded space enough for a courtyard that would be centered around a traditional ornamental rock.

Even before the old stone from the Ming dynasty Shao Yuan was found, named, and installed in the museum courtyard, the grounds of the Singing Crane Garden had found the breath of life again.

Ironically, life came back to stones and gardens faster than to the intellectuals who had suffered breakage on this same terrain. The post-Mao rehabilitation program brought out of hiding cultural treasures years before the men and women who knew the value of these shards could gain a truly new lease on life. In the first decade after Mao Zedong's death in 1976, it was easier and safer to blame all problems on the so-called Gang of Four. Headed by Mao's imprisoned wife, Jiang Qing, this small cohort was held responsible for all the pain inflicted across the land. Victims and perpetrators alike knew that millions had been involved in terror willingly. The fervor and the demonization, however, could not yet be denounced. Instead, authorities began the slow process of rehabilitating the castigated, distant past. At Beijing University, this involved taking out of storage archaeological remains once slotted for destruction. One of the genuine miracles of the museum in the garden was that there was actually enough art and archaeology to be exhibited when Arthur Sackler came up with the idea, and the funds, for cultural preservation.

Su Bai, a senior archaeologist delegated to conduct initial discussions with Dr. Sackler, was himself a victim of the Cultural Revolution. Born in 1922, he had been incarcerated in the very ox pens that were torn down for the new museum. He did not speak about this with the American donor. Instead, the plans for the preservation and exhibition of ancient artifacts were discussed, while recent history remained a shadowy witness. Like the old garden surrounding the museum site, the Cultural Revolution remained rooted in a silent soil.

After the building of the Sackler Museum, I asked Su Bai about the relatively large volume of archaeological artifacts salvaged on the Beida campus. He replied with an ironic smile: "In those days it was easier to save objects than people.... One small character sufficed to sequester our collection from the hands of the Red Guards. We packed everything in boxes and marked them *feng* [sealed]. This implied that they were dangerous, 'feudal' remains and should be kept out of sight. . . . The boxes survived, but many of our colleagues did not."[3] The official history of the department of archaeology at Beijing University makes no mention of this ruse. Compiled in order to publicize the collection of the Sackler Museum, this chronological record is markedly reticent about the years of terror. There are no entries between

February 1966 (when archaeology graduate students were sent to labor on the grounds of the Ming dynasty tombs) to August 1970 (when "the first group of graduate students came back to school").[4] The missing four years have not been forgotten. They are the real reason why the Sackler Museum means so much to a department, and to a university once marked by hatred of the past. The museum itself does not memorialize the lives lost or the memories that are still raw. Instead, it is an indirect nod to the terrain where scholars were once punished for the very knowledge now promoted inside the Sackler institution at Beida.

The historian who would grasp the meanings of silence on the grounds of Ming He Yuan has to make sense of the space between broken shards. One urn inside the Sackler Museum has been a mirror of this process for me. When I first viewed the clay pot in October 1993 I had not yet understood the confused history it contained. Dating from the Xia dynasty (as its label suggests), this *gang* could have been made any time between the twenty-first and the sixteenth centuries before the common era. It was discovered in Henan province. Today, this large vessel is a lacework of cracks. Like the scholars and intellectuals who come to occupy the garden, this *gang* shows its brokenness without apology. Ragged shards have been glued together, much like the lives of those who now recall the destruction of the Singing Crane Garden and of the Cultural Revolution. Broken yet whole, this vase invites an open-ended reckoning with the past. Its artfully molded lip suggests that beauty was never far from utilitarian concerns. If the ancient potter could shape such a graceful container, surely the historian can try to fathom the broken past with a similarly artful eye.

Gaston Bachelard, in a very different context, pointed out the need to listen carefully to the "wellspring in a sealed vase." Even without the aid of a Chinese *gang*, the French philosopher knew the importance of remains from the past that hold great significance for those willing to listen when "waves repeatedly echo against the sides of this vase, filled with sonority."[5] Bachelard argued that these sonorous waves reveal the genuine tonality of life—and we may add, of the garden and of historical memory in this much-tortured corner of Beijing. Such a "tonality" may also be glimpsed in a photograph that accompanied an exhibit about the history of archaeology at Beida. This image shows Professor Su Bingqi (1952–1983) carefully touching an ancient vase. The knowing gaze, the light imprint of fingers upon a fragment that survived millennia is enough to underscore the survival of the aged intellectual as well. A professor of history who had special expertise in archaeological matters, Su suffered along with eminent communist experts such as Jian Bozan. Perhaps it was the "wellspring" in this vase—the knowledge that the ancient past would outlast the harsh idiocies of the Red Guards—that kept Su Bingqi from taking his own life during the decade of the niu peng. The establishment of the museum in the garden validated this faith in the endurance of historical memory. While urns fared better than the battered bodies, there was enough expertise and enough material remains lingering after the Cultural Revolution for Arthur Sackler to seed a new garden at Beida. This would be a new kind of yuan dedicated explicitly to cherishing China's historical memory.

To Study the Past Was a Cardinal Sin

The observable past had to be shrunk and sanitized for the opening exhibition at the Sackler Museum in May 1993. Yet its very presence created a spaciousness once denied in the niu peng. Much like the Singing Crane Garden in its times of flourishing, so too the Sackler Museum framed possibilities for cultural reflection. Dr. Sackler's gift to Beida aided the revival of historical consciousness after the Cultural Revolution. In this task, the museum shared the mission of other institutions dedicated to the enlargement of public memory. In the words of Susan Crane, a historian of museology, the display of art objects provides an opportunity for the coming together of subjectivities and objectivities alike: "Museums are flexible mirrors whose convex potential for multiple interpretations and participation (that is, by those who have either kind of personal historical consciousness: as veterans and survivors, or as historians) will continue to make them appropriate venues for active memory work, either on site or in the minds of those whose historical consciousness has been activated, nourished, challenged, and revived."[6] Like Jorge Luis Borges, Crane appeals to the metaphor of the mirror to describe how the museum reflects and augments the past. By evoking a wide range of recollections beyond the objects in the glass case, the Sackler Museum at Beida undertook this memory work as well.

The challenge of recollection begins even before one enters the elaborately carved doors that mirror the Yenching style. Outside the museum, the front courtyard brings to mind the sense of symmetry that reigned here when the Ninde Hall for Religious Studies was first erected in the 1920s. Unlike more recent Beida buildings dedicated to computers and applied sciences, there is a choice on this site in favor of grace and harmony. Instead of cement towers, the Qing dynasty sundial marks the entrance to a museum dedicated to illuminating history. To the left of the sundial rises the gray mass of the modern Ming He Yuan stone. A new boulder mounted on a marble pedestal, this simple monument links the museum directly to the Singing Crane Garden and to the generosity of Sackler's widow, Jill Sackler. On the pedestal, university officials found it fitting to recall the princely past that preceded their (reluctant) acceptance of the gift of a new garden from foreign donors.

The boulder is inscribed with three large characters naming the garden of Prince Mianyu. A lost world of landscaped spaces is brought to life here through the vivacious calligraphy of Qigong, an artist who is a direct descendant of the Manchu princes of the nineteenth century. Qigong's name and seal appear, as convention requires, in a small square below the words for "Singing Crane Garden." For visitors who know the history of the Qing dynasty, and who recall the atrocities of the Cultural Revolution, Qigong's name suffices as a poignant memorial. A cousin of the last emperor, Puyi, Qigong was severely attacked during the 1960s. As a professor of traditional calligraphy, this Manchu nobleman suffered violent beatings and incarceration in the ox pens. While the former ruler Puyi was paraded in the streets, his cousin languished in several different prison camps. Puyi was a grandson of Yihuan, and Qigong was his great-nephew. Both were forced to do menial labor that lowly servants once carried out for garden owners in northwest Beijing. After Mao's death, Qigong found some solace in writing his memoirs.[7] Now, he is allowed to carve in stone again the name of a garden once recalled in secret and in terror.

Inside the Sackler Museum, a similar response is being crafted by archaeologists who salvaged the ancient past from the will to ruination that characterized the Red Guards. As Su Bai recalls: "During the Cultural Revolution people were treated worse than objects. To study the past was itself a cardinal sin. Now we have the opportunity to treat objects with tender care. If relics can be honored, perhaps we can restore the dignity of those who suffered for the love of history as well."[8] Conservation techniques inaugurated by the Sackler Museum of Art and Archaeology are in this context not merely advances in museum science. They represent a profound rehabilitation of the love of history itself. Attachment to the past was once a crime. Thoughtful cherishment of it now is almost a public virtue.

Cherishment of the past, however, had not yet become widespread when Arthur Sackler first approached Beijing University officials with the idea of an art museum in the early 1980s. Archaeologists and historians, working under the direction of the Communist Party, were still involved in complex deliberations about what was "progressive" and what was "reactionary" about the past. Criticism was still more important than scholarship and preservation. As a result, Sackler's initiative was squelched almost before it began. What moved the project along was Sackler's keen grasp of China's cultural politics. He understood perfectly well that Chinese authorities needed to buttress their claim to power with a nationalistic affirmation of the imperial past. Therefore, he brought to China a gift. In an official, high-profile visit in August 1980, seven years before the museum idea took root in the garden terrain, Arthur Sackler landed in Beijing with a throne that had belonged to the Qianlong emperor. Famous as a collector, Sackler was bringing history back to a country traumatized by the Cultural Revolution. He also knew that the humiliating defeat of 1860 had left a longing for objects of Qing provenance. The return of an imperial treasure from the looted grounds of the Yuan Ming Yuan had the potential to change the political climate.

Sackler's speech at the Palace Museum was a marvel of diplomatic tact. In the presence of the American ambassador Leonard Woodcock and the minister of public health, Qian Xinzhong—an aged well-known physician who also suffered in the niu peng—Sackler spoke about the "genius" of Chinese culture: "We present, as a token of our esteem, respect and affection, this work of Chinese genius and culture. In the past, it marked the rule of an emperor. Today, it represents the sovereignty of a people. And, for the future, it signifies a new era in the history of China, of my nation, and of the world. It is given as a tribute and as a new symbol, as a friendship throne."[9] Talk of "friendship" between China and the United States smoothed the path for further collaboration, including the building of the museum at Beida. It also masked, for a while, the passions of the collector who cherished cultural reconstruction and would make sure it became legitimate once again in China after Mao.

The Role of the Donor Is to Doan

Arthur M. Sackler was born on August 22, 1913, to immigrant Jewish parents in Brooklyn. The fact that he became one of the most renowned collectors of

Chinese art in the twentieth century is just as remarkable as the widespread net of his philanthropic activities. He ended up building art museums at Harvard and the Smithsonian, at Beijing University as well as at the Royal Academy of Art in London. This geographical reach did not come easily to those born poor. Sackler's father, Isaac, emigrated from Russian-occupied Poland and sought to give his three sons the best education America could offer. The success of his effort can be seen in the marble plaque that adorns the entrance of the Sackler Medical School in Tel Aviv. It reads: "Dedicated to Mankind for the Health of All People in Honor of Our Parents, Isaac and Sophie Sackler by Raymond R. Sackler, MD; Mortimer D. Sackler, MD; Arthur M. Sackler, MD."[10]

To look at another philanthropic family, the fact that John D. Rockefeller's children went on to amass great collections of Chinese art and endow medical schools should not surprise us. They were following a path of wealthy, culturally informed philanthropy. For the offspring of Jewish immigrants to undertake similarly wide-ranging projects required an extra measure of will and moral idealism. The Rockefellers' Peking United Medical College, opened in 1921, was dedicated to "the best that is known to Western Civilization not only in medical sciences but in mental and spiritual culture."[11] The Sackler Medical School in Tel Aviv, by contrast, is both more modest and more ambitious. Completed in 1966, it aims to take medical learning beyond the boundaries of the Jewish state. Far from dwelling on Western civilization, this institution as well as all other institutions subsidized by Arthur Sackler pay homage to world culture in a nonjudgmental fashion. In February 1986, speaking at the dedication of the Arthur M. Sackler Health Communications Center at Tufts University in Massachusetts, this son of Jewish immigrants from Poland expressed his credo as follows: "At a time when the accumulated nuclear arsenals deriving from the most brilliant minds of science and technology can destroy the world, . . . we need more than ever to build links of understanding and mutual respect between peoples of different civilizations. All, in our mutual interest, must seek to reach a goal which can best be fulfilled through the building of the most important bridges between civilized men and women of culture, of all cultures—the arts, the sciences and the humanities."[12] As these words make clear, Sackler saw himself as bridge builder, as a man who was gifted with wealth that could be used to increase links of understanding and mutual respect between different civilizations.

Not coming from a family with traditions of ownership and entitlement made him particularly alert to the responsibilities of a donor. While the Rockefellers had a reservoir of Christian beliefs concerning charity and benevolence, Arthur Sackler is on record as stating that he hated the word "philanthropy":

For good reasons, I cringe when I hear it applied to me. I am no philanthropist. To be able to establish an institution dedicated to the arts, or post-graduate humanistic studies, or medical schools to advance science and the preservation of health and life, is a privilege. To be able to establish communication media or centers devoted to the dissemination of ideas and knowledge is not an act of charity. It is a privilege. . . . In our society I find money obscures the true value of people, of life and of art. It is only when I woke up and realized what a lever it was to advance worthwhile goals, in building edifices dedicated to the beauty of the arts, temples dedicated to knowledge, schools dedicated to science that I began to get a better balance. Perhaps some would say a more realistic perspective. I found it could give life to new concepts, even bring "dead things" to life.[13]

Bringing dead things to life was not just a metaphorical undertaking on the campus of Beijing University. It was Sackler's homage both to the Chinese and the Jewish past. Sackler chose to see his activities as a form of sharing what was not his to keep in the first place. The deepest root of this outlook may be found in the Jewish concept of *Tzedaka*—best translated as "righteousness" as opposed to more common notions of charity. According to Maimonides, the great medieval commentator, there are eight ascending degrees of engagement with the world for those bent upon practicing this path of Tzedaka.[14] The lowest rung of the giving ladder is occupied by those who have wealth but shared it grudgingly. The highest is reserved for those who provide others with concrete options for furthering their own goals.

Although Arthur Sackler did not often refer to Jewish texts in his giving, it is clear he was aware of them and informed by their standards. Interviewed by a *Washington Post* journalist after the news of his generous donation to the Smithsonian had spread worldwide, he remarked: "The role of the donor is to doan. . . . Great art doesn't belong to anyone. Never will. The more successful your collections are, the more they cease to be your property."[15] Playing upon the Latin root for the word "donor," Sackler made it clear that he was in the business of returning "gifts." He did not see himself as the sole owner of the art he had amassed with great effort (and great pleasure). The obligation to return to the public benefits obtained in private is essentially a Jewish idea. Meir Meyer, the acquisition director of the Israel Museum, confirmed this. After extensive dealings with the Sackler brothers, he became convinced that they were "genuinely broad minded men who stand in a direct lineage with the Rambam [Maimonides]."[16]

For Arthur Sackler, the commitment to doan came after he finished medical school, after he turned away from the possibility of becoming an artist himself, after poverty left a permanent mark on his consciousness. As an undergraduate at New York University in the 1930s, he had experienced the Great Depression firsthand. What little security his parents gained though rental properties in Brooklyn in the 1920s was lost in the stock market crash. The young man who had taken painting and sculpture courses at Cooper Union in the evening found himself suddenly penniless. Early encounters with poverty made Arthur Sackler identify with China in the first place. Half a century before he built the museum at Beida, he took the Canadian doctor Norman Bethune as his moral exemplar. In the 1930s, Bethune was in China enduring hardships along with the Red Army. In the most difficult circumstances of war and revolution, he sought to heal the wounds of the poor. In New York City, Arthur Sackler (a budding physician) heard about Bethune's work and rose to support it with enthusiasm. He even went as far as to collect money for the idealist Canadian serving in China. Many decades later, when he first went to China to sponsor medical conferences, nothing pleased Sackler more than to be honored as a "present-day Bethune."[17]

After his early fund-raising effort in the depression-stricken city, Arthur Sackler began to savor the rewards of a successful medical career. His intellectual—and financial—breakthrough began in 1950. This was the year in which he first presented several research papers arguing for the neuro-endocrinal foundation of psychosis. These conjectures caused a revolution in medical thinking about the chemical factors that affect schizophrenia and led the Sackler brothers to pioneer some of the first medications for the disease. The profits from these medications provided an opening for a new taste in art. In the early 1950s, Arthur Sackler came upon some Chinese ceremonial objects and Ming dynasty furniture that would permanently alter his aesthetic sensibility. Whereas he had previously begun collecting American and then PreColumbian art, he now turned his attention to the intricacies of Asian creativity.

Just as his professional work became more deeply immersed in the biomedical manufacturing of drugs for psychiatric disorders, his passion for the civilization of ancient China grew more intense as well. By 1958, the Sackler brothers were turning new medical research into a profitable enterprise.

Further income was generated by their pioneering work in ultrasound technology—called in these early days "ultra sonometry." Taken all together, these experimental advances provided the wealth necessary for the Sackler brothers to invest in art. New terminology was not reserved for the laboratory alone. Arthur Sackler, who had bought the McAdam Medical Advertising firm in 1942, now used it to launch a much more ambitious project: a journal that would reach, he hoped, every single medical practitioner in the United States.[18] This vision became the *Medical Tribune*, a digest of recent research for doctors all over the world. International subdivisions of the *Medical Tribune* began to generate substantial income. This enabled the Sackler brothers to begin large-scale philanthropic projects.

The Tel Aviv medical school was the first of their joint enterprises. Later, the brothers collaborated in raising funds needed for the Dandur Temple at the Metropolitan Museum of Art in New York. The idea of three Jewish doctors paying for the largest Egyptian temple outside of Africa was an irony that was not lost upon the then-director of museum, Thomas Hoving. In his memoir, *Making the Mummies Dance*, Hoving took delight in "unmasking" the pretensions of these Park Avenue practitioners, so unlike the Rockefellers and the Astors, who were more "congenial" colleagues on the board of directors of the Met. Discounting the Sacklers' sensitivity to anti-Semitism as historically conditioned phobia, Hoving's memoir portrays Arthur Sackler as a greedy, vulgar multimillionaire, a curmudgeon fit for delicious gossip:

One story had it that when he and his two brothers—also medical doctors, both, like Arthur, married to doctors—were about to graduate from Columbia's Physicians and Surgeons College, they held a conference about what they wanted to do next. Private practice didn't much appeal, and one of the Sackler brothers suggested they invent something or make something better. They pounced upon Argyrol, a disinfectant created by the art collector Albert Barnes, which was in general used in the twenties and thirties. They succeeded in removing the toxic properties in the solution and patented it as Betadyne, which became the surgical scrub used in virtually every modern operating room worldwide. The Sacklers made millions.

Arthur started collecting art as soon as he'd made his first one hundred thousand. He retired in his fifties, an exceptionally wealthy man. In a month he was bored. In the middle of the night he awoke with the revelation that there was no medical newspaper in the United States. He started one and became even wealthier. With part of his wealth he collected Oriental art, although he had some respectable old masters, a classical bronze from Turkey, and a few Impressionists. In less than ten years, with advice from the top specialists in Chinese and Japanese art, Sackler had accumulated a huge collection.[19]

What is missing in this tale about Argyrol and Betadyne is any sense of the passion that animated the collecting life of Arthur Sackler. There is no credit here for the idealism of a bridge builder, for a Jewish doctor whose China work was inspired by the selfless dedication of Norman Bethune.

In China, unlike at the Met, Sackler's generosity had a significant historical context. Even while prejudice against Western "capitalists" still lingered after the death of Mao, Sackler was seen as unique. More like his Canadian predecessor, the American doctor was hailed for his love of China. At a ceremonial banquet in Beijing, Arthur Sackler was welcomed not as a rich Jew trying to buy his way into the sacred palace of high art, but as a doctor eager to serve beyond the illness of the body: "He loves China dearly since China is the ancient country where human civilization originated and he is willing to be the Norman Bethune of the day by making contributions to the country that has all his admiration."[20] The exuberance of these words reveals the eagerness of party officials to gain the support of a friend of China. They were praising their own culture as well as the doctor who loved it enough to collect and preserve its artistic treasures.

I Collect as a Biologist

As a "friend of China," Arthur Sackler organized conferences on nutrition and set up the China *Medical Tribune* so that doctors attacked during the Cultural Revolution might have access to information denied to them over a decade of atrocities. Even the return of the Qianlong throne was carried out with a ceremony meant to consolidate ties between China and the United States. As a bridge builder, Sackler was energetic and self-confident. As a collector, he had an avid and keen eye all his own.

His art collection was not only unique but was also intended to justify a distinctive way of looking at the world. Some curators and collectors had nothing but contempt for Sackler's approach. In their eyes he was a "hoarder of the most ancient Chinese bronzes," "the most disliked donor at the Met," "the most skilled practitioner of medical advertisements," "the largest shareholder in Boston's State Street Bank."[21] These assessments weighed heavily on the mind of a man who sought to gather beautiful objects and then use them to build a better world. When he finally explained himself in his own words, it was not to the art world but to Lon Tuck, a *Washington Post* journalist who listened to Sackler's story with a nonjudgmental ear. It is in this conversation with Tuck that we finally hear the person beyond the persona. In simple words, Sackler confessed: "I collect as a biologist. To understand a civilization, a society, you must have a large enough corpus of data."[22]

The quest for large amounts of information about a specific civilization led Arthur Sackler to collect in bulk. To critics of the Sackler approach to art, this was simply a justification for buying up large collections. "Buying in bulk" was a favorite expression in anti-Semitic literature that dwells on money-hungry merchants from the Lower East Side. Since Arthur Sackler began collecting Asian art at a time before it became fashionable (and therefore it was less expensive than European art) some critics assumed that he was drawn by the bargain-basement mentality.

Quite a different view emerges from the perspective of Lois Katz, the curator of the Brooklyn Museum who was persuaded to join Sackler's efforts and became the exceptionally knowledgeable curator of the Sackler collection: "When Dr. Sackler acquired art from large private collections destined to be sold or dispersed, he often tried to keep those collections intact."[23] The leap from the objects he cherished to the principles he lived by was shorter for Arthur Sackler than for most other collectors. As a medical doctor and research biologist, he saw no conflict with the art of collecting. As a collector, Sackler also took it upon himself to study and to sponsor scholarship on objects in his care. In the preface to a volume on connoisseurship supported by the Sackler Foundation, he articulated a key component of his own creed that went beyond the arts to culture more broadly: "For me, a pre-eminent function of collecting has been the reconstruction of civilizations, of different cultures, and this goal can only be achieved through scholarly studies. In collection, as in the sciences, when a large corpus of materials has been gathered a representative as well as a true reconstruction of the past can be attempted."[24]

The reconstruction of civilization had been a goal in Beijing ever since the missionaries established universities for the comparative study of culture. Now, a Jewish physician had the means to set up an institution to bring these ideals into practice. If Sackler's words could have been heard or read by inmates of the ox pens, they would have brought great solace indeed. Imagine not being indicted as a criminal for one's scholarly studies, but being actively involved in a reconstruction of the past. While Red Guards continued their rampage, an American-Jewish psychiatrist in New York already envisaged the possibility of a recomposition of cultural remains in a way that would produce a true mirror for civilization.

No single item in the Sackler collection reflects the uniqueness of the owner's vision more than the famous Chu silk manuscript. One of the oldest pieces of evidence (ca. 800 B.C.E.) for the evolution of Chinese writing, it was acquired by Arthur Sackler as a single fragment. More-cautious collectors doubted its antiquity until a series of conferences verified through extensive scholarship the instinct that made the initial purchase seem like an act of madness. As word of the historic significance of the Chu silk manuscript spread all over the world, officials at Beijing University expressed their hope that Sackler would donate this precious artifact at the opening ceremonies for the museum that occupied a corner of the old Singing Crane Garden. Sackler's sudden death in 1987 and ensuing legal conflict, as well as reservations about the status of conservation technology in China, has kept the piece of silk in the United States. Nonetheless, its uniqueness, longevity, and complex fate make it symbolic of the Sackler vision. When the Beida Museum finally opened in 1993, the Sackler Foundation sponsored a large conference on "Chinese Archeology in the Twenty-first Century." In light of the intellectual and spiritual decimation of the 1960s, this was a project as bold as the purchase of the Chu manuscript had it been in its own time.

Sackler's efforts to foster a renewed appreciation of cultural politics was aided by his translator and friend Tommy Hu. Dr. Hu had been a cosmetic surgeon who dedicated his talents to healing victims of burning before the Cultural Revolution. Demoted and deported from his position in Beijing, Tommy Hu spent the years of terror in the harsh northwest. It was in this exile that he learned about his father's suicide in 1968. By employing Hu, as a translator first and later as editor of the Chinese *Medical Tribune*, Arthur Sackler displayed an awareness that talent and ravaged spirits can be mobilized for new goals.

Hu made great progress in spreading new medical information in China in the 1980s. Ideas about cultural conservation were harder to get off the ground. Arthur Sackler did not live to see the opening of his museum at Beijing University. Nonetheless, the vision of history which he developed through his collection and essays created a distinctive framework for reflection. A Jew who never turned away from his parents' immigrant experiences or from the nagging reality of anti-Semitism after the Holocaust, Sackler took China's suffering seriously. Art and archaeology became Sackler's slanted light. As with Oswald Siren's camera during the civil war, the museum became a link between past and present, between what could be exhibited and what remained yet to be understood. In this project, Arthur Sackler acted quite consciously as a "culture broker"—taking from different worlds elements of beauty that needed re-appreciation.[25] When necessary, he could also be a shrewd bargainer who knew how to clinch deals that enhanced international understanding.

You Have a Chance to Bring Back Part of the Past

Negotiations for an art museum at Beijing University tested Sackler's brokering skills in the extreme. Knowing when to speak and when to keep silent, when to bribe and when to plead, when to give and when to withhold funds was part of his talent. A century after Lord Elgin, he came to initiate cultural preservation on a site where destruction held dominion. Arthur Sackler plotted his way to the museum idea slowly, with care. At the height of the Cultural Revolution in China, he was already working on a new art museum at Harvard—to give youth an opportunity to re-appreciate the past in a setting of grace and scholarly understanding. The Beijing opportunity emerged later. After his first trip to China in 1976 (when memories of the Cultural Revolution were still raw and unmentionable), Sackler returned five more times before gaining a letter of understanding from Beijing University officials concerning the idea of the museum. Medicine was the key that opened doors previously shut to cultural memory and to the idea of conservation. In August 1980, the ceremonial Qianlong throne helped begin conversations about museology. Political resistance to foreign involvement in China's internal cultural affairs, however, remained strong. Undaunted, Arthur Sackler pursued other avenues of helping China. One year after the throne gift, he gained the trust and friendship of Qian Xinzhong, minister of public health. After the success of the 1981 conference on nutrition, the ground was ripe for a new initiative. The establishment of the Chinese *Medical Tribune* in 1983 gave Arthur Sackler access to a huge readership—and a new position for Tommy Hu, as well. Aided by Chinese advisers, Sackler sent his lawyer, Michael Sonnereich, and his negotiator, Curtis Cutter, back to China to begin conversations with Beijing University about the possibility of a museum.

The results of these meetings in 1984 were mixed, but encouraging. Sackler was invited back for the October celebrations marking the thirty-fifth anniversary of the founding of the People's Republic. It was in this intensely political setting that the museum idea got its final blessing from party authorities. Reluctant officials at Beijing University had been outmaneuvered by the Ministry of Public Health. A letter of agreement was signed on March 7, 1985, by Arthur Sackler and Ding Shisun, president of Beida. The university agreed "to designate a location for the construction of the Museum within the campus of the University of Beijing at a mutually agreed upon location suitable for the purpose."[26]

The vision of the museum evolved along with the site. Sackler and his representatives did not dwell on the political significance of reconstructing historical studies after the ravage of the Cultural Revolution. Beida's representatives did not share their dark memories of the dilapidated shacks on the grounds of the Singing Crane Garden. Later, the official history of the Sackler Museum would read as follows: "In response to Dr. Sackler's kindness, we have chosen the most beautiful part of our campus as the location of the museum. We also decided that the style should conform to the other buildings around it, but the interior should be designed to meet the needs of a modern museum."[27] These words were written by Wen Zhong—an economist who had himself suffered greatly in the ox pens. Unwilling to dwell on the dark past, Wen Zhong wished instead to portray Beida as the champion of cultural conservation. "The most beautiful part of [the] campus" had been the most traumatized. The Yenching buildings surrounding the Sackler Museum had been the outer boundaries of the niu peng. Not mentioning this history allowed negotiations to proceed.

The two years between the signing of the letter of intent in 1985 and the death of Arthur Sackler on May 26, 1987, were marked by wrangling over the design of the museum in Beijing. Lo Yi Chan made sure that Sackler's vision was embedded in the aesthetic traditions of the Singing Crane Garden. Like Henry Murphy in the 1920s, this American-Chinese architect fought many battles with the school authorities. The goal remained the same: to accommodate a modern institution in a framework that had a meaningful connection to traditional landscape design. Lo Yi Chan was chosen by Sackler upon the recommendation of I. M. Pei, who turned down the opportunity to work on the museum project after a disheartening experience with the Huangshan Hotel farther west of Haidian. Pei, too, had sought to combine traditional and modern garden aesthetics. The wrangling over materials and the disrepair that followed the opening of the lovely hotel did not make him eager to take on another project (until the 2006 Suzhou Museum brought I. M. Pei back to native ground).

Lo Yi Chan was younger and more hopeful than I. M. Pei. The son of the well-known professor of Confucian philosophy Wingtsit Chan, he came from a family that took pride in its contributions to Chinese nationalism before "liberation." Lo Yi Chan's previous success with the Seed Bank project in Beijing made him eager to take on the Sackler Museum. Building on seeds and Confucianism, he took Sackler's ideas in a direction quite unexpected by Beida's party officials. They had planned for a small, innocuous building. Lo Yi Chan argued for an expansive space centered around the courtyard model. The groundbreaking ceremony on September 8, 1986—like the Qianlong throne presentation—was marked by politics. The new American ambassador Winston Lord stood by the side of Beida president Ding Shisun as Arthur and Jill Sackler took hold of a shovel (figure 37). It would be one of their most joyous photo opportunities before his death, less than one year later. Lo Yi Chan's role emerged only in the winter of 1986–87. Though he had limited time with the visionary sponsor of the project, Chan embraced the idea of cultural conservation. He knew that Sackler's vision of the museum at Beida could never be fitted into the narrow space designated by the initial agreement. Neither the amount of land nor the design of the old Yenching buildings accommodated Sackler's dream.

By January 1987, a new vision was born: behind the facade of a Yenching-

Figure 37. Groundbreaking ceremony for the Arthur M. Sackler Museum, September 8, 1986. From left to right, Winston Lord (the U.S. ambassador), Jill Sackler, Arthur M. Sackler, Qian Xinzhong (minister of health), Ding Shisun (president of Beijing University), Curtis Cutter. Photo courtesy of Curtis Cutter.

style structure, the museum would enclose a circular space, not unlike the partially open verandas of former princes and scholars. Like these predecessors, the Sackler Museum courtyard centered on an artificial rock. With the help of Wang Xizu, the manager most familiar with the Sackler project as well as the ravaged campus of Beida, a huge buried boulder was uncovered. Rumors spread by pre–Cultural Revolution era workers suggested that this was the very rock that had adorned the Ming dynasty veranda of Mi Wanzhong's Ladle Garden (Shao Yuan). Later, rumor became fact. Professor of geology Yang Chengyun identified the Sackler rock directly with the Mi Shi You— "the stone that was Mi's Friend." With this organic link, museum and garden became allies in bringing the past back to life.

Lo Yi Chan's plan for a courtyard-centered museum met with strong support from Sackler. Together they argued for a unique extension. The argument was won over the objections of Beida officials. By February 1987, however, Sackler wanted even more: He argued that the garden motif had to prevail in front of the museum as well. Looking for a formal way to incorporate the Beida Museum in a tribute to his wife, Jill Sackler, he obtained an agreement from the university to build a sculpture garden: "The Jill Sackler Sculpture Court and Garden will be created on the west side of the museum. The University will be responsible for the costs of preparing the garden, except that any foreign landscape architects hired as consultants will be paid for by the Sackler Foundation."[28] This agreement was signed by Jill Sackler on behalf of the Arthur Sackler Foundation on May 20, 1987—six days before Sackler's death. It became one of the most contested documents of the many that delayed the official opening of the museum until May 1993.

Sackler's death and the crackdown that followed the democracy movement of 1989 made matters worse. In April 1989, when Jill Sackler and Curtis Cutter had toured the area surrounding the Sackler Museum, they had received assurances that costs and planning for the garden were still on track. During the next month, these plans along with the hopes of China were dramatically derailed. Student demonstrations and the events of June 4 brought bloodshed back to Beijing. Fears of chaos that had shadowed China's capital during the Cultural Revolution surfaced once again. Aged party rulers dreaded another wave of Red Guard anarchism. Students born long after 1949 had little personal familiarity with the demonology of the Mao era. They took to the streets confident that their shouts and songs were thoroughly "democratic." Instead, as often before, violence prevailed.

On the Beida campus, where Arthur Sackler had envisioned a museum for the preservation of culture, another purge began. Officials in charge of dealing with students, as well as with the Sackler Foundation, became more rigid in their demands. Sickened by the killings of June 4, Lo Yi Chan was tempted to abandon the project altogether. He returned to China only because he "felt a moral obligation to bring to fruition the vision of Dr. Sackler."[29] He came back to a changed China. Not only was Sackler gone—and with him the charisma and high-level contacts that had smoothed the project at its inception—but Beida was trying to minimize the visibility of foreigners on campus as well.

Two battles had to be fought over the garden idea and the placard over the museum door. The original agreement included the provision that Sackler's name would appear over the entrance of the museum. This was clearly a troublesome prospect for Beijing University officials after 1989. They argued that "no foreigner's name" had ever been thus immortalized on the grounds of Beida. Lo Yi Chan pointed to the Edgar Snow memorial at the edge of Wei Ming Hu. "But he was a friend of China," was the angry retort. Sackler had been called a "friend" only on the plaque at the entrance of his Medical Tribune Building, not declared so by Chairman Mao himself. China's foremost educational institution could not afford the public visibility of the name of a prominent capitalist-collector. Lo Yi Chan remained adamant. The museum would open up with Sackler's name, or not at all. On May 27, 1993, a marble sign with golden letters was put in place. It reads—in both English and Chinese—"Arthur M. Sackler Museum of Art and Archaeology." Retrospectively, Wen Zhong insists that the placard is "too small, too awkward, too out of place. And what about the Sackler bust that was supposed to be inside the entrance?"[30] It was installed a decade later—a small clumsy image set to the side near the gift shop entrance.

Before the concession of the bronze bust, Lo Yi Chan fought fiercely for the Sackler name on the museum door. He also tried to resolve the issue of the Jill Sackler Garden. In September 1990, political battles over the garden around the museum intensified. The name of one foreign benefactor was already too much. The idea that Sackler's widow also wanted to be acknowledged in stone was too much. In a letter to university officials, Curtis Cutter sought to restate the idea, while adding the promise of additional funds. In the end, however, no sculptures were ever obtained or exhibited in the name of Jill Sackler. Instead, a difficult compromise was agreed upon: a space would be set aside on the west side of the museum for the eventuality of a sculpture garden. In the front of the museum, where Arthur Sackler's name was already displayed, there would be a different, more Chinese marker. The new boulder, to echo the older one within the museum courtyard, would be inscribed with the garden's traditional name: Ming He Yuan.

Professor of history and geography Hou Renzhi was consulted about this politically sensitive matter. He had extensive knowledge about the history of the terrain. After persecution as a rightist in 1957 and as a former inmate of the ox pens, Hou Renzhi knew how to smooth the ripples of controversy. For once, the simple truth sufficed. The Singing Crane Garden had been located on this site in the nineteenth century. Why not call the garden outside the Sackler Museum by this venerable name? Both Curtis Cutter and Jill Sackler liked the name. Cutter persuaded Mrs. Sackler to settle for having her name carved at the base of the new Ming He Yuan stone: "You have a chance to bring back to life part of the past," he told her.[31] With Curtis Cutter's diplomacy and Hou Renzhi's expertise, the Singing Crane Garden gained a new, posthumous life. The new boulder with Qigong's calligraphy created the impression of an unbroken past. There was, however, very little continuity in this corner of the campus of Beijing University. The Cultural Revolution had torn the life of intellectuals to bits. The Tian An Men massacre of 1989 almost severed the Sackler Museum project from its roots. The fact that the museum and the garden have a life at all is due to patient concessions and creative improvisation enacted under difficult circumstances. Unlike Lord Elgin in 1860, Arthur Sackler, Lo Yi Chan, Jill Sackler, and Curtis Cutter understood the wisdom of compromise.

When the Arthur M. Sackler Museum of Art and Archaeology opened in Beijing on the ninety-fourth anniversary of Beida, there was both anxiety and triumph. University officials were worried about the opening date's proximity to June 4. The gates of the university were locked and access tightly controlled during the opening ceremonies. Yet the opening did take place. The *New York Times* chose to dwell on the politically sensitive nature of the project that had come to fruition so close to the month of June. Frustrated by lack of journalistic access to the opening ceremonies, *Times* correspondent Sheryl WuDunn concluded:

While the Archaeology Department says it wants outsiders to visit, the university seems reluctant to ease its restrictions on visitors. In fact, university officials hesitated before allowing foreign reporters to attend the museum opening, and they escorted a restricted number of journalists in and out of the campus. . . . From the start, Chinese authorities said they considered the museum a sensitive project. Initially, the Government was even hesitant to accept the museum as a gift from Mr. Sackler, partly because it was generally suspicious of Westerners. The project finally got under way in 1986, but ran into many snags and the opening was delayed several times. One mundane, time-consuming task, for example, was to properly clean and repair the collection's 10,000 objects, many of which had never been restored.[32]

Restoring objects after the great hurt of the Cultural Revolution was difficult indeed. Sealed off, shards had survived in dusty boxes. They were unpacked and exhibited with the help of Heather Peters, an art historian with extensive experience in Cambodia after the Khmer Rouge. Before taking on the Sackler assignment in Beijing, Peters had worked on the restoration of the National Museum in Phnom Penh, where the ravage had been more concentrated in both the numbers killed and objects destroyed. From this scene of devastation, Peters came to the Sackler Museum of Art and Archaeology in Beijing intensely mindful of what the restoration of art objects can do for the healing of a bruised national soul.

In Cambodia, the reopening of the National Museum had enabled new rulers to display the greatness of the past and thereby deflect some of the grief that still shrouds the present. In China, the Sackler Museum built on the grounds of the niu peng performs a similar function. Communist Party officials at Beida were initially reluctant to take on the Sackler project and became even more cautious about its implications after the crackdown of 1989. In the end, however, this museum in the garden was able to nurture both national pride and genuine scholarship. The Sackler institution at Beida does not directly illuminate the pain of the recent past. It provides instead a space to move around relics once deemed evil and dangerous. It is a spacious container for unresolved sorrow.

A Museum to Take Off One's Face

The Sackler Museum at Beijing University is decidedly not a Cultural Revolution museum. Like the National Museum in Phnom Penh, it avoids pointing to either victims or victimizers. It speaks volumes about the richness of ancient history and remains silent about recent atrocities. In Cambodia, that silence has been broken. Shortly after the Vietnamese takeover (called "liberation"), it was deemed important to recall genocide more openly. In early 1979, the new Cambodia authorities commissioned Vietnamese experts trained in Poland to create a new genocide museum. Modeled after Auschwitz, the museum's purpose was to remind the Khmer people and the world community about what happened in Cambodia from 1975 to 1979. In China, no political regime has yet found it expedient to erect an official museum for the victims of the Cultural Revolution. Unlike in Cambodia, the Chinese atrocities did not leave behind a sea of skulls and bones. What remains is only a plethora of memories. In the garden setting of Beida, old stones and ancient relics are finding their place in courtyards and behind Plexiglas. Perhaps this is all that gardens can accomplish in societies where historical remembrance remains a hotly contested terrain.

China's first Cultural Revolution museum opened only recently—forty years after the revolution's outbreak at Beida in a corner of the country far away from official control. Embedded in a mountain setting near the town of Shantou, this is a structure that documents atrocity without naming the Communist Party as a culprit. Funded by Hong Kong businessman Li Ka-Shing, it is a place for visitors from the far south to contemplate the red terror in the "mirror of history."[33] Borges's image of a heap of broken mirrors is not the animating force here. Rather more traditional views of the past as a guide to moral government inspire the curator and visitors alike. The assumption is simple enough: If future generations of Chinese can be made aware of the pain inflicted upon senior intellectuals and party officials in the 1960s, then the socialist future may yet be established upon a firm foundation. Horrific images of teachers tortured by children are shown, along with the contorted face of a former opera star whose hair is being twisted off his head by Red Guards. About a thousand visitors a day come to this museum in the far south of China to contemplate crimes that remain officially uncommemorated in Beijing.

On the Web, more contentious survivors and scholars have established the "Virtual Museum of the Cultural Revolution."[34] Started in 1996, with the memory of the recent suppression of student movements still fresh in mind, this site uses a far broader range of materials and perspectives to paint the Cultural Revolution atrocities in their full horror. In Chinese and in English, one can access hundreds of documents, chronologies, interviews, memoirs— and even works of art inspired by the red nightmare. The animating vision behind this scrupulous—and thoroughly nonofficial effort—is the warning of Ba Jin, one of China's best-known writers, who was subjected to the indignities of the "Garden for Labor Reform" when he was in his late seventies. Almost alone among the victims of his generation, Ba Jin had insisted that China needed a physical reminder about the trauma of the Cultural Revolution: "We must build a museum, a museum for the sake of remembrance. . . .

It is crucial that each person fix in his mind all the words that were spoken, all the acts that he himself committed during that awful decade. This is not only to preserve wounds, but also to recall our own responsibility for what is now called simply 'the great catastrophe.' Whether one was a victim or perpetrator . . . whether dragon, phoenix, ox or horse, there must be a place where one can take off one's face, in the mirror, to see what he himself did during the Cultural Revolution."[35] This mirror image was not intended as an aid to better government. Instead, it was meant to remind both victim and victimizers alike that they share in culpability. Ba Jin's vision of a museum of the Cultural Revolution was not in terms of a garden of solace. Rather, he called for a place that would enable the abandonment of pretense.

In the absence of such a site, Ba Jin used his own essays to expose his own complicity in the horror that had engulfed China in the 1960s. The year 1986 marked the twentieth anniversary of the outbreak of the Cultural Revolution. For Ba Jin, it also marked twenty years of regret for the death of his wife, Xiao Shan, and his friend, Ye Yichun. These two were among the many inmates of the ox pens who had been humiliated by the Red Guards through beatings and senseless accusations. Looking back on his own behavior, Ba Jin passed a very harsh judgment indeed: "I was nothing more than a misshapen, docile ox. . . . I too raised my fist countless times to shout 'Long Live the Cultural Revolution.' . . . The ox pens can never be torn down. It is enough for me to feel 'handled' in any way, and I return to the experience of being an ox, behave as if I was incarcerated for the first time. My own fears bring me back, they are my eternal memorial of a time when I was weak, when I lacked courage."[36] Ba Jin describes here the shameful truth that marked the lives of all prominent victims of the Red Guards. What is unique in this essay is that Ba Jin called for a museum where there would be no subterfuge, even in victimization. Like Jewish victims of the Holocaust who helped build many museums without putting the burden of the past to rest, Ba Jin keeps asking: "What did I do to let this happen?"

One of Ba Jin's younger disciples, the philosopher Xu Youyu, has taken up the issue of memorialization in his own research and essays. Xu, like Ba Jin, writes about the absence of a site for truthful reflection about the Cultural Revolution. Ten years after the older writer had called for a museum where one could take off one's face, Xu Youyu dissected further China's reluctance to confront an unadorned version of the events of the 1960s: "Our compatriots are often unwilling to face the dark side of life. Some people have grown impatient with descriptions of 'house searches,' 'ox pens,' 'punishment

meetings,' and 'physical struggle.' . . . They take it as just so much bab-
bling. . . . I hope that the Cultural Revolution museum of the future will be
able to reflect painful truths and shatter the self deceptions so prevalent
today."[37] Xu Youyu's vision of the museum, like that of Ba Jin, centers upon
the revelation of dark complicities. If only words like *niu peng* could be burnt
into public consciousness, the dreadful past might somehow be put to rest.

The Sackler Museum built on the site of the Singing Crane Garden is
not known for its harsh lights. In fact, great effort was made to obtain subtle,
lateral lighting so that fragments of China's past could be exhibited more
gracefully. Bronze urns from the ancient Zhou period and Han dynasty mirrors now glisten in hushed galleries. These relics are more resilient than the
traumatized consciousness explored by Ba Jin and Xu Youyu. They link Sackler's efforts directly to a tradition of nationalist museology. The idea of the
museum in China originated with a double agenda: exhibition and preservation. Contradictions between the two became apparent over time. Originally,
the museum was a privileged space for the elites to explore works of art once
savored by emperors alone. As in the European tradition discussed by John
Dixon Hunt, public spaces for the contemplation of cultural beauty were also
inserted directly into landscaped spaces. An old imperial courtyard known
simply as the Garden for the Delight of Beauty (Le Shan Yuan) was transformed in the 1890s into the Garden of Ten Thousand Characteristics (Wan
Xing Yuan).[38] A century before the Sackler Museum sanctioned the dusting
off of archaeological artifacts, the idea of the garden was expanded to include
cultural objects that might foster a national consciousness.

In creating the Garden of Ten Thousand Characteristics, a semi-public
collection of art and artifacts, Chinese reformers were inspired by the Meiji
Restoration of 1868. They had tried to modernize the country by imitating
Japan's museum-building effort, which was seen as an important corollary to
nation building under state sponsorship. This initiative, undertaken with the
blessings of Yihuan's son (the Guangxu emperor), showed a new civic mind-
edness among the descendants of princes who had owned the Singing Crane
Garden and the Garden of Flourishing Grace. For Yihuan, the ruined gardens
of Haidian had served as a private memorial. The institution of the Garden
of Ten Thousand Characteristics, by contrast, exhibited and celebrated notions of grandeur that were meant to shore up Chinese identity in the last
decade of the Qing regime.

In Shanghai, another institution was gestating at the same time. It too
was part of the momentum for museum building in China. Shortly after the

Opium War of 1840–42, a French priest had already begun plans for a history museum. This, new institution, however, did not depend on the expanded meanings of a gardening tradition. By 1874, Lord Elgin's successors in Shanghai (including his brother Bruce, the British ambassador) were powerful enough to establish a "Museum of Asian Arts." Japanese diplomats and merchants followed suit, realizing that "museum" was a useful code word for smuggling rare and important artifacts out of China.[39] This foreign-sponsored museum stands in contrast to the nation-building efforts of Chinese scholar-officials who tried to maintain the reform movement after the failure of Guangxu's Hundred Days of Reform. In 1903, the classically trained scholar Zhang Qian visited Japan and was greatly impressed with museum-building projects there. Returning to China, he decided to use his own personal funds to launch the Nan Tong Museum—the first modern institution to consciously sever the bond between garden and museum.

Zhang Qian, like Arthur Sackler, was a cultured man who did not shy away from business concerns. His involvement in merchant activities enabled him to accumulate the funds necessary to start a public institution dedicated to teaching the public the latest information about archaeology, history, and the arts. Not content to build one museum, Zhang Qian went around the country speaking to different reform-minded groups about the importance of exhibiting the national past in order to build a better Chinese future. By 1912, Zhang Qian's credo had gained national hearing. With the collapse of the Manchu dynasty in 1911, the new republican government found it even more urgent to gain credibility through its support of national history. By 1936, the Chinese Museum Association listed no fewer than thirty-six institutions—most of them identified with the anti-Japanese war struggle. In 1949, however, there were only twenty-one museums left on the Chinese mainland, most of them quite reticent about art treasures, which would soon be labeled as "bourgeois" and "feudal."[40]

After "liberation," museums suffered the same fate as highly educated intellectuals: Originally welcomed into the project of socialist construction, they became a liability in the late Mao era. During the Cultural Revolution, the national past became an object of contestation. Objects from the imperial Confucian tradition, like the men and women who studied them, came to be seen as monstrous—something to be feared and eradicated. The museum became, at best, an instrument for objectification and of emotional distancing from the past. At worst, it became a threat to Mao's vision of a new proletarian culture. In the attack on art and traditional culture, the museum and the garden suffered a similar fate. Objects that had once been sequestered into museums and gardens had to be dragged out again, attacked again. Curators of the national past were demoted as "cremators." Writing in 1967, historian Joseph Levenson warned:

All kinds of relics are being treated as ominously significant for the here and now; they seem no longer safely dead, or put to death-in-life as simply historically significant. The fantastic drenching comes from a sense of danger, the danger of a war that cannot be left to experts, because they would not choose it and could not win it with their expertise alone. And it is this danger that gives the "cultural revolution" its dual target—the two cultures, western and traditional. . . . The god of history is a hidden god again. Relativistic historicism coolly accounting for one-time foes by giving them proper niches, is out of fashion. The dead are no longer monuments, but "ghosts and monsters" to be slain again.[41]

Joseph Levenson himself died before the end of the Cultural Revolution, before he could witness the reemergence of concern with historical memory in China, and in the West. Arthur Sackler, by contrast, lived long enough to seed the ground of the old Singing Crane Garden with the idea of a museum dedicated to conservation.

Sackler, like Levenson, brought to China an intense awareness of the lessons of the Holocaust. In an essay written in September 1974, fully a decade before he broached the subject of a new museum with the authorities at Beijing University, Sackler described his awe at Yad Vashem—the memorial to the victims of the Shoah in Jerusalem. Titled "Tears Alone Are Not Enough," this work revealed the grief of a doctor-collector who mourned for destroyed worlds and was committed to saving what was left over from the cremators of the past: "Yad Vashem brings from Jerusalem to the world a new message, a plea for the humanity of man. In God's name, if you have faith, how can you remain silent? In Man's name, if you want hope, then tears alone are not enough."[42] Sackler's appeal to God and Man would have rung hollow in the ears of Red Guards during the Cultural Revolution. In the heat of their ardor for Chairman Mao, they saw only evil in any talk of humanism and compassion. Never as well armed as the Khmer Rouge, not as indoctrinated as the SS troopers who guarded the death camps of Europe, these "little generals" nonetheless developed innovative techniques for the cultivation of historical amnesia. Their clumsy brutality pales in comparison to the gas chambers and the killing fields. Yet the spiritual wounds inflicted on several generations of Chinese intellectuals are deep enough that they cannot be readily healed.

The Sackler Museum is part of a slow-paced healing. Its spacious courtyard and surrounding lakes allow for a meandering walk through China's cultural past. New curators have received training in the West. Supported at the Smithsonian and Harvard by Sackler Foundation grants, Chinese experts in museology are returning home to train a new generation of graduate students to appreciate the past in all its concrete details. They are finding an academic climate more hospitable to expertise in preservation. In 1999, the Sackler Museum hosted a ceremony inaugurating the new Ph.D. program in archaeology at Beida. In the same corner of northwest Beijing where Elgin had burned princely gardens, where Red Guards had tortured professors for their knowledge about the past, a red banner announced the commemoration of fifty years of archaeological studies. For this ceremony, the Sackler name over the museum door was covered by the red banner. The Yenching legacy was hardly mentioned in the boisterous celebration of Beida's own accomplishments in the post-Mao era. The courtyard designed by Lo Yi Chan became transformed into a reception hall as tables were set up for refreshment, microphones to acknowledge the eminent scholars in the audience. Very few of the Chinese intellectuals present at this gathering had ever met Arthur Sackler. Fewer still were familiar with his ideas about beauty, science, art, and bridge building between cultures. They were simply beneficiaries of his vision. Like the Ming dynasty stone, Sackler has become part of the new "garden" culture at Beida. In a setting where learned contemplation had been nearly uprooted, stone and man alike had kept faith with the past. Together they are making room for the healing of historical memory in one corner of northwest Beijing.

Incompleteness Arouses in Us More Beauty

One of the reasons that the practice of cultural preservation could return to the terrain of the Ming He Yuan is that the idea of the yuan was never limited by space. To be sure, both garden and the museum were ideally suited for quieting the mind and for perusing dense layers of cultural inheritance. But even when the garden lay ruined and museums had been assaulted by war and revolution, writers like Zhu Guanqian held on to the idea of serene reflection. Even as China was being hurled into war with Japan in the 1930s, this European-trained philosopher insisted upon the value of art appreciation. Art, according to Zhu, facilitated a contemplative mind. Standing back from the tumult of the present was an intellectual and moral necessity. In one of his *Letters to Youth*, Zhu argued that all members of society should be urged to cultivate the garden-inspired perspective of jing—reflective stillness. Understanding the cultural past through art was not a matter of sentimental nostalgia. Rather, Zhu Guanqian insisted it required intellectual discipline and a willful separation from the clutter of mundane preoccupations: "Those who manage to create stillness about them will find it easier to develop a capacity for appreciation. . . . The calmness and sharpness I speak about here is that of the spiritual world. I am not referring here to the silence of the physical world, since the physical universe is never truly silent. My point is simply that the more calmness you create in your spiritual world, the more quiet you will feel in the physical world. . . . The achievement of jing is to help you remain calm in the midst of any great upheaval."[43] Zhu's reference to cataclysmic change foreshadows the destruction of cultural and physical space that took place before the building of the Sackler Museum at Beida. Of course, Zhu Guanqian had no way of anticipating how earthshaking the great upheaval of the Cultural Revolution would become in the 1960s. The worst he envisaged was war with Japan.

War came soon enough and drowned out all talk of spiritual calmness. As national salvation became an urgent call in late 1930s, Zhu Guanqian continued to advocate jing for a while longer. At the height of China's combat against Japan, Zhu returned to his earlier writings about education for an aesthetic worldview (*meigan jiaoyu*). Again and again he argued that skilled contemplation of art is not a property of the wealthy classes but rather a necessity for all social strata involved in the war effort. Such arguments could be made before 1949 because there was no single political authority in charge of the "well-being of the masses." Highly educated intellectuals could—and did—imagine themselves to be an integral part of the nation-building project and thus felt free to put forward various ideas about the best way to strengthen the spiritual fabric of China, even in times of war.

After the victory of the Communist Party on the mainland, however, such opinions were no longer welcomed. Philosophers, like other "mental workers," were expected to adjust their outlook to the Marxist-Leninist line. The burden for being "clear minded" (that is to say, of adopting an ideologically correct position) was now imposed by the state. Forced to conform to a framework of interpretation dictated from above, writers adopted a stiff, simple language in their essays about culture. The inner stillness and nuance that Zhu had sought to cultivate in the 1930s was now a liability in the eyes of his political handlers. As physical gardens fell into neglect, so too the words needed to make them live in the mind fell into disuse.

Even before he was dragged out of his home in the South Swallow Garden, Zhu had retreated from his commitment to jing. Although he still wrote about aesthetics, it was in a tightly managed materialist framework determined by the Marxist theory of class struggle. What was tragically lost in this narrowing of scholarly focus was Zhu's own understanding of the limitations of language and thought. When the garden ideal was still sanctioned in public spaces, expressive words were also free to meander, to suggest rather than name. In the 1930s, away from the reach of political dogmatism, Zhu Guanqian could still acknowledge that ordinary language was an imperfect vehicle for the mapping of beauty and interior peace: "The incompleteness of language arouses in us more beauty. We can taste more and more when language balks. . . . In music, too, the melody depends on prolonged silence. We can often sense spiritual sincerity and allow the imagination to wander toward beauty in these intervals between sounds. . . . Speechlessness does not mean not saying anything at all. It leaves room for what is implicit."[44] Zhu's idea of language as a "faint mirror of the senses" held out the possibility of slow-paced reflection. It left plenty of room for what is implicit and incomplete. It enabled the aged philosopher to make do with a fragmented view of the Yi Ran Ting during his incarceration in the niu peng. Even while Red Guards were demanding clear, self-incriminating speech, the old garden surrounding the ox pens provided the kind of solace that museums revived after the Cultural Revolution.

Walking around the Sackler Museum today, bits of Qing marble still accost one's steps (figures 38 and 39). Even if one does not have the intellectual tools to appreciate broken urns made thousands of years ago, a piece of arched marble or a horse mount leaning against a limber tree would suffice to bring back Zhu Guanqian's attentiveness to language that falters. Simply by being pieces of a larger past, these fragments suggest a world of beauty that may never be complete in words, or in thought. The speechlessness of shards augments their beauty, and our humility as well. Arthur Sackler understood this humility even as he developed his own vision of the museum as a beacon in dark times. He donated not only money but also ideas about conservation. In this way, he enabled Chinese intellectuals to lay claim to a buried past while making a meaningful homage to the tradition of the Singing Crane Garden. Without making a direct reference to traditions of Chinese garden-making, Arthur Sackler, too, wrote about the quest for beauty as if it were a spiritual necessity: "My conviction is that all art is an expression of man's faith. Although some caves of Dordogne, such as Lascaux,

Figure 38. Fragment of a Qing dynasty horse mount behind the Sackler Museum.

Figure 39. Fragment of a European-style bridge from the Summer Palace removed to the garden path around the Sackler Museum.

may have been a site of ritual, the presence of engravings and a few pieces of sculpture in other sites could speak to the possibility of aesthetic adornment of a cool, if not air-conditioned, habitat. I would also like to suggest that decorated places could have been the early 'museums' of man—or a comfortable spot where a group could gather in the presence of beauty, for non-religious social planning or intellectual functions."[45] Sackler's idea that caves were the earliest museums of man would certainly find no sympathy among the destroyers of the Yuan Ming Yuan or the Red Guards of the Cultural Revolution. Uninterested in residual bits of human creativity, they took their own values to be normative. Arthur Sackler, by contrast, was willing to step out of his own cultural assumptions. Beyond the parameters of the present, he glimpsed spaces of incompleteness that invite us to become more complete.

The museum is but only one kind of "garden" that facilitates cultural self-reflection. It is, at its best, a place uncluttered by labels so that the reflective mind may find its own mirror within. Even as he donated and designed several museum projects, Arthur Sackler understood that beauty could never be squeezed within any walled structure. It was, in his words, something evanescent and eternal, like the slanting light of an afternoon sun through a gourd-shaped gate. Although he never walked the paths of the Singing Crane Garden, Sackler was bold enough to envision art as rooted in nothing more than the soil of the imaginative mind: "Great art belongs to each and every human exposed to it . . . becomes part of our galaxies of memory banks and of the unconscious, continuous manifestations of our experience. And thus great art and culture belongs to all mankind."[46]

Conclusion
The Past's Tiered Continuum

A song of the rolling earth, and of words according,
Were you thinking that those were the words, those upright lines,
  Those curves, angles and dots?
No, those are not the words, the substantial words are in the ground . . .
All merges toward the presentation of the unspoken meanings of the earth.
—Walt Whitman, "A Song of the Rolling Earth"

The ground beneath the Singing Crane Garden has become over time a capacious repository for cultural memory. The ideal of *jing* (contemplation) combined with *dong* (shifting vistas) flourished in the garden, and later in the museum. In 1860, when violence broke out in this corner of China, and in the 1960s, when the ox pens swelled with educated inmates, the ground had to whisper its wisdom in nearly silent ways: the upturned roof of the Pavilion of Winged Eaves, curving paths leading to the old island of Benevolence and Blessing, a large ornamental rock hidden from public view. Souls were sustained in dark times by what Walt Whitman called, in another context, the "unspoken meanings of the earth."[1] For the optimistic American bard, the rolling earth contained exuberant wisdom. In northwest Beijing, by contrast, a darker cacophony prevailed. Pavilions, rocks, art works, books had not given themselves willingly to the passage of time. In the face of violent erasure, preservation required both courage and craft. Walt Whitman had celebrated optimistically the truths of the earth. In China, these verities were hard won. Even before the traumatic events that are the subject of this book, the late Ming landscape artist Ji Cheng had warned that gardens are places where sorrow reigns. The only hope he held out in the Yuan Ye was that a well-cultivated ground could "quench troubles along with your thirst."[2]

Ji Cheng's hope was fulfilled in the corner of China explored in this book. Ming He Yuan was but one of its names, one of the moments when Whitman-like words seeded the ground. Ravage, torture, revolution did not sap the vitality of hidden roots. Even after cranes fled and intellectuals were silenced, the soil (as it were) carried on a conversation with history. If we extend the metaphor of the garden to include not only place but time as well, we can better understand the resiliency of cultural memory. The garden, like cultural memory, is shaped by a willingness to live within the confines of the past. From its inception, the Singing Crane Garden did not turn its back on the landscaped spaces that preceded it in northwest Beijing. The ground kept its many names. Its complex genealogy was transmitted by poems and essays, by paintings and calligraphy. Scholars, architects, and visitors could access this history even when the garden itself fell into disrepair. Enough shards remained for those willing to engage in a dialogue with the past.

It is not only the soil beneath a few old pines that reminds visitors today of the beauty cherished here by Prince Mianyu. It is not only a marble plaque in front of the Yi Ran Ting that consolidates its dates and its link to Yenching University. It is not only the new, gray boulder in front of the Sackler Museum that brings to mind the sonorous name of Ming He Yuan. Even the faded, modest boulder marking the site of Red Lake (Hong Hu—a Cultural Revolution relic recalling ardor for Chairman Mao) has its spot beneath the Yi Ran Ting today (figure 40). The Beida campus in this northwest corner of China's capital has learned to make peace with its brutal past. There is room enough and time for the old lakes around Prince Gong's Lang Run Yuan to reflect speckled willows in the spring. The same shadows that so enchanted Dorothy Graham in the 1930s can be glimpsed on the withered water lilies in the fall (figure 41). The crisp winter shadows upon the white wall of the Sackler Museum are not accidental either. Lo Yi Chan knew enough of China's cultural history and the terrible fate of princely gardens in the nineteenth and twentieth centuries to create an internally stark yet many-layered landscape (figure 42).

Here, the history-conscious visitor is able to encounter many strata of the past illuminated by grace and loss. Writing in the south of France, far from China's history-littered terrain, Gustaf Sobin used the idea of "luminous debris" to describe vestiges of Provence and Languedoc. In these sun-drenched settings, luminosity is no metaphor. Nonetheless, it may be borrowed to shed light upon what was destroyed, and what was preserved, on the grounds of singing Crane Garden: "There's a need today, perhaps as never

Figure 40. Red Lake (Hung Hu)—stone marker from the Cultural Revolution beneath the Pavilion of Winged Eaves.

Figure 41. Lake in front of the Lang Run Yuan faculty housing compound on the campus of Beijing University.

Figure 42. Winter shadows on the eastern wall of the Sackler Museum of Art and Archaeology.

before, to reestablish contact with verticality: to feel ourselves rooted, not merely to the past in general but to our own specific moment within the past's tiered continuum. . . . We need to feel that this residency has been underwritten by antecedents: that we, the living are continuously accompanied by the presence no matter how remote, of predecessors. That we're not, finally, alone."[3] At Beida, this quest for "verticality" is embedded in both the mission and the architecture of the Sackler Museum. Without speaking about the niu peng directly, Lo Yi Chan's courtyard structure as well as the luminous artifacts on display inside the museum speak volumes about the past's tiered continuum.

In this corner of China, unlike in France, the links between past and present are most often textual. Words—fragile and abused—have been crafted into a memory vessel with as much as care the ancient urns of the Xia dynasty. Like the garden paths designed by Mianyu, these language bridges reveal an attachment to history that outlasts atrocity. They point toward the posthumous life of the garden in the mind, and in the eye of those who cherish cultural memory. This latter garden history is best understood through poetry. Yihuan's verses have been used in this study to capture the voice of the voiceless ground. This tenacious hold of gardens, especially in the wake of violent destruction, may also be glimpsed in the post-Holocaust writings of Zbigniew Herbert, a Polish poet who lived through the devastation of the war. Returning to his native land, he noted:

everyone here suffers from a loss of the sense of time
all we have left is the place the attachment to the place
we still rule over the ruins of temples specters of gardens and houses
if we lose the ruins nothing will be left.[4]

Herbert speaks about the inability to record history exactly as it happened. Trauma numbs the remembering mind. Nonetheless, the Polish poet insists, we must cling to ruins of gardens, and of houses. In these shattered bits lies the potential for renewal. How can a garden lead to rebirth? To answer this question, it is useful to recall how the very first Garden was fashioned as a site for the actualization of human potential. In the Hebrew Bible, this primal space is portrayed as growing out of God's own inexhaustible creativity. A landscaped corner in the larger universe of natural life, it is intended to be associated with delight: "And God made every tree grow out of the soil, delightful to the sight."[5] Soil and beauty are linked from the beginning of this narrative in order to sanction a dimension of beauty in human life. The garden could have been a place to satisfy more basic needs like nourishment and shelter. "Delightful to the sight" (*nachmad l'mareh*) goes beyond the urge for food and protection. Pleasing to the eye, this first Garden encourages humanity to enjoy beauty for its own sake. It proves, in the words of one biblical commentator, "what value the Creator lays on this aesthetic sense in the spiritual calling of Man."[6]

The Sheltering Garden

Sensitivity to beauty, according to the Jewish Bible, was supposed to protect humanity from brutalization. Adam's self-destructive choice and Abel's murder, however, show how the sense of aesthetics becomes blunted when violence rules supreme. The etymology of the word "atrocity" also reveals a willful destruction of life's fragile fibers. *Atro* comes from the Latin root for a very dark reddish-black color. Later, in old French, *atroce* gained the added connotation of fierce and cruel.[7] Combined, these roots point to a reality that is antithetical to the spacious reflectiveness nurtured by sheltering spaces.

At the same time, atrocity makes gardens more essential to human survival and healing. In northwest Beijing today, healing is taking many forms. The Sackler Museum is but one of its manifestations. Another, more wistful image may be found a tourist booklet about the ruined gardens of Yuan Ming Yuan. It shows the slashed stele behind the Sackler Museum in a soft autumn light. Beneath the violated stone, a field of wheat bends into the setting sun. The legend identifies this Qing remnant as a piece of marble that used to adorn the Crescent Terrace of the old Summer Palace. "It was a place for the Qing emperors to admire the moon, because when the moon was bright in the Mid-Autumn Festival, the scene was like what was described in one of Li Bai's poems. The stone table is now found at Peking University."[8] Not a word here about the gashes. No mention of the great hurt that sun-drenched wheat is meant to encircle with muted grief.

If one knew nothing of the layered history beneath the grounds of Peking University, one might imagine that the stele was brutalized by the same fires that destroyed the Summer Palace in 1860. By calling to mind the repeated atrocities committed here, however, both wheat and stone acquire greater depth. Their "conversation" mirrors a complex search for understanding in the very sites where loss and wordlessness prevail. After the nightmarish events of September 11, 2001, this search gained added intensity in a part of the Western world that seems at first glance so far removed from the Singing Crane Garden. Yet, as the weight of atrocity settled into public consciousness in New York, the questions of how landscaped spaces may help heal a wounded community came to the fore once again. Faced with a mind-numbing event, political discourse proved itself brittle to the point of sense-lessness. If thought is to have a second chance on Ground Zero, Sherwin Nuland has argued, it cannot be housed in glass or steel alone. Instead, the Yale-trained physician proposed a garden. After watching hundreds of people walking, standing, and gazing silently into sixteen acres of destroyed lives and vanished bodies, he suggested that New York build "a garden of quiet thought, a green space to renew ourselves."[9] Nuland's vision of the garden is indebted both to Chinese traditions of jing and dong, as well as to his own medical experience with the body's journey toward healing after trauma. The green space proposed for Ground Zero was supposed to aid healing by liter-ally incorporating into the memorial "the scar, which is an ongoing reminder of what has been endured."[10] Like sheaves of wheat encircling the gashed stele, so too the human mind needs room to reveal and to veil its trauma. The mind, according to Nuland, is like other wounded organs. It is never quite the same after atrocity. It heals very slowly, if at all. The garden is a space for po-tential healing—or more likely, as Nuland points out, a place to keep on mourning both privately and communally.

The winning design for Ground Zero did incorporate the idea of such a garden. Daniel Libeskind's imaginative structures had called for a rising spi-ral in which visitors and mourners alike would gain access to a sheltering en-closure. This garden was to have been built inside a glass tower, not low to the ground as Nuland has suggested. Nonetheless, it might have anchored the eye, the mind, and the heart in a contemplative space in which disaster can be confronted more directly.

While the fate of cultural memory remains in limbo in New York, the lessons of ravage in Haidian may grow more urgent with time. The site of Ming He Yuan continues to reveal how a garden may stretch quite literally beyond its physical and temporal boundaries. To dwell in the garden enables one to inhabit space more mindfully, to bring out the potential of spacious-ness within the very limits of human experience. In the words of Maggie Keswick, the classical yuan was to be a "liminal zone" in which the eye and the mind were informed about human rootedness in sacred time: "Religious or spiritual places seek to break across everyday social time, disrupt the nor-mal flow of events with an abnormal, sacred event. The sacred event must of course take place in real time and space, but it marks a shift in status, which is instantaneous and timeless and may even be experienced as being without duration. In a convincing Chinese garden, as much as in an effective play, one's sense of discrete, ordered intervals is transcended by a new order—that of the events themselves."[11] The Singing Crane Garden was such a space where the flow of events was ordered anew. Even after it was ruined, it continued to frame historical occurrences in northwest Beijing, to give them deeper meaning.

The Beauty of Speechlessness

Ming He Yuan, in its time, was but one corner of China, nothing more than one of many princely retreats. With its history fleshed out beyond the garden's perimeter, it becomes a site that reveals enduring dilemmas about the utility of art in times of trauma. An inventory of the garden thus becomes an inventory of wheat and stone, of poetry and fire, of slow-paced reflection and the niu peng. This kind of inventory mirrors the Chinese views of the past with its awareness of impermanence. Victor Segalen, a twentieth-century poet and sinologist, described this as a consciousness of time "in all its voracity." In a poem dedicated to the Chinese cherishment of "ten thousand things" he describes how history swallows material remains again and again:

Si le temps ne s'attaque à l'oeuvre, c'est l'ouvrier qu'il mord. Qu'on le rassasie: ces troncs pleins de sève, ces couleurs vivantes, ces ors que la pluie lave et que le soleil éteint . . .
Point de révolte: honorons les âges dans leurs chutes successives et le temps dans sa voracité.[12]

In this poem, a French admirer of Chinese culture argues for giving in to the teeth of time. Unlike "barbarians" who strive for the eternity of stone, the true guardian of historical memory accepts the inevitability of loss. Segalen's work rails against the arrogance of bronze. There is no point in rebelling against erasure. Honor the past because it is past, a voracious consumer of things best remembered in words.

Just how powerful words can be in containing the ravage of history became clear to me in May 1999 as I attended the conference celebrating the centenary of Beijing University. The commentator chosen for my presentation was Gong Wenxiang, a researcher in the literature department. Professor Gong, I learned later, was a veteran of the ox pens. During a break in our formal meeting, he spoke to me about the striking serenity exhibited by Zhu Guanqian during his incarceration in the niu peng. When we returned to the conference table, Gong made reference to the "beauty of speechlessness" that I had discussed in my essay. Then, he proceeded to rephrase a passage from Zhu Guanqian. I can do no better than let his words stand as a final testament to the resiliency of both language and history in this corner of China: "The beauty of history may be found not only in the limited sense possible in language, but even more so in boundless imagination. To a great extent the beauty of history may be found in its implicitness and incompleteness."[13] Fragmented—and at times suppressed—the history of the Singing Crane Garden remains a gateway for the imagination. In the slanted light of its voracious past, an informed visitor may still encounter the beauty of incompleteness.

Dramatis Personae

Individuals are listed in chronological order.

Mi Wanzhong (1570–1628), Ming dynasty scholar-official, one of the most famous painters of his generation. Mi Wanzhong ran into political trouble with eunuchs at court in 1600 and was removed from active politics. In 1612, he began to design, build, and paint the Shao Yuan garden in the hamlet of Haidian, site of the princely gardens of the Qing dynasty and of Yenching and Beijing Universities in the twentieth century.

Ji Cheng (1582–1642), Ming dynasty garden designer. Born near Suzhou, Ji Cheng designed some of the most well-known gardens of South China. In his later years he summarized his experience with landscape design in *Yuan Ye* (The Craft of Gardens), published in 1631.

Jean Denis Attiret (1702–1768), Jesuit painter and missionary to China. Attiret studied art in Rome and painted cathedrals before arriving in China in 1737. Favored by the Qianlong emperor (1711–1795), Attiret became a court painter and eventually adopted Chinese brush techniques for capturing the emperor's favorite vistas in the Summer Palace of Yuan Ming Yuan.

He Shen (1750–1796), Manchu official who rose from imperial bodyguard to become the favorite of the Qianlong emperor. He Shen ended up controlling the Boards of Revenue and the Civil Council, amassing a huge fortune supposedly equal to fifteen years of Qing imperial revenues. After his son married the emperor's favorite daughter, He Shen was granted a large garden compound adjacent to the Summer Palace. Called Gentle Spring Garden (Shu Chun Yuan), it was located on the grounds of the old Shao Yuan. After Qianlong's death in 1795, He Shen was executed for crimes against the empire by the Jiaqing emperor (1760–1820).

James Bruce, Eighth Earl Elgin (1811–1863), high commissioner to China on behalf of the British Empire. Born to Seventh Lord Elgin, famed as a collector and donor of the "Elgin Marbles," James had a distinguished diplomatic career starting with his 1842 appointment as governor of Jamaica. In 1847, he became governor-general of Canada and was successful in dealing with the 1849 rebellion in Quebec. In 1857, Lord Elgin was appointed as high commissioner to China and signed the Treaty of Tianjin, along with the French plenipotentiary Baron Gros in 1858. In the wake of the Arrow incident in Canton, Elgin returned to China in the summer of 1860 with Baron Gros. He launched a military expedition to the north under the command of General Hope Grant to force the dynasty to implement the Treaty of Tianjin and allow diplomatic representation in the imperial capital. In October 1860—after the capture and torture of western emissaries—James Elgin ordered the burning of the Summer Palace of Yuan Ming Yuan.

Mianyu, Prince Hui (1814–1865), owner of Ming He Yuan, the Singing Crane Garden. Born as the fifth son of the Jiaqing emperor, Mianyu became prince of the first rank in 1839. At the same time, he was granted a garden estate on the grounds confiscated from He Shen by his brother, the Daoguang emperor (1782–1850). More actively involved in national affairs than many of his imperial kin, Mianyu rose to become commander in chief of the forces defending north China from Taiping rebels in 1853. Having successfully rescued Beijing and Tianjin, he was granted the title of general who rescued the Mandate of Heaven (Feng ming da jiang jun). His studio name was Hall of the Seeker of Radiant Virtue (Cheng Hui Tang) to signal his devotion both to the Manchu language and military arts as well as to Confucian values and poetry. After his death, Mianyu was canonized as Duan (upright). He left a collection of poems called *Ai ri zhai ji* (Collection from the Studio of Cherished Days).

Thomas William Bowlby (1817–1860), correspondent for the *Times* of London. Having served as captain in the royal artillery and after working as a solicitor and inventor, Bowlby gained the opportunity to accompany Lord Elgin and Baron Gros to China in 1860. He traveled with the diplomats through Egypt, gaining their admiration for his wide cultural knowledge. He wrote a series of long essays for the *Times* during summer and early fall of 1860 describing various aspects of Chinese life as well as the progress of the military expedition to the north. Captured on September 14, along with Elgin's emissary Harry Parkes (1828–1885), Bowlby's tortured body was returned to the British camp on October 17, 1860, one day before the burning of the Summer Palace.

Yixin, Prince Gong (1833–1898), head of the Zongli Yamen, official in contact with the Western powers and supporter of the dynasty's self-strengthening movement in the 1870s and 1880s. Born as the sixth son of the Daoguang emperor, he became an adviser to his fourth brother, the Xianfeng emperor (1831–1861). In 1859 he became prince of the first rank and was granted a garden near the Summer Palace, the Garden of Moonlit Fertility (Lang Run Yuan). In 1860, as Western armies approached Beijing, Yixin was left in charge of negotiations. He signed the 1860 treaties with Lord Elgin and Baron Gros. In the decades that followed, Yixin had several major conflicts with Empress Dowager Cixi (1835–1908) over succession to the throne and the rebuilding of the Summer Palace.

Yihuan, Prince Chun (1840–1891), owner of the Garden of Flourishing Grace (Wei Xiu Yuan). Born as the seventh son of the Daoguang emperor, Yihuan became a favorite of his fourth brother, the Xianfeng emperor. In 1859 he became prince of the first rank, married the sister of the emperor's favorite concubine (Cixi), and was granted the Wei Xiu Yuan near the Summer Palace. After the burning of the Yuan Ming Yuan, Yihuan became a frequent visitor to the ravaged terrain of Haidian, writing many poems recalling life in the princely gardens. His position at court rose higher and higher, especially after 1875 when Empress Dowager Cixi took Yihuan's son to be the next boy emperor (Guangxu, 1871–1908).

Yihuan left two major collections of writings: *Jiu si tang shigao* (Poems from the Studio of Nine Reflections) and *Jiu si tang shigao xubian* (Additional Verses from the Studio of Nine Reflections).

John Leighton Stuart (1876–1962), president of Yenching University. Born to Presbyterian missionary parents in China, Stuart went on to a distinguished career in education and diplomacy. He was appointed as president of Yenching in 1919 and went on to serve as American ambassador from 1946 to 1949. As a representative of the liberal American vision of China, Stuart earned the contempt of the communists, especially Mao Zedong.

Henry K. Murphy (1877–1954), American architect who designed Yenching University in the 1920s. Trained at Yale, Murphy began to get commissions in China for missionary college in the 1910s. In 1919, he met with John Leighton Stuart, the new president of Yenching, and began the planning of a garden style campus in Haidian. This was Murphy's key opportunity to explore his theories about "adaptive architecture" while combining Western and Chinese materials and design.

Lu Zhiwei (1894–1970), well-known psychologist and linguist who served as president of Yenching University during the time of transition to the communist regime in 1940. In 1920, Lu returned to China after obtaining a doctoral degree in psychology from Columbia University. After teaching at Nanjing University for awhile, he was invited by John Leighton Stuart to Yenching in 1927. Starting in the 1950s, Lu came under severe attack for his close association with Yenching and was eventually transferred to the Chinese Academy of Science. He came under severe persecution once again during the Cultural Revolution and died due to mistreatment and illness on November 21, 1970.

Zhu Guanqian (1897–1986), pioneering scholar in Chinese philosophy of aesthetics. Member of the student generation that promoted new culture in 1919, Zhu went on to earn a doctoral degree in Europe with a thesis entitled "The Psychology of Tragedy." Returning to China in 1933, he became a distinguished professor of philosophy, adopting increasingly Marxist views after 1949. During the Cultural Revolution, Zhu Guanqian became one of the most prominent victims of Red Guard persecution at Beijing University. He survived and continued his scholarly work with a major study of Giambattista Vico.

Ji Xianlin (b. 1911), noted scholar of Indian religions and languages at Beijing University. Ji began his academic studies in Western literature at Shandong and Qinghua universities before going to Germany in 1935. At Göttingen, he focused on Sanskrit and Pali and earned a doctoral degree in 1941. Returning to China in 1946, Ji Xianlin became a distinguished professor of comparative religions. After being severely attacked during the Cultural Revolution, he wrote a memoir of his time in the "ox pens."

Arthur M. Sackler (1913–1987), physician, researcher, collector, and major philanthropist. Born to poor Jewish parents, Arthur Sackler went on to become a major researcher in the new field of psychobiology. He was also the founder of the international *Medical Tribune*, as well as a major art collector and philanthropist. Sackler built museums and other educational institutions at Harvard

University, Tufts University, and Beijing University as well as at the Royal Academy of Arts and the Smithsonian. The groundbreaking ceremony for the Beijing University museum took place in September 1986, with a design by Lo Yi Chan. The museum opened in 1994.

Shi Lu (1919–1982), painter, calligrapher, and prominent victim of the Cultural Revolution in Xian. Born into a traditional Confucian family, Shi Lu became a cultural radical and gained national attention for his 1956 portrait of Mao Zedong ("fighting in Northern Shaanxi"). During the Cultural Revolution, Shi Lu was repeatedly beaten and put into solitary confinement. He suffered a mental breakdown, but continued to practice calligraphy and to paint in secret. His boldest, most visionary works were produced at this time.

Hou Renzhi (b. 1924), professor of historical geography at Beijing University with expertise in the history of Beijing. Hou Renzhi received his bachelor's degree from Yenching University and went on to earn a doctoral degree from Liverpool University in 1949. Returning to China, he became a pioneer in the field of historical geography. Persecuted first in 1957, Hou was once again attacked during the Cultural Revolution. He survived and went on to become a distinguished researcher in the history of Beijing and of the imperial gardens of Haidian. He was consulted by Beijing University officials concerning the Singing Crane Garden (Ming He Yuan) that occupied the grounds connected to the Arthur M. Sackler Museum of Art and Archaeology.

Glossary of Chinese Terms

Ci Ji Si (慈濟寺 / 慈济寺)　Shrine of Abundant Kindness, Qing period fragment on the Beijing University campus, also known as Hua Shen Miao (花神廟 / 花神庙)— Temple of Flowering Angels.

cong hai sang tian (滄海桑田)　Literally "dark sea mulberry field," an expression used to describe world-changing events. It also conveys dismay about such occurrences because they bring about destruction and historical trauma.

Da Xue Tang (大學堂 / 大学堂)　Hall of Great Learning, the name of the Imperial University founded in 1898.

dong (動 / 动)　Literally "motion," used here as changing vistas of the garden as one moves from a sedentary position to slow-paced ambulation.

Haidian (海淀)　Literally "shallow sea."

he li ji qun (鶴立雞群 / 鹤立鸡群)　Literally "like a crane standing among chickens." This expression is used to describe the morally high-minded gentlemen amid a more selfish, politically manipulative generation.

he ming zhi shi (鶴鳴之士 / 鹤鸣之士)　Literally "crane crying / singing scholar," an expression to describe virtuous and well-respected intellectuals who refuse to serve corrupted regimes.

Heibang Dayuan (黑幫大院 / 黑帮大院)　"Compound for Black Elements," official term for incarceration chambers of the Cultural Revolution.

jing (靜)　Motionless and stillness, used in garden lore to describe views obtained from a stationary point of view.

jing (靖)　Tranquility, describing the state of mind obtained from contemplation. Also, to "pacify" or suppress rebellion.

Lang Run Yuan (朗潤園 / 朗润园)　Literally "light/clear and moist/smooth garden," used here as Dorothy Graham suggested, "Garden of Moonlit Fertility."

lao gai yuan (勞改園(院) / 劳改园(院))　Labor reform camp. See below for "garden" and "courtyard."

Ming He Yuan (鳴鶴園 / 鸣鹤园)　Literally "Singing Crane Garden," "Ming (鳴 / 鸣)" can connote both "singing" and "crying."

niu gui she shen (牛鬼蛇神)　Literally "ox ghosts and snake spirits," a term used to criticize and torture high-level intellectuals and cadres during the Cultural Revolution.

niu peng (牛棚)　Ox pen, a place of incarceration for intellectuals during the Cultural Revolution.

Shu Chun Yuan (淑春園 / 淑春园)   Gentle Spring Garden, owned by the eighteenth-century Manchu favorite, He Shen (和珅).

Wei Xiu Yuan (蔚秀園 / 蔚秀园)   Literally "flourishing grace garden," used here as Garden of Flourishing Grace.

Xiao Jing Ting (校景庭)   Literally "School Scenes Pavilion." Originally called Yi Ran Ting (翼然亭), this pavilion is the only piece of architecture left of Ming He Yuan (鳴鶴園 / 鸣鹤园) of the Qing dynasty that was part of Shu Chun Yuan (淑春園 / 淑春园). The pavilion was modified after Yan Jing (燕京 / 燕京) University moved to here in 1926. There are more than ten paintings of the campus in the pavilion, so it is called the "School Scenes Pavilion." The pavilion was repaired in 1984.

yao ru huang he (杳如黄鶴 / 杳如黄鹤)   To disappear without a trace like the yellow crane.

Yi He Yuan (頤和園 /颐和园)   The Joyfully Harmonious Garden.

Yi Ran Ting (翼然亭)   Literally "soaring thus pavilion," used here as "Pavilion of Winged Eaves."

yuan (園 / 园)   Garden. Inside the large enclosure, elements of tree, water, and earth.

yuan (院)   Courtyard, compound, public office. The term for "labor reform camp"—lao gai yuan (勞改園(院)/ 劳改园(院)) —plays with both "garden" and "courtyard."

Yuan Ming Yuan (圓明園 / 圆明园)   Literally "round/complete bright garden," used here as the Garden of Perfect Brightness.

Notes

Introduction

1. Denis E. Cosgrove, *Social Formation and Symbolic Landscape* (Madison, Wis., 1998), p. 1.

2. Feng Jin, "Jing, The Concept of Scenery in Texts on the Traditional Chinese Garden: An Initial Exploration," *Studies in the History of Gardens and Designed Landscapes* 18, no. 4 (Winter 1998): 339–365.

3. Yang Lian, "Apologia—To a Ruin," quoted in Chinese and English in Barmé, "The Garden of Perfect Brightness," p. 67. I am greatly indebted to Geremie Barmé for his help in working on this project, especially his photographs of the remnant of the Singing Crane Garden that appeared with my essay "Garden and Museum: The Shadows of Memory at Peking University," *East Asian History*, no. 17 (December 1999).

4. Yang Lian, "Apologia—To a Ruin."

5. The translation is my own.

6. Primo Levi, "Voices," trans. Ruth Feldman in Forché, ed., *Against Forgetting*, p. 377.

7. Hou Renzhi, *Yan Yuan Shihua*, p. 131.

8. Ji Xianlin, "Ta shixian le shenming de jiazhi," pp. 28–29.

9. Owen, *Remembrances*, p. 28.

10. Ou Yangxiu, "Zui wen ting ji," p. 231.

11. For further discussion of Qianlong's poetry as well as his garden building practices, see Philippe Forêt, *Mapping Chengde: The Qing Landscape Enterprise* (Honolulu, 2000), pp. 47–99.

12. This 1747 poem is quoted in full in Jiao Xiong, *Beijing xibu zhai yuan ji*, p. 102. This translation is my own.

13. R. H. Matthews, *Chinese-English Dictionary* (Cambridge, 1969), p. 458.

14. Bachelard, *The Poetics of Space*, p. xxxii.

15. Schama, *Landscape and Memory*, p. 19.

16. Hummel, *Eminent Chinese of the Ch'ing Period*, p. 968.

17. Mianyu, *Ai ri zhai ji* (Collection from the Studio of Cherished Days), folio edition (Beijing, 1871), p. 1.

18. Clunas, *Fruitful Sites*, p. 13.

19. Hunt, *Greater Perfections*, p. 15.

20. Ibid., pp. 19–20.

21. For a further discussion on the impact of Confucius upon garden practice, see Hu, "The Shao Garden of Mi Wanzhong (1770–1628)," p. 336.

22. Quoted in Hu, *The Way of the Virtuous*, p. 5.

23. Ibid., p. 11.

24. Graham, *Chinese Gardens*, p. 6.

25. Chen Congzhou, *Shuo yuan/On Chinese Gardens*, p. 51.

26. Ji Cheng, *The Craft of Gardens*, p. 13.

27. Fung, "Here and There in the Yuan Ye," p. 43.

28. Li and Lim, "Poetics of Gardening: A Holistic Approach Towards Chinese Landscape Cultivation Based on the Case Study of Yuan Ye," 229–249.

29. Ibid., p. 267.

30. Minford, "The Chinese Garden," p. 267.

31. Casey, *The Fate of Place*, p. 339.

32. Hou Renzhi, *Yan Yuan Shihua*, p. 167.

33. Ibid., p. 171.

34. Yihuan, "Jie jiu di zhi Ming He Yuan zhi gan" (Reflections Upon Visiting Singing Crane Garden with My Ninth Brother), in *Jiu Si Tang shigao xubian* (Additional Verses from the Hall of Nine Reflections) (1874), quoted in Chinese in Hou Renzhi, *Yan Yuan Shihua*, p. 43. This translation is my own and was first published under the title "A Lesson in Mourning," *Resonance* (May 2001): 37.

35. Frederick Mote's studies of Chinese historiography are cited and discussed at length in Ryckmans, "The Chinese Attitude Towards the Past," p. 11.

36. Laub and Podell, "Art and Trauma," p. 995.

Chapter 1. Singing Cranes and Manchu Princes

1. Siren, *Gardens of China*, p. 46.

2. Casey, *Getting Back into Place*, pp. 168–170.

3. Jean Denis Attiret, "A Particular Account of the Emperor of China's Gardens Near Peking," in *The Genius of Place*, ed. Hunt, p. 149.

4. Chang Chi-yun, ed., *Zongwen da cidian* (The Encyclopedic Dictionary of Chinese Language), 10:16848.

5. Peng Zhizhong, *Ming he yu yin* (The Veiled Music of Singing Cranes). I am very grateful to Xie Yinghai, a former student from Wesleyan who obtained this collection of Daoist poems from the Hong Kong University Library.

6. Translation by John M. Ortinau, in Liu and Lo, eds., *Sunflower Splendor*, pp. 238–239.

7. Wu, "The Chinese Pictorial Art: Its Format and Program," pp. 129–130.

8. Personal interview with Yue Shengyang, Beijing, May 18, 1998.

9. For a description of this encounter, see Schwarcz, *Long Road Home*, p. 82.

10. Ibid., p. 147.

11. Personal interview with Dai Chung, widow of Wang Yao, Beijing, May 10, 1998.

12. Jiao Xiong, *Beijing xibu zhai yuan ji*, p. 247. This work also describes the placard that adorned Mianyu's library with the message: "cleanse the wind, take note of wonders."

13. For a further discussion of the religious significance of *zhai*, see Wong, *A Paradise Lost*, pp. 37–42.

14. Yihuan, "Ou cheng" (By Accident), *Jiu Si Tang shigao xubian*, 7 (date?): 34.

15. Hou Renzhi, *Yan Yuan Shihua*, p. 117.

16. Tuan Yi-Fu, *Cosmos and Hearth*, p. 203.

17. Ji Cheng, *The Craft of Gardens*, p. 111.

18. Liang Ssu-Cheng, *A Pictorial History of Chinese Architecture*, p. 48.

19. Hu, "The Shao Garden of Mi Wanzhong," p. 417.

20. Ibid., p. 422.

21. Yang Chengyun and XiaoDongfu, *Gu yuan cong heng*, p. 15.

22. Hu, "The Shao Garden of Mi Wanzhong," p. 422.

23. T. S. Eliot, "The Waste Land," in *The New Oxford Book of American Verse*, pp. 595–609.

24. Mukerji, *Territorial Ambitions and the Gardens of Versailles*, p. 278.

25. Quoted in Keswick, *The Chinese Garden*, p. 17.

26. Ibid., p. 60.

27. I am indebted to John Finlay for clarifying the name of this eleventh image in the "forty views" commissioned by the Qianlong emperor of the Yuan Ming Yuan.

28. Wong, *A Paradise Lost*, p. 67.

29. Hung, "Ho Shen and Shu-ch'un-yuan," p. 103.

30. This is my rendition from the poem quoted in Hou Renzhi, *Yan Yuan Shihua*, p. 161.

31. Crossley, *A Translucent Mirror*, p. 62. The Manchu ideal of manliness is also discussed in Eliott, *The Manchu Way*.

32. Rawski, *The Last Emperors*, p. 169.

33. Ibid., p. 211.

34. Jiao Xiong, *Beijing xibu zhai yuan ji*, p. 67. This translation is my own.

35. Hou Renzhi, "Xiao yuan shigao" (Draft History of the Gardens of Our School), 9.

36. Jiao Xiong, *Beijing xibu zhai yuan ji*, p. 69.

37. Ibid., p. 70.

38. Yihuan, "Jie jiu di zhi Ming He Yuan zhi gan" (Reflections Upon Visiting Singing Crane Garden with My Ninth Brother), *Jiu Si Tang shigao* (1876) 5: 72. This translation is my own.

39. Mianyu, *Ai ri zhai ji*, p. 4.

40. Ibid., pp. 7–9.

41. Ovid, *Ovid's Poetry of Exile*, trans. David Slavitt (Baltimore, 1990), 273.

42. Hou Renzhi, *Yan Yuan Shihua*, p. 197.

43. Graham, *Chinese Gardens*, p. 158.

44. Yihuan, "Wei Xiu Yuan er lu" (Two Songs in Praise of the Garden of Flourishing Grace), *Jiu Si Tang shigao xubian*, 5:21. My rendition was published under the title "Twenty Autumns Later" in *Pointed Circle* (Spring 2001): 20.

45. Graham, *Chinese Gardens*, p. 148.

46. Yixin, *Cui jin yin* (Collection of Elegant Fragments), 3:193.

47. Ibid., 5:2123. This rendition from the original Chinese is my own.

48. Mianyu, *Ai ri zhai ji*, p. 26.

49. Yixin, "Shen ren qin" (Diligence of a Sage), in Mianyu, *Ai ri zhai ji*, p. 38. This translation is my own.

Chapter 2. War Invades the Garden

1. Olson, *Cranes on Dying River*, p. 70. Lawrence Olson, an eminent historian of Japan, was also my colleague for some years at Wesleyan University. His poetry, like his scholarship, has guided key aspects of this work.

2. Crossley, *A Translucent Mirror*, p. 206.

3. Walrond, *Letters and Journals of James, Eighth Earl of Elgin*, pp. 149–150.

4. Ronald Bowlby, "A Times Man in War-Torn China," *Times* online (September 14, 2006), p. 1.

5. Ibid.

6. "Obituary: Thomas William Bowlby," *Illustrated London Times* (December 29, 1860), p. 14.

7. For further discussion of this term as it was used in nineteenth-century China, see Thiriez, *Barbarian Lens*, pp. 20–25.

8. Knollys, *Incidents of the China War of 1860*, p. 209.

9. Yihuan, "Zheng yue shi jiu ri" (The Nineteenth Day of the New Month), *Jiu Si Tang shigao*, vol. 2, p. 53.

10. Cameron, *Barbarians and Mandarins*, pp. 345–347.

11. Mackerras, *Modern China*, p. 81.

12. Wong, *A Paradise Lost*, p. 65.

13. Hurd, *The Arrow War*, p. 219.

14. Wong, *A Paradise Lost*, pp. 83–84.

15. Ibid., p. 88.

16. Ibid., p. 89.

17. Treue, *Art Plunder*, p. 134.

18. Ibid., p. 135.

19. Walrond, *Letters and Journals of James, Eighth Earl of Elgin*, pp. 97–98.

20. Ibid., p. 332.

21. *Dictionnaire Universelle* (Paris, 1978), s.v. "Jean-Baptiste Louis Gros," p. 210.

22. Walrond, *Letters and Journals of James, Eighth Earl of Elgin*, pp. 109–110.

23. Thomas William Bowlby, "Letters from China" (September 1860). I am indebted to Reverend Ronald Bowlby for sharing with me an original transcript of Thomas William Bowlby's China writings.

24. Ibid.

25. Lucy, *Lettres intimes sur la campagne de Chine*, p. 3.

26. Hurd, *The Arrow War*, p. 178.

27. Wong, *Deadly Dreams*, p. xi.

28. Hurd, *The Arrow War*, p. 205.

29. Quoted in ibid., p. 213.

30. Walrond, *Letters and Journals of James, Eighth Earl of Elgin*, p. 350.

31. MacFarquhar and Fairbank, eds., *The Cambridge History of China*, 10:257.

32. Walrond, *Letters and Journals of James, Eighth Earl of Elgin*, p. 357.

33. Hurd, *The Arrow War*, p. 226.

34. Walrond, *Letters and Journals of James, Eighth Earl of Elgin*, p. 359.

35. Wolseley, *Narrative of the War with China*, pp. 212–224.

36. Swinhoe, *Narrative of the North China Campaign*, p. 29.

37. Ibid., p. 299.

38. Walrond, *Letters and Journals of James, Eighth Earl of Elgin*, p. 362.

39. Wolseley, *Narrative of the War with China*, pp. 224–225.

40. Ibid., p. 226.

41. Swinhoe, *Narrative of the North China Campaign*, pp. 305–306.

42. Ibid., p. 307.

43. "A cry of horror could be heard throughout the allies' camp. The appearance of the recovered bodies, the state of the prisoners who survived testify in a most brutal fashion as to the abominable treatment heaped upon the martyrs of Pe-King and Youen-Min-Youen. These Chinese atrocities cannot be left unpunished; no doubt whatsoever must be left in this regard; whoever was the instigator and main culprit of these crimes—even if it points to such a lofty personage as the Emperor. But Hien-Foung escaped to Djehol. The English, with good reasons, want to personally punish this notable criminal; general Grant and Lord Elgin believe that they can strike back at him in a way that will be noticed by destroying Youen-Min-Youen; I do not think this is a good solution; we will give the Chinese the impression that we are truly Barbarians—furthermore, one does not wreak vengeance upon stones for blood unjustly spilled. The French find themselves in disagreement with their Allies on this point: pillagers but not arsonists." Cordier, *Expédition de Chine de 1860*, pp. 384–385. For a fictional recreation of the French involvement with the destruction of the Yuan Ming Yuan and Haidian, see Pierre-Jean Rémy, *Le sac du Palais d'été* (Paris, 1971).

44. Quoted in Barmé, "The Garden of Perfect Brightness," pp. 134–135.

45. "Why have French soldiers pillaged and burned the emperor's Summer palace? France is a civilized empire, her soldiers are subject to discipline, how then could they, on their own authority, set to flame to emperor's palace? This is something about which your Excellency seems to be unaware." Cordier, *Expédition de Chine de 1860*, p. 364.

46. Swinhoe, *Narrative of the North China Campaign*, p. 319.

47. Ibid., pp. 320–321.

48. Walrond, *Letters and Journals of James, Eighth Earl Elgin*, pp. 364–365.

49. Quoted in Knollys, *Incidents of the China War of 1860*, p. 203.

50. Swinhoe, *Narrative of the North China Campaign*, pp. 336–337.

51. Ibid., p. 406.

52. Yihuan, "Wei Xiu Yuan xiao qi gan jiu si shou" (Four verses upon resting in the Garden of Flourishing Grace), *Jiu Si Tang shigao xubian*, 4:15.

53. Quoted in Knollys, *Incidents of the China War of 1860*, p. 209.

54. "Mark well this date and remember it, because it will be inscribed in world history. More prestigious than any other, the glory that comes after the great Failure of West for many centuries, all that erased completely. . . . We entered with some 2,500 the boundaries of Pe-King and there peace was signed." Lucy, *Lettres intimes sur la campagne de Chine*, p. 125.

Chapter 3. Consciousness in the Dark Earth

1. Chang Chi-yun, ed., *Zhongwen da cidian*, 4:1517.

2. Yihuan, "Deng jia shan wang Ming He Yuan you gan" (Ascent to an Artificial Hill to Record Emotions upon Gazing at Singing Crane Garden), in *Jiu Si Tang shigao xubian*, 7:32. This English translation comes from Hou Renzhi, *Yan Yuan Shihua*, p. 167.

3. Yang and Xiao, *Gu yuan cong heng*, p. 342.

4. Glück, *Proofs and Theories*, p. 75.

5. Quoted in Wong, *Paradise Lost*, pp. 163–164.

6. Macaulay, *The Pleasure of Ruins*, p. 40.

7. Hung, *Transience*, p.80.

8. Thiriez, *Barbarian Lens*, p. 72.

9. Yihuan, "Wei Xiu Yuan er lu" (Two Poems About the Garden of Flourishing Grace), *Jiu Si Tang shigao xubian* 6:62. My rendition, titled "No Rest in Supple Verse," was published in *Parting Gifts* (December 2002): 72.

10. Yihuan, "Jie jiu di zhi Ming He Yuan zhi gan" (Reflections Upon Visiting Singing Crane Garden with My Ninth Brother), in *Jiu Si Tang shigao xubian* (Additional Verses from the Hall of Nine Reflections) (1874), quoted in Chinese in Hou Renzhi, *Yan Yuan Shihua*, p. 43. This translation is my own and was first published under the title "A Lesson in Mourning," *Resonance* (May 2001): 37.

11. For a further discussion of Ge Hong's usage of *cang hai sang tian*, see Schwarcz, "White Mulberries and the Blackest Sea," pp. 17–19.

12. Wong, *Paradise Lost*, pp. 83–84.

13. Yihuan, "Wei Xiu Yuan er lu" (Two Songs in Praise of the Garden of Flourishing Grace), *Ji Si Tang shigao xubian*, 5:21. My rendition was published under the title "Twenty Autumns Later" in *Pointed Circle* (Spring 2001): 20.

14. Maleuvre, *Museum Memories*, p. 275.

15. Quoted in Treue, *Art Plunder*, p. 127.

16. Quoted in ibid., p. 142.

17. Ovenden, *John Thomson*.

18. Chen Congzhou, *On Chinese Gardens*, p. 172.

19. Tang Keyang, "From Ruined Gardens to Yan Yuan," pp. 150–172.

20. Edwards, *Yenching University*, p. 27. For a fuller discussion of Stuart's decision to take on the presidency of Yenching, see West, *Yenching University and Sino-Western Relations*, p. 173.

21. Galt, *Yenching University*, p. 62.

22. Stuart, *Fifty Years in China*, p. 49.

23. Quoted in Cody, *Building in China*, p. 157.

24. Quoted in ibid., p. 247.

25. Quoted in ibid., p. 248.

26. Quoted in ibid., p. 161.

27. Quoted in Widmer, "Importing Alma Mater," p. 30. I am indebted to Ellen Widmer, my colleague at Wesleyan, for sharing with me her wealth of knowledge about Christian colleges in China, and especially the architectural history of Yenching.

28. Quoted in David Barboza, "I. M. Pei in China, Revisiting Roots," *New York Times*, October 9, 2006, pp. B1 and B7.

29. Tang, "From Ruined Gardens," p. 164.

30. Ibid., p. 167.

31. For a fuller discussion of the scholarly interests of William Hung, see Egan, *A Latter Day Confucian*.

32. Hung, "Ho Shen and Shu-Ch'un-Yuan," p. 8.

33. Hung Ye (William Hung), "Wei Xiu Yuan Xiaoshi," pp. 39–45.

34. Lee, *Book of My Nights*, p. 97.

35. Galt, *Yenching University*, 57.

36. Mao Zedong, "Farewell, Leighton Stuart!" in *Selected Works of Mao Zedong* (Beijing, 1959), 4:437–439.

37. Quoted in West, *Yenching University*, pp. 213–214.

38. Quoted in Egan, *A Latter Day Confucian*, p. 137.

39. Ibid., p. 240.

40. Ibid.

41. Ibid.

42. Chang, "The Great Proletarian Cultural Revolution," p. 18.

Chapter 4. Red Terror on the Site of Ming He Yuan

1. Primo Levi, "Voices," trans. Ruth Feldman in Forché, ed., *Against Forgetting*, p. 377.

2. Ji Xianlin, *Niu peng zayi* (Recollections of the Ox Pens), p. 78.

3. See "Introduction" for more discussion of this ravaged site.

4. Feng Jicai, *Ten Years of Madness*, p. 23.

5. Xu Youyu, *Zhen mian lishi*, pp. 20–31.

6. For a historical analysis of the connection between the May Fourth Movement of 1919 and the Cultural Revolution, see Ci Jiwei, *Dialectic of the Chinese Revolution* (Stanford, Calif., 1994).

7. Hao, "Synopsis of Several Incidents," p. 160.

8. *Za Lan* (Mash and Pulp) (September 1966). I am grateful to Shelley Hawks, who made this unique publication available to me.

9. Chang, "The Great Proletarian Cultural Revolution," p. 23.

10. Quoted in Schoenhals, ed., *China's Cultural Revolution*, p. 235.

11. Ibid.

12. Ibid., p. 252.

13. Ibid.

14. Hao, "Synopsis of Several Incidents," p. 161.

15. Ibid., p. 168.

16. Yang, *Lost in the Crowd*, pp. 15–16.

17. Hao, "Synopsis of Several Incidents," p. 135.

18. Personal interview with Ji Xianlin, October 26, 1993.

19. Hao, "Synopsis of Several Incidents," p. 158.

20. Ibid., p. 160.

21. Ji Xianlin, *Niu peng zayi*, p. 95. The translation is my own.

22. Xu Youyu, "Tan Wenge," pp. 32–36.

23. Ji Xianlin, *Niu peng zayi*, p. 104.

24. Personal interview with Zhao Baoxu, May 6, 1999.

25. Ibid.

26. Ji Xianlin, *Niu peng zayi*, p. 56.

27. Ibid., pp. 66–67.

28. Yue Daiyun, "Dajiang kuo qianli," p. 21.

29. Personal interview with Zhou Yiliang, October 29, 1993.

30. Personal interview with Chen Yuezeng, October 28, 1993.

31. Feng Youlan, "Zi zhuan" (Autobiography), p. 307.

32. Yue Daiyun, ed., *Jinian Wang Yao xiansheng*, pp. 272–73.

33. Hao Ping, "Synopsis of Several Incidents," p. 142.

34. Li Yigui, "Jian Bozan de yuanhun" (The Unappeased Soul of Jian Bozan), in Shi Xiang, ed., *Wenhua de Zhaoyi*, p. 226.

35. Ibid., p. 227.

36. Personal interview with Zhou Yiling, October 29, 1993.

37. Yue and Wakeman, *To the Storm*, p. 236.

38. Wang Xuezhen, ed., *Beijing Daxue jishi*, 2:675–676. The translation is my own.

39. Tian Yuqing, "Wei shixue changjin jinli."

40. I am grateful to several colleagues at Beijing University who shared details of the Cultural Revolution years. I respect their desire for anonymity.

41. This is my translation of the explanatory materials at the Beijing University Museum's inaugural exhibition.

42. Quoted in Hawks, *Painting by Candlelight*, p. 483. I am greatly indebted to this work and to its author for much information about the life and work of Shi Lu.

43. Zhu Guanqian, "Ziwo jiantao" (Self-investigation), *Zhu Guanqian chuanjii* 9 (1993): 5.

44. Chu Kwang-Tsien, *The Psychology of Tragedy*, p. 234.

45. Quoted in Hawks, *Painting by Candlelight*, p. 349.

46. Edwards, *Yenching University*, p. 132.

Chapter 5. Spaciousness Regained in the Museum

1. John Dixon Hunt, "Curiosities to Adorn Cabinets and Gardens," p. 199.

2. Bachelard, *The Poetics of Space*, p. 184.

3. Personal interview with Su Bai, November 1, 1993.

4. *Beijing Daxue kaogu xi de lishi* (History of the Archaeology Department of Beijing University) (Arthur M. Sackler Museum at Beijing University, 1997), p. 5.

5. Bachelard, *The Poetics of Space*, p. 203.

6. Crane, "Memory, Distortion, and History in the Museum," pp. 46 and 53.

7. Qigong, *Xu yu*, p. 132.

8. Personal interview with Su Bai, November 1, 1993.

9. Sackler, *One Man and Medicine*, p. 279.

10. I am indebted to Simon Gitter, dean of the Sackler Medical School in Tel Aviv, who gave me a tour of the building and shared its institutional history with me on June 13, 1994.

11. Bullock, *An American Transplant*, p. 47.

12. Sackler, *One Man and Medicine*, p. 58.

13. I am indebted to Dr. Sackler's daughter, Elizabeth Sackler, who shared with me this unpublished manuscript, entitled "Some Thoughts on Philanthropy," in personal correspondence dated June 5, 1995.

14. Salamon, *Rambam's Ladder*, p. 20.

15. Tuck, "Convictions of a Collector," p. 21.

16. Personal interview with Meir Meyer in Jerusalem, June 15, 1994.

17. Yang Yuli, "U.S. Doctor's Generosity to China," pp. 32–34.

18. Castagnoli, "There Were Giants in Those Days," pp. 3–8.

19. Hoving, *Making the Mummies Dance*, p. 118.

20. Qian Xinzhong, "To Be the Norman Bethune of the Day," in Spens, ed., *Studio International,* p. 96.

21. Kornbluth, "The Temple of Sackler," pp. 81–83.

22. Tuck, "Convictions of a Collector."

23. Katz, "The Arthur M. Sackler Collections," in Spens, ed., *Studio International,* p. 49.

24. Arthur Sackler, preface to Sheng Fu, *Studies in Connoisseurship* (Princeton, N.J., 1987), pp. ix–x.

25. Richard Kunin, *Reflections of a Culture Broker* (Washington, D.C., 1997), p. 13.

26. I am greatly indebted to Curtis Cutter, Dr. Sackler's longtime associate and representative, for compiling for me a chronology of Sackler's activities in China. Curtis Cutter, "Chronology," unpublished document (1999), p. 4.

27. Wen Zhong, "In Memory of Dr. Arthur M. Sackler," in Spens, ed., "Dr. Arthur M. Sackler Special Issue," *Studio International* (1987), p. 95.

28. Cutter, "Chronology," p. 5.

29. Personal interview with Lo Yi Chan, May 21, 1996.

30. Personal interview with Wen Zhong at Beijing University, February 5, 1997.

31. Personal interview with Curtis Cutter, October 12, 1999.

32. WuDunn, "New Museum Is in Beijing, but Who Will See It?"

33. Coonan, "China's First Cultural Revolution Museum," pp. 2–3.

34. Chen Chao and Hua Xinmin, "Virtual Museum of the Cultural Revolution," *www.end.org.* Accessed April 27, 2007.

35. Ba Jin, "Ji nian" (Remembering), in *Suigan lu*, p. 782.

36. Ba Jin, "Ershi nian qian" (Twenty Years Ago), in *Suigan lu*, p. 827.

37. Xu Youyu, "Wenge bowuguan?" pp. 10–12.

38. Zhonguo ziran kexue bowuguan shehui bian (Society for Chinese Natural History Museums), ed., *Bowuguan xue xin bian*, p. 35. I am indebted to Tong Enzheng, a specialist in Chinese archeology and museum studies, who shared with me this source as well as his own experience in the ox pens.

39. Ibid., p. 13.

40. Ibid., p. 19.

41. Levenson, "Curators and Cremators," p. 9. I am indebted to Lyman VanSlyke for making this manuscript available to me during my graduate studies at Stanford University, more than thirty years ago.

42. Arthur Sackler, "Tears Alone Are Not Enough," *One Man and Medicine*, pp. 230–233.

43. Zhu Guanqian, "Shengming" (Life), *Zhu Guanqian chuanji*, 9:274.

44. Zhu Guanqian, "Wu yan zhi mei" (The Beauty of Speechlessness), *Zhu Guanqian chuanji*, 1:157.

45. Arthur Sackler, "Museums: Caves, Cathedrals and Complexes-All a Bridge Between Peoples," address to the Edinburgh Festival Symposium, August 19, 1983, in Spens, ed., "Dr. Arthur M. Sackler Special Issue," *Studio International* (1987), p. 100.

46. Quoted in Elizabeth Sackler's foreword to Jessica Rawson, *Western Zhou Ritual Bronzes from the Arthur M. Sackler Collections* (Cambridge, 1990), p. 9.

Conclusion

1. Whitman, "Song of the Rolling Earth," in *Collected Works of Walt Whitman*, p. 283.

2. Ji Cheng, *The Craft of Gardens*, p. 74.

3. Sobin, *Luminous Debris*, p. 278.

4. Herbert, "Report from the Besieged City," in Forché, ed., *Against Forgetting*, p. 462.

5. Hirsch, ed., *The Pentateuch Translated and Explained*, 1:57. For further discussion of the biblical paradigm, see Prest, *The Garden of Eden*.

6. Hirsch, ed., *The Pentateuch Translated and Explained*, 1:42.

7. *Oxford English Dictionary* (Oxford, 1978), 1:541.

8. Lan Peijing, ed., *Yuan Ming Yuan Garden*, p. 66.

9. Quoted in Libeskind, Wieseltier, and Nuland, eds., *Monument and Memory*, p. 41.

10. Ibid., p. 39.

11. Keswick, *The Chinese Garden*, p. 198.

12. "If time does not assault the work, it is the artisan who dies. One has to satiate them: these limbs full of sap, their vivid colors, and their golds washed by rain, dimmed by the sun. . . . No point in resisting: let us pay homage to past ages in their successive collapse, and to time for its voracity." Segalen, *Stèles*, pp. 29–31.

13. Gong Wenxiang's remarks were delivered orally. He was kind enough to give me a written version after our meeting, which was incorporated into my essay "Through and Against the Tide of History: Zhu Guanqian and the Legacy of May Fourth," *China Studies*, no. 5 (1999): 10.

Bibliography

Ackerman, Diane. *Cultivating Delight: A Natural History of My Garden.* New York, 2001.

Appleton, William. *A Cycle of Cathay: The Chinese Vogue in England During the Seventeenth and Eighteenth Centuries.* New York, 1951.

Attiret, Jean Denis. "A Particular Account of the Emperor of China's Gardens near Peking." *The Genius of the Place.* Ed. John Dixon Hunt. New York, 1982. 120–130.

Ba Jin. *Suigan lu* (Random Reflections). Beijing, 1996.

Bachelard, Gaston. *The Poetics of Space.* Trans. Maria Jolas. New York, 1964.

Barmée, Geremie. "The Garden of Perfect Brightness: A Life in Ruins." *East Asian History*, no. 11 (June 1966: 63–82.

Beijing Daxue kaogu xi de lishi (The History of the Archaeology Department of Beijing University). Arthur M. Sackler Museum at Beijing University, 1997.

Berkowitz, Alan J. "The Moral Hero: A Pattern of Reclusion in Traditional China." *Monumenta Serica* 40 (1992): 43–57.

Berry, Wendell. *The Selected Poems of Wendell Berry.* Washington, D.C., 1998.

Bloch, Ariel, and Chana Bloch. *The Song of Songs: A New Translation.* New York, 1995.

Bowlby, Ronald. "A Time, Man in War-Torn China." *TimesOnline*, September 14, 2006.

Bredon, Juliet. *Peking: A Historical Description of Its Chief Places of Interest.* Shanghai, 1922.

Bullock, Mary Brown. *An American Transplant: The Rockefeller Foundation and Peking Union Medical College.* Berkeley, Calif., 1980.

Butler, Thomas, ed. *Memory: History, Culture, and the Mind.* Oxford, 1989.

Cai Yuanpei. *Cai Yuanpei meixue wenxuan* (Cai Yuanpei's Selected Essays on Aesthetics). Beijing, 1983.

Cai Zongqi. *A Chinese Literary Mind: Culture, Creativity and Rhetoric in Wenxin Diaolong.* Stanford, Calif., 2001.

Cameron, Nigel. *Barbarians and Mandarins: Thirteen Centuries of Western Travelers in China.* Chicago, 1970.

Cao Xueqin. *Hong Lou Meng* (Dream of the Red Chamber). 2 vols. Beijing, 1976.

Caruth, Cathy. *Unclaimed Experience: Trauma, Narrative and History.* Baltimore, 1996.

Casey, Edward S. *The Fate of Place: A Philosophical Inquiry.* Berkeley, Calif., 1997.

———. *Getting Back into Place: Toward a Renewed Understanding of the Place-World.* Bloomington, Ind., 1993.

———. "Smooth Spaces and Rough-Edged Places: The Hidden History of Place." *Review of Metaphysics.* 1, no. 2 (December 1977).

Castagnoli, William G. "There Were Giants in Those Days: The Early History of Medical Advertising." *Medical Marketing and Media* (March 1997): 1–9.

Chang Chi-yun, ed. *Zhongwen da cidan* (The Encyclopedic Dictionary of Chinese Language). 10 vols. Taipei, 1973.

Chang H. C. "The Great Proletarian Cultural Revolution: A Terminological Study." *Studies in Chinese Communist Terminology* 12 (1967).

Chen Chao and Hua Xinmin. "Virtual Museum of the Cultural Revolution." *www.end.org.*

Chen Congzhou. *Shuo yuan/On Chinese Gardens.* Translated by Chen Congzhou. Shanghai, 1990.

Chen H. S. and G. N. Kates. "Prince Kung's Palace and Its Adjoining Garden in Peking." *Monumenta Serica* 5 (1940): 140–158.

Chen Lifang and Yu Sianglin. *The Garden Art of China.* Portland, Ore., 1986.

Chen Zhi. "*Zaoyuan* ciyi de chanshu" ("Interpretation of the Word zao yuan"). *Jianzhu lishi yu lilun,* Academic Committee of Chinese Garden History. Nanjing, 1981, 127–141.

Chu Kwang-Tsien. *The Psychology of Tragedy.* Hong Kong, 1988.

Clunas, Craig. *Fruitful Sites: Garden Culture in Ming Dynasty China.* Durham, N.C., 1996.

Cody, Jeffrey W. *Building in China: Henry K. Murphy's "Adaptive Architecture," 1914–1935.* Hong Kong, 2001.

Coonan, Clifford. "China's First Cultural Revolution Museum." *The Independent,* February 21, 2006, 2–3.

Cordier, Henri. *L'expédition de Chine de 1860: Histoire diplomatique, notes et documents.* Paris, 1906.

Cosgrove, Denis, and Stephen Daniels. *The Iconography of Landscape.* Cambridge, 1988.

Crane, Susan. "Memory, Distortion, and History in the Museum." *History and Theory* 36, no. 4 (December 1997): 40–55.

———. *Museums and Memory.* Stanford, Calif., 2000.

Crealock, Henry Hope. *Chinese War: Sketches of the Allied Expedition to Pekin.* 2 vols. London, 1861.

Crossley, Pamela K. *A Translucent Mirror: History and Identity in Qing Imperial Ideology.* Berkeley, Calif., 1999.

Cutter, Curtis. "Chronology of Sackler Museum in Beijing." Unpublished manuscript. 1999.

Danby, Hope. *The Garden of Perfect Brightness: The History of the Yuan Ming Yuan and of the Emperors Who Lived There.* Chicago, 1950.

Delbanco, Dawn Ho. *Art from Ritual: Ancient Bronze Vessels from the Arthur M. Sackler Collection.* Washington, D.C., 1983.

Duan Liancheng, ed. *Dalu cang ru* (Convulsions on the Mainland). Hong Kong, 1990.

Edwards, Dwight. *Yenching University.* New York, 1959.

Egan, Susan. *A Latter Day Confucian: Reminiscences of William Hung.* Cambridge, 1988.

"Elgin and Kincardine, Earls." *Encyclopedia Britannica.* Chicago, 1969.

Eliot, T. S. *Four Quartets.* New York, 1943.

———. "The Waste Land." *The New Oxford Book of American Verse.* Ed. Richard Ellmann. New York, 1976, 595–609.

Elliott, Mark C. *The Manchu Way: The Eight Banners and Ethnic Identity in Late Imperial China.* Stanford, Calif., 2001.

Feng Jicai. *Ten Years of Madness: Oral Histories of the Cultural Revolution.* San Francisco, Calif., 1996.

Feng Li, *Landscape and Power in Early China.* The Crisis and Fall of the Western Zhou. Cambridge, 2006.

Feng Youlan. "Zi zhuan" (Autobiography). *San song tang quanji* (Collected Essays from the Three Pine Studio). 13 vols. Beijing, 1999.

Forché, Carolyn, ed. *Against Forgetting: Twentieth-Century Poetry of Witness.* New York, 1993.

Fountain, Henry. "After 9,000 Years the Oldest Playable Flute Is Heard Again." *New York Times.* September 28, 1999, A20.

Fu Sheng. *Studies in Connoisseurship.* Princeton, N.J. 1987.

Fu Xinian et al. *Chinese Architecture.* New Haven, 2002.

Fuller, Michael. *The Road to East Slope: The Development of Su Shi's Poetic Voice.* Stanford, Calif., 1990.

Fung, Stanislaus. "Here and There in the Yuan Ye." *Studies in the History of Gardens and Designed Landscapes* 19 (1999): 440–452.

Fung, Stanislaus, and John Makeham. *Chinese Gardens: In Honor of Professor Chen Congzhou of Shanghai.* Special issue of *Studies in the History of Gardens and Designed Landscapes* 18 (1998).

Gaddis, John Lewis. *The Landscape of History: How Historians Map the Past.* Oxford, 2002.

Galt, Howard S. *Yenching University.* Cambridge, 1939.

Glück, Louise. *Proofs and Theories: Essays on Poetry.* Hopewell, N.J., 1994.

———. *Wild Iris.* Hopewell, N.J., 1991.

Graham, Dorothy, *Chinese Gardens.* New York, 1938.

Gussow, Mel. "The Art of Aftermath Distilled in Memory." *New York Times*, November 14, 2001, p. 4.

Han Pao-te. *The Story of Chinese Landscape Design: External Forms and Internal Visions.* Trans. Carl Shen. Taipei, 1992.

Hao Ping, "Synopsis of Several Incidents During the Great Proletarian Cultural Revolution at Peking University." *Chinese Studies* 29 (Autumn 1966): 156–174.

Hardie, Alison. "Yuan Huan: Records of the Hall Surrounded by Jade of Master-in-Seclusion." *Studies in the History of Gardens and Designed Landscapes* 25, no. 1 (2005): 32–41.

Harrist, Robert E. "Site Names and Their Meaning in the Garden of Solitary Enjoyment." *Journal of Garden History* 13 (1993): 53–60.

Hawks, Shelley Drake. "Painting by Candlelight During the Cultural Revolution: Defending Autonomy, Authenticity and Intellectual Claims to Leadership in the People's Republic of China." Ph.D. dissertation, Brown University, 2003.

Hegel, G. W. F. *The Philosophy of Hegel.* Ed. Carl Friedrich. New York, 1954.

Hirsch, Rabbi Samson Raphael, ed. *The Pentateuch Translated and Explained*. New York, 1971.

Hou Renzhi. "Xiaoyuan shigao: Ming He Yuan, Jing Chun Yuan" (Draft History of the Gardens of Our School: Pure Spring Garden, Singing Crane Garden). *Beijing Daxue xuebao* (*Beijing University Journal*) (May 1957): 9.

———. *Yan Yuan Shihua* (Tales from Yan Yuan Garden). Beijing, 1988.

Hoving, Thomas. *Making the Mummies Dance: Inside the Metropolitan Museum of Art*. New York, 1993.

Hu Dongchu. *The Way of the Virtuous: The Influence of Art and Philosophy on Chinese Garden Design*. Beijing, 1991.

Hu, Philip. "The Shao Garden of Mi Wanzhong (1770–1628): Revisiting a Late Ming Landscape Through Visual and Literary Sources." *Studies in the History of Gardens and Designed Landscapes* 19 (1999): 410–422.

Hubbard, Elbert. *Little Journeys to the Homes of the Great: Eminent Artists*. New York, 1928.

Hummel, Arthur W. *Eminent Chinese of the Ch'ing Period (1644–1912)*. Taipei, 1970.

Hung, William. "Ho Shen and Shu-ch'un-yuan: An Episode in the Past of the Yenching Campus." *Yenching Studies*. Vol. 1. Peking, 1934, 100–110.

Hung Ye (William Hung). "Wei Xiu Yuan Xiaoshi" (Brief History of the Garden of Flourishing Grace). *Ping xibao* (January 1932.): 39–45.

Hung, Wu. "Ruins in Chinese Art: Site, Trace, Fragment." Paper presented to the Ruins in Chinese Visual Culture symposium, University of Chicago, May 17, 1999.

———. *Transience: Chinese Experimental Art at the End of the Twentieth Century*. Chicago, 1999.

Hunt, John Dixon. "Curiosities to Adorn Cabinets and Gardens." In *The Origins of Museums: The Cabinet of Curiosities in Sixteenth and Seventeenth Century Europe*, edited by Oliver Impey and Arthur MacGregor. Oxford, 1985, 199.

———. *Greater Perfections: The Practice of Garden Theory*. Philadelphia, 2000.

Hurd, Douglas. *The Arrow War: An Anglo-Chinese Confusion, 1856–1860*. New York, 1967.

Impey, Oliver, and MacGregor, Arthur, eds. *The Origins of Museums: The Cabinet of Curiosities*. Oxford, 1985.

Ji Cheng. *The Craft of Gardens (Yuan Ye)*. Trans. Alison Hardie. New Haven, 1988.

Ji Xianlin. "Meng suo Wei Ming Hu" (Bound Eternally to Unnamed Lake). *Jingsheng de meili* (Enchantments of the spirit). Beijing, 1998.

———. *Niu peng zai yi* (Recollections of the Ox Pen). Beijing, 1998.

———. *Suigan lu* (Random Reflections). Beijing, 1996.

———. "Ta shixian le shenming de jiazhi" (He realized the value of life). *Zhu Guanqian jinian ji* (Commemorating Zhu Guanqian). Anhui, 1987, 26–30.

———. "Wang" (Forgetting). *Da Gong Bao*. (February 5, 1993).

Jiao Xiong. *Beijing xibu zhai yuan ji* (Notes on the residences and gardens of west Beijing). Beijing, 1996.

Jing Mei. *Ru meng ru yan Gong Wang Fu* (Dreams and mist: The garden of Prince Gong). Beijing, 2004.

Johnsgard, Paul. *Crane Music: A Natural History of American Cranes.* Washington, D.C., 1991.

Johnston, R. Stewart. *Scholar Gardens of China: A Study and Analysis of the Spatial Design of the Chinese Private Garden.* Cambridge, 1991.

Kaplan, Flora, ed. *Museums and the Making of "Ourselves": The Role of Objects in National Identity.* London, 1994.

Keswick, Maggie. *The Chinese Garden.* New York, 1986.

Knollys, Henry. *Incidents of the China War of 1860 (Compiled from the Private Journals of General Sir Hope Grant).* London, 1875.

Kornbluth, Jesse. "The Temple of Sackler." *Vanity Fair* (September 1987): 80–84.

Kurin, Richard. *Reflections of a Culture Broker: A View from the Smithsonian.* Washington, D.C., 1997.

Lan Peijing, ed., *Yuan Ming Yuan Garden.* Beijing, 2000.

Laub, Dori, and Daniel Podell. "Art and Trauma." *International Journal of Psycho-Analysis* 76 (1995): 991–1004.

Lawton, Thomas, and Lentz, Thomas. "Beyond the Legacy." *Anniversary Acquisitions for the Freer Gallery and the Arthur M. Sackler Gallery.* Washington, D.C., 1998, 132–160.

Lee Li-Young. *Book of My Nights.* New York, 2001.

Levenson, Joseph R. *Confucian China and Its Modern Fate: A Trilogy.* Berkeley, Calif., 1965.

———. "Curators and Cremators: More Reflections on What Is Happening in China." Unpublished ms. based on a talk given in Hong Kong on July 1, 1967.

Li Jianzhong. "Yu he gong tian, ren sheng ru ge" (Dancing with Cranes: Seeing Life as a Song) *Renmin ribao (People's Daily)* (November 2000), 4.

Li Yong. "Canku puohui shehui er si" (Suffered Cruelly and Died from Injustice). *Wenhua de zhaoyi* (The Morass of Culture). Ed. Shi Xiang. Changchun, 1994.

Li Xiaodong and Felicia Lim. "Poetics of Gardening: A Holistic Approach Towards Chinese Landscape Cultivation Based on the Case Study of Yuan Ye." *Studies in the History of Gardens and Designed Landscapes* 24, no. 3 (2006): 229–249.

Lian Lihu, ed. *Wang Yao xiansheng jinianji (Remembering Professor Wang Yao).* Tianjin, 1990.

Liang, Ellen Johnston. "Qiu Ying's Depiction of Sima Guang's Duluo Yuan and the View from the Chinese Garden." *Oriental Art* 33 (1987): 120–138.

Liang Ssu-Ch'eng. *A Pictorial History of Chinese Architecture: A Study of the Development of Its Structural System and the Evolution of Its Types.* Cambridge, 1984.

Libeskind, Daniel, Leon Wieseltier, and Sherwin Nuland, eds. *Monument and Memory.* New York, 2002.

Liu Wu-Chi and Lo, Irving Yucheng Lo, eds. *Sunflower Splendor: Three Thousand Years of Chinese Poetry.* Trans. John M. Orthinau. New York, 1975.

Liu Xiuzi and Hardie, Alison. "The Garden of Perfect Brightness." *Studies in the History of Gardens and Designed Landscapes* 25, no. 1 (2005): 792–810.

Loch, Henry Broughman. *Personal Narrative of Occurrences During Lord Elgin's Second Embassy to China in 1860.* London, 1900; reprint, 2002.

Lord, Bette Bao. *Legacies: A Chinese Mosaic.* New York, 1990.

Lu Xun. *Collected Works.* Trans. Gladys Yang. Beijing, 1988.

Lucy, Armand. *Lettres intimes sur la campagne de Chine.* Marseille, 1861.

Macaulay, Rose. *The Pleasure of Ruins.* New York, 1953.

MacFarquhar, Roderick, and John K. Fairbank, eds. *The Cambridge History of China.* Cambridge, 1978.

Mackerras, Colin. *Modern China: A Chronology from 1842 to the Present.* San Francisco, 1982.

Maleuvre, Didier. *Museum Memories: History, Technology, Art.* Stanford, Calif., 1999.

Malley, Therese, ed. *Elysium Britannicum and European Gardening.* Washington, D.C., 1999.

Malone, Carroll B. *History of the Peking Summer Palaces Under the Ch'ing Dynasty.* New York, 1966.

Matsuda, Matt K. *The Memory of the Modern.* New York, 1996.

Messenger, Phyllis, ed. *The Ethics of Collecting Cultural Property.* Albuquerque, 1999.

Mianyu, Prince Hui. *Ai ri zhai ji (Collection from the Studio of Cherished Days)* Beijing, 1871.

Minford, John. "The Chinese Garden: Death of a Symbol." *Studies in the History of Gardens and Designed Landscapes* 18, no. 3 (1998): 260–275.

Moore, Charles, William J. Mitchell, and William Turnbull, Jr. *The Poetics of Gardens.* Cambridge, Mass., 1988.

Morris, Edwin T. *The Gardens of China.* New York, 1983.

Mukerji, Chandra. *Territorial Ambitions and the Gardens of Versailles.* Cambridge, 1997.

Munakata, Kiyohiko. "Mysterious Heavens and Chinese Classical Gardens." *Res* 15 (1988): 72–80.

Mydans, Seth. "Skulls Still Speak in Cambodia to Both Victim and Victimizer." *New York Times,* May 27, 1996, 10.

Naquin, Susan. *Peking: Temples and City Life, 1400–1600.* Berkeley, Calif., 2000.

Olson, Lawrence. *Cranes on Dying River.* New York, 1947.

Ou Yangxiu. "Zui weng ting ji" (Jottings by the Pavilion of the Drunk Old Man). *K'ui yeh chi (Sunflower Splendor).* Ed. Wu-Chi Liu and Irving Lo. Bloomington, Ind., 1976, 231–232.

Ovenden, Richard. *John Thomson (1831–1921) Photographer.* Edinburgh, 1997.

Owen, Stephen. *Remembrances: The Experience of the Past in Classical Chinese Literature.* Cambridge, 1986.

Pajin, Dusan. "Symbolism of Chinese Gardens." *Journal of Oriental Studies* 34, no. 1 (1996): 17–33.

Pan, Stephen. *Peking's Red Guards.* New York, 1968.

Paz, Octavio. *A Tale of Two Gardens: Poems from India, 1952–1995.* Trans. Eliot Weinberger. New York, 1997.

Pearce, Susan. *Museums, Objects, and Collections: A Cultural Study.* Washington, D.C., 1992.

Peng Zhizhong. *Ming he yu yin* (The Veiled Music of Singing Cranes). Taiwan, 1962.

Peters, Heather. "Cultural Heritage of the National Museum of Cambodia." *Expedition,* 37, no. 3 (1995).

————. "Presentations and Representation of Historical and Cultural Identity in the National Museum of Cambodia." Unpublished ms. presented at the Annual Meeting of American Association of Museums, April 1998.

Pirazzoli-Serstevens, Michèle. "The Emperor Qianlong's European Palaces." *Orientations* (November 1998): 61–71.

Prest, John. *The Garden of Eden.* New Haven, 1981.

Qi Gong. *Xu yu (Idle Chatter).* Beijing, 1994.

Rawski, Evelyn S. *The Last Emperors: A Social History of Qing Imperial Institutions.* Berkeley, Calif., 1998.

Reid, John Gilbert, *The Manchu Abdication and the Powers, 1908–1912.* New York, 1936.

Rilke, Rainer Maria. *Duino Elegies and the Sonnets to Orpheus.* Trans. A. Poulin, Jr. Boston, 1975.

Ripley, S. Dillon. *The Sacred Grove: Essays on Museums.* Washington, D.C., 1969.

Rose, Gilbert J. *Trauma and Mastery in Life and Art.* New Haven, 1987.

Ryckmans, Pierre. "The Chinese Attitude Towards the Past." *Papers on Far Eastern History* 39 (1989): 1–16.

Sackler, Arthur M. *One Man and Medicine.* New York, 1983.

Sackler, Elizabeth. Foreword to *Western Zhou Ritual Bronzes from the Arthur M. Sackler Collections.* Ed. Jessica Rawson. Cambridge, Mass., 1990.

Salamon, Julie. *Rambam's Ladder: A Meditation on Generosity and Why It Is Necessary to Give.* New York, 2003.

Sals, Florence S. *Letter from Peking Union Medical College.* Chinese Academy of Science, 1989.

Salva, Alex. "Desire for Words—Exhibition Review." *Orientations* (Hong Kong) 10, no. 3 (1992): 10.

Schafer, Edward. H. "Cosmos in Miniature: The Tradition of the Chinese Gardens." *Landscapes* 12 (1963): 94–102.

Schama, Simon. *Landscape and Memory.* New York, 1995.

Schmidt, J. D. *Harmony Garden: The Life, Literary Criticism and Poetry of Yuan Mei.* London, 2003.

Schoenhals, Michael, ed. *China's Cultural Revolution, 1966–1969: Not a Dinner Party.* Armonk, N.Y., 1996.

Schwarcz, Vera. "The Garden in Its Time: Visions of Refuge in One Corner of Beijing." *Studies in the History of Gardens and Designed Landscapes* 22, no. 4 (March 2003): 265–292.

————. *Long Road Home: A China Journal.* New Haven, 1984.

————. "Through and Against the Tide of History: Zhu Guanqian and the Legacy of May Fourth." *China Studies* 5 (1999): 78–98.

————. "White Mulberries and the Blackest Sea: Metaphors for Historical Trauma in Nineteenth-Century China." *Resonance* (2002): 22–26.

Segalen, Victor. *Steles.* Paris, 1922.

Shenstone, William. "Unconnected Thoughts on Gardening." In *The Genius of the Place: The English Landscape Garden.* Ed. John Dixon Hunt and Peter Willis. New York, 1982, 246–250.

Shi Xiang, ed. *Wenhua de zhaoyi* (The Morass of Culture). Changchun, 1994.

Silbergeld, Jerome. "Beyond Suzhou: Region and Memory in the Gardens of Sichuan." *Art Bulletin* 86, no. 2 (June 2004): 2097–2227.

Siren, Oswald. *Gardens of China.* New York, 1949.

Sobin, Gustaf. *Luminous Debris: Reflecting on Vestige in Provence and Languedoc.* Berkeley, Calif., 1999.

Spens, Michael, ed. "Dr. Arthur M. Sackler Special Issue." *Studio International* 200, supp. 1 (1987).

Spring, Madeline. "The Celebrated Poems of Po Chu-i." *Journal of the American Oriental Society* 111, no. 1 (January–March 1991): 363–372.

Stanford, Ann. *Dreaming the Garden.* Los Angeles, 2000.

Stuart, John L. *Fifty Years in China: The Memoirs of John Leighton Stuart, Missionary and Ambassador.* New York, 1954.

Swinhoe, Robert. *Narrative of the North China Campaign of 1860.* London, 1871.

Szymborska, Wislawa. *Poems: New and Collected, 1957–1997.* Trans. Stanislaw Baranczak and Clare Cavanagh. New York, 1998.

Tang Keyang. "From Ruined Gardens to Yan Yuan—A Transformed Vision of the 'Chinese Garden': A Discussion of Henry K. Murphy's Yenching University Campus Planning." *Studies in the History of Gardens and Designed Landscapes* 24, no. 2 (2004): 150–172.

Tian Yuqing. "Wei shixue changjin jinli" (Renew Commitment to the Investigation of Historical Studies) *Beijing Daxue xin kan (Beijing University News).* October 20, 1992.

Thiriez, Régine. *Barbarian Lens: Western Photographers of the Qianlong Emperor's European Palaces.* Amsterdam, 1998.

Treue, Wilhelm. *Art Plunder: The Fate of Works of Art in War and Unrest.* Trans. Basil Creighton. New York, 1961.

Tsu, Frances Ya-sing. *Landscape Design in Chinese Gardens.* New York, 1988.

Tuan Yi-Fu. *Cosmos and Hearth: A Cosmopolite's Viewpoint.* Minneapolis, 1996.

Tuck, Lon. "Convictions of a Collector." *Washington Post,* September 21, 1986.

Valder, Peter. *Gardens in China.* Portland, Ore., 2002.

Valéry, Paul. "Le Cimetière Marin." *Oeuvres.* Paris, 1960, 86–90.

Vergo, Peter. *The New Museology.* London, 1989.

Walrond, Theodore, ed. *Letters and Journals of James, Eighth Earl of Elgin.* New York, 1969.

Wang Meng. "Huai nian liu shi nian dai?" (Missing the Sixties?). *Dong fang* [East] 5 (1995): 37–40.

Wang Wenguan, *The Classic Beauty of Yan Yuan.* Beijing, 1999.

Wang Xuezhen, ed. *Beijing Daxue jishi* (Chronology of Beijing University). Beijing, 1997.

Wang Youqin, *Wenge shounan zhe* (Victims of the Cultural Revolution). Hong Kong, 2004.

Wang Yushan. *Shi Lu.* Beijing, 1996.

Wang Zhenming, ed. *Haidian guzhen jengwu zhilu* (Record of the Traditional Scenery of Haidian Village). Beijing, 2000.

Wee, Rebecca Liv. *Uncertain Grace.* Port Townsend, Wash., 2001.

Weil, Stephen. *A Cabinet of Curiosities: Inquiries into Museums and Their Prospects.* Washington, D.C., 1995.

Weng, Wan-go. *Gardens in Chinese Art.* New York, 1988.

Weschler, Lawrence. "Inventing Peace: What Can Vermeer Teach Us About Bosnia? A Three-Hundred-Year-Old Lesson About Fashioning Order in a World of Chaos." *New Yorker,* November 20, 1995, 64–68.

West, Paul. *Yenching University and Sino-Western Relations, 1916–1952.* Cambridge, 1976.

Whitman, Walt. *Collected Works of Walt Whitman.* New York, 1989.

Widmer, Ellen. "Importing Alma Mater: Yenching in the Context of China's Christian Colleges and Their Counterparts Abroad." Unpublished essay.

Winchester, Simon. *The River and the Center of the World: A Journey Up the Yangtze and Back in Chinese Time.* New York, 1996.

Wolseley, Garnet J. *Narrative of the War with China in 1860.* Wilmington, Del., 1972.

Wong, J. Y. *Deadly Dreams: Opium, Imperialism, and the Arrow War (1856–1860) in China.* Cambridge, 1998.

Wong Young-Tsu. *A Paradise Lost: The Imperial Garden Yuan Ming Yuan.* Honolulu, 2001.

Wu, Nelson. "The Chinese Pictorial Art: Its Format and Program." In *The Translation of Art: Essays on Chinese Painting and Poetry.* Ed. James C. Y. Watt. Hong Kong, 1976, 127–139.

Wu Youqin, "Da daoshi he da tongxue zhi jian." (Between Beating Teachers and Beating Students). *Ershiyi shiji* (Twenty-first Century), October, 1996, 35–42.

WuDunn, Sheryl. "New Museum Is in Beijing, but Who Will See It?" *New York Times,* June 30, 1993, section C15, p. 1.

Xu Youyu. "Minzu de jiyi yu shenming" (A Nation's Memory and Fate). Unpublished ms. Courtesy of the author. 1997.

———. "Tan Wenge" (Discussing the Cultural Revolution). *Ming liu fang tan* (Popular Themes Today) 2 (1994): 31–33.

———. "Wenge bowuguan?" (A Cultural Revolution Museum?) *Qingnian baokan shijie* (World of Youth) (January 1986): 10–12.

———. *Zhen mian li shi* (Facing History). Beijing, 2000.

Yang Chengyun and Xiao Dongfu. *Gu yuan cong heng* (The Journey of an Ancient Garden). Beijing, 1998.

Yang Hongxun. *The Classical Gardens of China: History and Design Techniques.* Trans. Wang Huimin. New York , 1982.

Yang Jiang. *Lost in the Crowd: A Cultural Revolution Memoir.* Trans. Geremie Barmée. London, 1986.

Yang Lian. *Non-Person Singular: Selected Poems of Yang Lian.* Trans. Brian Holton and Mabel Lee. London, 1994.

Yang Yuli. "U.S. Doctor's Generosity to China." *Beijing Review,* May 13–19, 1992, 29–34.

Ye Jian. "Art Is Valued for Its Originality—An Account of the Chinese Eccentric Painter Shi Lu." *Shi Lu shu hua ji.* Beijing, 1990.

Yeh Wen-hsin. *Landscape, Culture and Power in Chinese Society.* Berkeley 1998.

Yihuan, Prince Chun. *Jiu Si Tang shigao* (Verses from the Studio of Nine Reflections). Vols. 1–9. Folio edition. Beijing, 1876.

———. *Jiu Si Tang shigao xubian* (Additional Verses from the Studio of Nine Reflections). Vols. 1–7. Folio edition. Beijing, 1891.

Yixin. Prince Gong. *Cui jin yin* (Collection of Elegant Fragments). Folio edition. Vols. 1–5. Beijing, 1896.

Young, James. *The Texture of Memory: Holocaust Memorials and Meaning.* New Haven, 1993.

Yue Daiyun. "Dajiang kuo qianli." (The River Is Mighty and Broad). In *Renge de guili: Weiming xuezhe Ji Xianlin* (The Force of One Man's Integrity: The Venerable Scholar Ji Xianlin). Ed. Jia Rui. Beijing, 1997.

———. *Jinian Wang Yao Xiansheng* (Remembering Mr. Wang Yao). Beijing, 1990.

Yue Daiyun and Carolyn Wakeman. *To the Storm: The Odyssey of a Revolutionary Chinese Woman.* Berkeley, Calif., 1985.

Yun Qiao, ed. *Classical Chinese Gardens.* Beijing, 1982.

Za Lan (Mash and Pulp). Special Cultural Revolution Periodical About "Black Art." September 1966.

Zhang Longxi. "Tanqiu mei er wanshan de jingshen: Huainian Zhu Guanqian xiansheng" (The Drive to Pursue Beauty and to Perfect the World: Commemorating Mr. Zhu Guanqian). *Zhu Guanqian jinian ji (Remembrances of Zhu Guanqian.)* Anhui, 1987.

Zhonguo ziran kexue bowuguan shehui bian (Society for Chinese Natural History Museums), ed. *Bowuguan xue xin bian* (New Essays in Museology). Jiangxi, 1982.

Zhou Shifang, ed. *Zhu Guangian zongbai hualun (Essays in Honor of Zhu Guanqian).* Hong Kong, 1987.

Zhu Chen. "Fuqin de xin kai" (Father's Joy and Grief) *Zhu Guanqian jinian ji* (Essays in Memory of Zhu Guanqian). Anhui, 1987.

Zhu Guanqian. *Zhu Guanqian chuanji* (Collected Works of Zhu Guanqian). 19 vols. Anhui, 1993.

Zhu Jie. *Yuan ming yuan.* Beijing, 2000.

Index